Vessels *of* Meaning

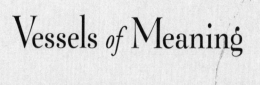

Vessels *of* Meaning

Women's Bodies, Gender Norms, and

Class Bias from Richardson to Lawrence

Laura Fasick

ᴍ Northern Illinois University Press DeKalb 1997

© 1997 by Northern Illinois University Press

Published by the Northern Illinois University Press,

DeKalb, Illinois 60115

Manufactured in the United States using acid-free paper ∞

All Rights Reserved

Design by Julia Fauci

Library of Congress Cataloging-in-Publication Data

Fasick, Laura.

    Vessels of meaning : women's bodies, gender norms, and

class bias from Richardson to Lawrence / Laura Fasick.

      p. cm.

    Includes bibliographical references and index.

    ISBN 0-87580-221-4 (alk. paper)

    1. English fiction—History and criticism. 2. Women and

literature—Great Britain—History. 3. Social classes in litera-

ture. 4. Body, Human, in literature. 5. Sex role in literature. I.

Title.

PR830.W6F37 1997

823.009'352042—dc20   96-43943

                  CIP

Portions of chapter 1 originally appeared in *South Atlantic
Review* 58 (1993) and are reprinted with permission of the
publisher.

Portions of chapter 1 originally appeared in *Essays in Literature*
19 (1992) and are reprinted with permission of the publisher.

This book is dedicated to

Frank, Adele, Pamela, and Julie Fasick

with thanks for everything,

especially that ticket to San Francisco.

Contents

Acknowledgments

PERHAPS THE MOST pleasant part of the generally pleasant process of writing this book is to acknowledge help received along the way.

First, I record my appreciation of the two release-time awards that I received from the administration of Moorhead State University. For two years I taught only eight courses annually instead of nine. The resulting gain in research time was invaluable.

I thank the many able people at Northern Illinois University Press whose talents have helped in this book's production as well as the two anonymous readers whose generous and helpful comments guided my revision.

Mary Burgan and Adele Fasick, two model academics, read and improved individual chapters. I am grateful to them both.

Moorhead State University is blessed with skillful and hard-working librarians, and I have benefited immeasurably from their abilities. Special thanks, however, must go to Dianne Schmidt, MSU's incomparable interlibrary loan librarian, who routinely performs miracles.

I have learned from the experience of many faculty members at Moorhead State University. One individual stands out in particular: Betty Moraghan, who not only loves but embodies poetry, imparts its magic to the lives of everyone fortunate enough to meet her—even those whose preferred genre is the novel. She has illuminated my endeavors, as she has those of many others, with the radiance of her strength, wisdom, and profound grace.

Perhaps we no longer believe in domestic angels, but Margaret Goscilo and Donald Gray are proof that academic angels do indeed exist. Margaret has been a crucial figure in every stage of this project's development. She read tirelessly and commented with insight on draft after draft. It would take an enormous volume to do justice to her extraordinary kindness, consideration, and unflagging encouragement, and another at least as long to detail sufficiently her intellectual caliber. Her combination of professional advice and personal encouragement has enriched this manuscript and my life. Donald Gray gave characteristically generous and perceptive counsel on key chapters. Well before this book was ever conceived, however, he first introduced me to the pleasure and practice of literary research and guided me through my first forays into scholarship. For that and for more I will always be in his debt.

Finally, and in a category all their own, Simone, Marcel, and Guy deserve the best care I can provide in return for the delight, beauty, and inspiration they have provided ever since they entered my life. Without their supportive presence the completion of this book would have been possible but never so much fun.

All those named above have contributed to whatever merit this book possesses. Its faults are entirely my responsibility.

Vessels *of* Meaning

Introduction

RECENT LITERARY SCHOLARSHIP has devoted much attention to the idealization of nurturant femininity that began during the mid-eighteenth century, gained momentum during the nineteenth, and continues—albeit in drastically modified form—during the twentieth. Idealization of women has been a consistent theme in Western literature, of course, concurrent with their denigration. But the deliberately distanced adoration of the courtly lover and the rhetorical conventions of Elizabethan sonneteers, for example, postulate a romance that precludes consummation, much less the ongoing dailiness of domestic life. The eighteenth century saw the emergence of something new: an emphasis on the virtuous wife and mother—the bourgeois housekeeping woman—as the embodiment of human goodness and as a link between the human and the divine. Perhaps it is no accident that this new emphasis on women's spiritual authority emerged simultaneously with a growing interest in the rewards and responsibilities of affective familial life. As the extended kinship household shrank to the smaller-scale and tighter-knit home, the importance of relationships within that home intensified, and its mistress became the monitor and guardian of those relationships. In the literary imagination, at least, human connections assumed both the purifying and the comforting functions as well as the spiritual significance of quasi-religious experiences. Such sanctification of domestic relations, Alexander Welsh has argued persuasively in *The City of Dickens,* was a response to the secularization of society. In Welsh's reading of Dickensian heroines, Charles Dickens is representative of Victorians who staved off fear of death and uncertainty about human immortality by recourse to the figure of the angelic woman.[1] The result is to place an almost intolerable weight of responsibility upon that figure. As Welsh remarks in a later book, Dickens constructs "a highly elaborated but basically simple myth of human—or at least male—existence. . . . But it is important to acknowledge how heavily both the personal and the social claims of this myth depend on the exaggerated powers of the heroine, who is enlisted to save personal identity and to make tolerable the course of history."[2] The socially disenfranchised Victorian woman thus assumes enormous powers in fiction, a fact that critic Nina Auerbach has celebrated in *Woman and the Demon*.[3] But Welsh notes ominously that, although Dickens "wishes to embrace . . . the myth of women who possess such powers without any threatening aspect," those powers can equally well arouse "the actual hostility of the male to the female eidolon he has created" (*From Copyright* 98–99). We need not see this process of mingled reverence and rage at the salvic yet somehow sinister female as originating with the Victorians, however; like many of the characteristic tropes of nineteenth-century literature, it was already employed in the eighteenth.

As the conventions of courtly love coexisted with far more pragmatic medieval marriage practices, so the exalted authority of the domestic woman operated more as a set of cultural conventions than as guidelines for relations between actual men and women. Although Nancy Armstrong has argued that the domestic woman gained discursive power through the cult of virtuous femininity, economic and social arrangements severely circumscribed women's material authority.[4] Indeed, the very disparity between the rhetoric of virtuous femininity and the situation of real women—their own behavior and men's attitudes toward them—was surely responsible for some of the particular tensions and ambiguities in texts that most showcase such rhetoric.

Many critics, among them Bram Dijkstra in *Idols of Perversity,* Helena Michie in *The Flesh Made Word,* and Amanda Anderson in *Tainted Souls and Painted Faces*,[5] have focused on sexuality as the central issue in eighteenth- and nineteenth-century discussions about female virtue and nature. Certainly the rhetoric of purity and "fallenness" is a consistent thread in those discussions. Yet sexuality is only one, not necessarily the supreme, arena in which women can act out (or deny) the all-encompassing aspects of ideal femininity: nurture and service. These aspects are more crucial than specific sexual prescriptions and proscriptions. The assumption that women are "giving" in a way that men are not—that nurture comes naturally to females—dictates that women devote themselves to others even while it ostensibly praises women for doing so already. At the same time, because this nurture supposedly *is* naturally feminine, men are largely exempt from its responsibilities. Thus for their caregiving of others, women receive praise predicated partially upon the impossibility of reciprocal nurture from men.

Arguments for women's nurturant natures often originate in the structure and arrangement of the female body. From time immemorial, the physical differences between the sexes have served as the basis for assuming that women and men experience different psychological, intellectual, and emotional processes. Although we are currently most familiar with the idea that the relative slightness and weakness of the female body accompany moral elevation, historically there have been times when this frailty has meant primarily humiliation. For example, the humbled Katharina in *The Taming of the Shrew* rhetorically asks women

> Why are our bodies soft, and weak, and smooth,
> Unapt to toil and trouble in the world,
> But that our soft conditions, and our hearts,
> Should well agree with our external parts?
> (5.2.165–68)

A man must "commi[t] his body / To painful labour" (5.2.148, 149) from which a woman's "weakness past compare" (5.2.175) exempts her, and her "love, fair looks, and true obedience — / [are] Too little payment for so great a debt" (5.2.153–54). In Katharina's (and Shakespeare's) terms, women's physical fragility necessitates their dependence on men, which in turn should ensure their docility, obedience, and subservience. These normative female qualities, far from being proof of a morally sensitive nature that can correct and control men's coarser sensibilities, are women's payment for men's protection in a frank trade-off of goods and services. Yet in succeeding centuries, the trade-off becomes swathed in ideology as the assumed refinement, delicacy, and grace of the ideal female body become more constructed as signifiers of a precious feminine spirituality.

Thomas Laqueur's argument in *Making Sex* is relevant here. According to Laqueur, the eighteenth century moved from a centuries-old vision of women as underdeveloped versions of men to a new view of them as radically different but complementary beings.[6] In the earlier model of thought, women were by definition imperfect because incomplete, manhood being the state of fullest human development. Thus Shakespeare's Katharina, like the other women of her time, must learn to accept subordination as the legitimate consequence of her biologically ordained inability to "measure up" to a single (male) standard of excellence. In the later model, women could develop as fully as men but only in a different direction: their perfection was entirely distinct from men's. Their uniquely female development therefore fitted them for an equally distinct brand of authority, which, however, paradoxically mandated the self-abnegation that justified women having any authority at all. Whereas men supposedly fulfilled themselves through individualistic striving, women completed their "natural" development through the self-effacing processes of marital devotion and maternal nurture. Thus, the imperatives of human biology underwrote social arrangements that decreed women should serve others. Jill L. Matus wittily paraphrases one Victorian version of this theory: "Characteristically self-sacrificing, female development is geared to the good of the species; ambitious and self-interested, the male perfects himself."[7] What power Victorian women were supposed to possess arose ostensibly out of an extreme version of the Christian paradox that he who humbles himself shall be exalted. The problem, of course, is that authority restricted to the domestic and affective realms can often seem ineffectual—indeed, impotent—in comparison to that which controls political, economic, and social functions. Moreover, the argument that women's greater moral purity depends upon their separation from the rough-and-tumble male world requires that women sacrifice material power for the sake of their putative moral stature.

The ideology of moral feminine superiority has never received unanimous support. Both men and women have pointed out, sometimes acidly, its logical weaknesses and self-contradictions. Sometimes rejection of this ideology has accompanied arguments to allow women entry into positions of practical power. Yet more striking, some branches of feminism consistently have co-opted ideas of women's moral superiority to justify the expansion of women's political, economic, and other practical authority. Thus some suffragettes argued that women's votes would have a purifying and elevating effect upon the nations that enfranchised women. More recently, some feminists have organized all-female pacifist and social justice movements at least partly on the grounds that women are largely innocent of the violent and exploitative tendencies shown by men throughout history.[8] Yet these attempts to draw upon "traditional women's culture" complicate feminist attempts to dismantle "the rigidity of male and female roles." Thus Adrienne Harris and Ynestra King can argue for feminist "critique of stereotypes" and on the same page refer to "the powers of a particularly female imagination."[9] What does it mean to assign gender to the imagination in this way? Is the reader to assume that this "female imagination" is an attribute common to all women or a result of gendered socialization among women of a particular time and place? And, if socialization for any group of women is uniform, can we assume the results also will be uniform and therefore predictable? Some explorations of female socialization have postulated results that are regular—indeed, apparently inevitable and inescapable.[10] Thus psychologists Carol Gilligan and Nancy Chodorow hypothesize a reliance on relationship, connection, and nurture as characteristically female and as leading to a distinctive female personality with a sex-specific moral code.[11] Gilligan began the studies in this area (which made her famous) as a way to challenge the depreciation of female development arising from Piaget's male-based theories of moral growth. Yet neither her work nor Chodorow's necessarily endorse the circumstances that facilitate this female moral character, no matter how valuable some aspects of that character might be. For Chodorow, as for Dorothy Dinnerstein, women's almost total responsibility for early child care is crucial in shaping gender roles and thus influencing social arrangements seemingly far removed from gender—but is a heavily malign influence for both men and women.[12] In Dinnerstein's argument "patriarchal and masculine assertions of domination and control" are one form of the rebellion against earlier childhood dependence on and resentment (as well as love) toward "a mother who seems both endlessly bountiful and all powerful" (Harris and King 6). Only men's integration into child care can stem aggression that otherwise could destroy the world.

In addition to encouraging the idea that we should merge and blend gender roles, however, formulations of a distinctive female character can lead toward celebration of femaleness as something essentially, not just socially, different from male identity. In this celebration, it is possible to separate—and to exonerate—women from the weight of aggression and pain that male-dominated culture has produced. Thus feminist theorists from Susan Griffin to Mary Daly have argued for the existence of a specifically female ethos that nourishes life and defies a patriarchal order intent on death. Daly declares that her book *Gyn/Ecology* is "written on the edge of a culture that is killing itself and all of sentient life. . . . The Godfather insatiably demands more sacrifices, and the fundamental sacrifices of sadospiritual religion are female."[13] Griffin, meanwhile, blends women and nature—apparently all "material beings" aside from men—in a single "embodied . . . and an impassioned [voice]." As the female voice is "embodied," so she declares that the "paternal voice" of "recognized opinion" causes "reactions I experienced in my female body," again making the female body the site and signifier of a consciousness opposed to that different type of consciousness possessed by "civilized man."[14] Daly, Griffin, and others like them sponsor roles and possibilities for women far beyond those advocated by eighteenth- and nineteenth-century proponents of domestic femininity. Yet one similarity remains: the idea that women *as women* possess a special moral stature. As Daly puts it,

> Within this anti-pollutant, purifying, moving O-Zone, the aura of gynocentric consciousness, life-loving feminists have the power to affirm the basic Gyn/Ecological principle that everything is connected with everything else. It is this holistic process of knowing that can make Gyn/Ecology the O-logy of all the -ologies, encircling them, spinning around and through them, unmasking their emptiness. . . . It can free the flow of their "courses" and overcome their necrophiliac circles, their self-enclosed procession, through spiraling creative process. (11)

The "eternal feminine"—evident in Daly's linking of women through the ages—here remains as much a redemptive force as it was, say, for Goethe, even though the form of redemption Daly proposes probably would have been unrecognizable to him. And just as the ideology of domestic femininity dismissed aberrant females as not "true women," Daly describes male-identified women as artificial and mechanical rather than flesh-and-blood females. They are "malfunctioning machine[s], . . . dutiful, dim-witted 'Daughter[s]' gone beserk, . . . failed fembot[s]" of the "Male Mother" (14). Daly's distinction here is reminiscent of the way in which Hélène Cixous refuses to accept all writing by women as "women's writing." For Cixous, as "women's writing" demonstrates specific linguistic and structural qualities quite distinct from the sex of its author, womanhood entails a set of special—and very impressive—psychological attributes. The result is a description of femaleness as prescriptive as anything from an eighteenth-century conduct book. Cixous declares that "the first voice of love . . . is alive in every woman" and that "[i]n women there is always more or less of the mother who makes everything all right, who nourishes, and who stands up against separation: a force that will not be cut off but will knock the wind out of the codes."[15] Above all, Cixous assures us, this monolithic "she" gives. "She doesn't know what she's giving, she doesn't measure it; she gives though, neither a counterfeit impression nor something she hasn't got. She gives more, with no assurance that she'll get back even some unexpected profit from what she puts out. She gives that there may be life, thought, transformation" (92). The basis for this female generosity appears to be an equation between the nurturing female body and the inexhaustible female spirit. Cixous, insisting that "[m]ore so than men . . . , women are body" (87), ecstatically urges Woman to reclaim "her native strength . . . her goods, her pleasures, her organs, her immense bodily territories" (81–82).

The celebration of "Woman" in Cixous's words doubtless is meant to be uplifting, but it is possible for individual women to feel as far removed from the terms of her paean as they are from the raptures of Samuel Richardson over Clarissa or of Charles Dickens over Amy Dorrit. One can argue, indeed, that this reinterpretation of women's physicality and psychology is potentially as constricting as previous visions because it is as total and as totalizing. The intention may be to empower the previously powerless and to give voice to the formerly silenced, but—as in the most patriarchal constructions of femininity—individual variations vanish within a universalizing whole, as in Griffin's single voice for all of women and nature. That both Cixous and Griffin explicitly reject most previous (male-authored) generalizations about women does not obscure their own universalizing tendencies. To give another example of such continued essentialism, human reproductive processes in the past have served as a reason to exclude women from decision making about social structures. Women presumably were too drained by those processes to have the intellectual energy for public policy. On the other hand, Barbara Love and Elizabeth Shanklin argue that gestation justifies matriarchy, "in which women, those who produce the next generation, define motherhood, determine the conditions of motherhood, and determine the environment in which the next generation is reared."[16] For Love and Shanklin, a matriarchal society will inevitably and necessarily be a nurturant one. They write, "By 'matriarchy' we mean a society in which all relationships are modeled on the nurturant relationship between a mother and her child" (279) apparently without feeling any need to prove that mother/child relationships invariably are nurturant. They go on to describe how "deep nurturance and nurturant social structures" would produce "a genuinely harmonious society, a society of self-regulating, positive individuals" (279–80). Their argument therefore equates women's power with supposedly innate nurturant capabilities arising from women's biological capacity for motherhood.

What does it mean to assume that women are specially equipped to nurture and that emotional generosity is inscribed in their very bodies? More broadly, how do conceptions of the body and theories of "innate" female characteristics work together? Given that "masculinity" and "femininity" are often offered as opposites, how does novelists' use of gender constructions reinforce, blur, or otherwise complicate this binary pair? Literary representations of bodies, particularly female bodies, help expose, whether consciously or not, the ambiguities that underlie our ideas about gender and its meaning. To illuminate some of those ambiguities, this book examines the way representations of the body in novels by authors ranging from Samuel Richardson to D. H. Lawrence attempt to "naturalize" various behavioral and affective norms and looks at the resulting implications for power relations between the sexes. As a secondary consideration it explores how class status further complicates those relations. This examination of gender and class clarifies that, as women have often been expected to operate by values different from men's, different classes too are often subject to different norms. The perception of women as a sex with a distinctively different set of needs, imperatives, and desires than men greatly facilitates understanding of similar "distancing" perceptions of other groups. In particular, the Victorian idealization of women can be remarkably similar to the same period's sentimentality over the "deserving poor," a parallel worthy of attention. Negative stereotypes are not always the most damaging: both women and those members of the working classes singled out for praise frequently suffer further constriction from the terms in which they are celebrated. They are set apart as separate and unequal in a supposed superiority that too often translates into practical inferiority. The danger therefore is not so much of one class or sex attempting to impose alien values upon another as its insisting that the other remain different in its internalized norms as well as its material conditions—the better to continue serving the interests of the dominant group.

Any study of the body in literature runs the risk of being overwhelmed by the mass of material available. From its inception fiction has partaken of and implicitly conveyed a series of wide-ranging ideas about the treatment of the body—how to feed it, discipline it, display it. Moreover, although some subjects have undoubtedly inspired an equal amount of descriptive and prescriptive writing, no subject has inspired a larger *quantity* of writing than the human body has. In particular, everything from medical theories to theological and moral models to folk beliefs to the individual quirks and fetishes of authors has helped shape the treatment of women's bodies in the novel and thereby the novel's assignment of meaning and value to women themselves. In choosing the authors studied here, I have considered both the centrality of the body to their works and the fruitfulness of placing these same works side by side. Thus Samuel Richardson forms a natural pair with Frances Burney rather than with, say, Jane Austen, partly because of Richardson's and Burney's common indulgence in what many consider faults: a fussy, indeed nervous, novelistic insistence upon female decorum and a correspondingly heightened sense of the male potential for sexual aggression. A feeling of sexual panic links Richardson's and Burney's novels, yet the differences in handling the shared theme are instructive indeed. Likewise, Dickens and Thackeray are naturally joined by their richly ambivalent fictional embrace of domesticity and a shared obsession with maternally inflected love interests. Dickens and Thackeray, moreover, are central figures in the novelistic treatment of male maturation: David Copperfield, Arthur Pendennis, Arthur Clennam, and Philip Firmin attest to their creators' eagerness to explore the growth of boys into men and to examine the women who shape that growth. Charlotte Brontë and Elizabeth Gaskell, on the other hand, provide an illuminating comparison with the two male authors and also with each other. The critical tradition, only recently challenged, of ascribing cosiness to Gaskell and stormy passion to Brontë should not disguise the limitations both women build into the happiness and self-sufficiency of even their most seemingly independent because least attached heroines. Their perspectives on the cult of feminine nurturance, although differing from those of Dickens and Thackeray, emerge from apparent intellectual and cultural similarities.[17] Finally, D. H. Lawrence, the one twentieth-century author discussed here, continues the moral didacticism and reformist intentions that characterize all the writers who precede him in the pages of this book. Like them, he most commonly expresses his sense of social and individual health or malaise through his presentation of the romantic—and in his case often specifically sexual—connections between his characters.

The mention of sexuality points to a distinctive feature about this book. Some discussion of the subject is inevitable in a work about gender and body, but I focus on other bodily appetites and functions, putting them in the context of contemporary ideas and norms. A variety of didactic and editorial writings from authors as diverse as Jean-Jacques Rousseau and anonymous contributors to Victorian periodicals helps provide a framework in which the novelists' fictional representations of the body can be understood better.

My abiding concern is to do justice to the number of variations and the multiplicity of meanings that representations of the body afford. The same facts of female physiology have resulted in widely different deductions as to women's "natural" spheres of power, from Victorian doctors' insistence that women's reproductive functions unfitted them for public life to Love and Shanklin's belief that the same functions justify women's control of social arrangements and structure.[18] Thus although I am tracing certain themes from Richardson to Lawrence, I am emphatically concerned with ambiguities, differentiations, fusions, and nuances at all levels. To begin with, I discuss the novels in relation to the apparent consensus of overtly didactic materials such as conduct books, newspaper "editorials," and sermons: if gender and class expectations seem simple and absolute there, they quickly become far less so when authors incorporate and challenge them and otherwise react to them in fiction. Then, authors' apparent meaning for the body can become more complicated as well when juxtaposed with peers' views, whether oppositional or not. This book therefore pairs some of its primary authors, then re-pairs them with different emphasis. It uses subsidiary figures to contextualize the others, complicating as well as clarifying, for instance, Richardson's views through Fielding, Lawrence's through Gissing. Finally, this book is alert to the conflicting schemes possibly at work within an individual text, which result in cross-pollination that may be either fruitful or frustrating, depending upon the skill of the author and the desires of the reader.

To illustrate the polyphony possible even in the oeuvre of one author, the first chapter of this book examines the novels of Samuel Richardson from three distinct though overlapping perspectives, provided by contemporary theories of sensibility, maternity, and what we now call anorexia. This chapter is concerned with exploring the tension between Richardson's exaltation of his compelling heroines and his overt allegiance to gender hierarchy. While he clearly is fascinated with the splendor of feminine virtue, he just as clearly is disturbed by the power with which it theoretically *should* invest women. Only by using bodily differences as a rationale for distinct duties and virtues for men and women can Richardson avoid the subversive implications of his own heroine worship.

The second chapter, the only other devoted to a single author, examines Frances Burney's novels as a response to and corrective of conduct-book ideas about feminine delicacy. Conduct books typically attributed to the modest woman the ability to repel masculine aggression and indecency through the dignity of her presence. Developing the theory of differing physical strength between the sexes into one of complementary roles, they asserted that masculine strength enabled men to defend modest women, while feminine delicacy impelled that defense as a tribute to women's charms. Burney demolishes both the reliance on the forceful male body as an instrument of defense and the belief in the easy interpretability of feminine "presence." She shows that the physical manifestations of feeling typically characterized as feminine—blushes, tears, heart palpitations, trembling limbs, and even swooning—are as easily subject to misreading by rakes as they are to accurate interpretation by decent men. Indeed the ability—a rare one—to read the meanings of physical presence correctly proves invaluable for real communication. Modesty, presented by conduct books of the time as a specifically female attribute, turns out to be an essential characteristic for all parties engaged in communication, since too strong a confidence in the body's self-evident rights and powers prevents any recognition of the bodily, emotional, or social rights and powers of others. Burney thereby demolishes the differences between male and female virtue that Richardson struggled to maintain.

The third and fourth chapters move into the Victorian period with an examination of women's relations to food first in novels by Charles Dickens and William Makepeace Thackeray and then in Elizabeth Gaskell's *Cranford* and Charlotte Brontë's *Villette*. Although critics from Sandra Gilbert and Susan Gubar to Bram Djikstra to Helena Michie have suggested that the Victorians idealized female anorexia, the third chapter argues that the sickly female body was not a nineteenth-century object of reverence. Dickens and Thackeray applaud the woman who feeds others, not the one who starves herself, and their strongest condemnation falls upon the woman who denies and frustrates (usually male) appetites. Eating, which Helena Michie among others equates with sexual activity, seems more important here as a metonymy for general nurture, and thus it is not female sexuality that inspires horror so much as female cruelty.

Whereas Dickens and Thackeray dramatize women's relations to food as a way to show that women *should* nourish the men in their lives (yet often fail to do so), Gaskell and Brontë use food imagery in their novels about spinsters to help explain the nourishment that women themselves need. Whereas Dickens and Thackeray imagine a feminine bounty that women could offer men if only they would, Gaskell and Brontë perceive no such plentitude built into the feminine spirit. Rather, they realistically question the ability of women to satisfy even themselves and frankly acknowledge the material as well as emotional importance of men to women's lives. The result is to demystify femaleness, which emerges as neither demonic nor angelic but human in its limitations as well as its potential.

As chapters 3 and 4 question the current critical notion that the Victorians admired female anorexia, chapter 5 opposes the accompanying belief that the Victorians idealized female debility generally by examining the issue of strength and service in women's domestic work. Marriage, of course, was the standard Victorian "career" for women. The importance of "service" as an aspect of marriage meant that a debility that potentially interfered with service was actually the target of moral reproach. The condemnation of female invalidism and exaltation of service form the focus of the fifth chapter, which also examines the related issue of the need to differentiate the lady who kept a home from the female domestic who worked there. The treatment of the body provided a means of distinction: the servant's body typically was constructed as comic, sometimes neuter or ambiguously gendered; the lady's was always refined, enhanced by sensibility. Moreover, members of the working classes undergo further "desexing" through the corollary imposition of loyalty to the employer that diverted them from standard roles of patriarch, wife, and dependent child. Instead many loyal servants figure as semifamilial appendages of the class above them, neither encouraged nor able to mirror the arrangement of gender roles accepted by their "superiors."

Richardson's first novel, *Pamela,* the earliest work included, reappears in the final chapter, where it is paired with D. H. Lawrence's *Lady Chatterley's Lover,* the only twentieth-century novel discussed here. While the first chapter scrutinizes primarily Richardson's gender constructions, the final chapter broadens the perspective to consider the interplay of gender and class and to speculate on the significance of the two authors' differing treatments of those two categories. This chapter also balances the preceding one by continuing the examination of tension between gender and class roles. Here we see an interesting historical shift from Richardson to Lawrence in their parallel cross-class romances. It is far more important for Richardson to prove that his servant heroine Pamela is physically a "lady" than to establish that she is a "woman." Her gender identity is never under debate, even as she battles sexual experience; her ability to become a recognizable member of the upper classes, however, is crucial to her story. By the time of Lawrence's Lady Chatterley these priorities, as well as the sex of the servant figure, have been reversed; it is insignificant whether Constance is a lady (or Lady), but it is vital that she be a woman—for physical femaleness (or maleness) is no longer sufficient to prove sexual selfhood. As Constance discovers her womanhood, she becomes the servant of her servant, since to be a woman, for Lawrence, is to serve a man. For men, on other hand, virility, rather than gentility, now signals the possession of leadership qualities. Richardson's Mr. B must learn to chasten his sexuality before he is fit to exercise the political power his position offers him. Lawrence's Mellors, however, demonstrates his fitness to lead (in contrast to the physically impotent and politically regressive Sir Clifford) through his masculinity—figured with almost embarrassing directness through his capacity for erection.

The conclusion to this book suggests that the emergence of a new idea of feminine "virtue" as essentially maternal is intertwined with the evolving form of the novel. The result is a tendency toward literary idealization of "types"— both domestic women and worthy members of the working class—not previously the subjects of much sentimentality. Both "good" women and the "good" working class embody the idea of service to others, yet the form of their service precludes its mutuality: the devotion that should motivate them should also prevent them from expecting or desiring reciprocity. Thus a moral code is established whereby it is both natural and good for some to offer service and for others to accept it.

This book provides a new perspectives to the recent proliferation of scholarship on the body. To mention only a few instances, Thomas Laqueur's *Making Sex* provides a theoretical precedent in examining ideas about the body as social constructions but does so without reference to literature. Likewise Ornella Moscucci, in *The Science of Woman,*[19] gives an historical overview of the nineteenth-century medical profession's views on gender but without a literary component. Both Margaret Homans's *Bearing the Word* and Peter Gay's multivolume *The Bourgeois Experience: Victoria to Freud* [20] are psychoanalytic—the former Lacanian, the latter strictly Freudian—while my study concentrates on the cultural and social rather than the psychological. Helena Michie in *The Flesh Made Word* explores some similar territory but privileges sexuality as the body's most important meaning. Elaine Showalter's *Sexual Anarchy* [21] concentrates exclusively on the fin de siècle, while this book covers other periods as well. In *The Servant's Hand* Bruce Robbins examines servants in British fiction but without serious consideration of gender, which also holds for Peter Keating in *The Working Classes in Victorian Fiction,*[22] a work that also confines itself to a handful of turn-of-the-century writers.

Although this book clearly is indebted to Michel Foucault's work on representation as a form of power and to Nancy Armstrong's *Desire and Domestic Fiction,* one of the most interesting Foucauldian studies of gender in literature, it differs from both by being grounded in an acceptance of a reality—social and otherwise—prior to representation. As a result, it treats literary works as showing ways in which social practices are reflected, challenged, endorsed, or questioned, and not as exclusively determining those social practices.

The structure of this book, with themes that run throughout but receive varying emphases at different points, mirrors its argument: that there is a need for greater specificity and recognition of individual variation in the claims we make about bodies and fictional representations of them. While not ignoring the extent to which authors share the misogyny and/or classism of their times, we can also see when their writings expose the oppressiveness of certain class and gender expectations. Discerning the implications of those expectations may also lead us to reexamine our own ideas about the behaviors and affects that arise "naturally" from the bodies we inhabit.

1 | Sentimental Authority
The Female Body in the Novels of
Samuel Richardson

RECENTLY THE EIGHTEENTH CENTURY has received much attention as an exceptionally significant moment in the formation of modern ideas of gender. According to most current historical accounts, it was during this period that the doctrine of separate spheres for the two sexes began to emerge. Companionate marriage became a new ideal,[1] and motherhood achieved an unprecedented status. At this time, according to Nancy Armstrong, the "domestic woman" rose to ascendancy, and, according to Thomas Laqueur, there was a new "scientific" belief in the incommensurability of the sexes: in men and women being complementary and different rather than in women being inferior versions of men.[2]

Two of the most striking cultural phenomena of this century were the increased glorification of maternity and the rising cult of sensibility. Although influencing each other, the two remained separate in many ways, yet both had a dramatic impact on ideas about women and womanhood. Both, for example, broke with previous theories that female nature was insatiably sexual (theories that of course remained in operation alongside new ideas of female purity). Proponents of both claimed to respect and appreciate women. And finally, both have come under intense scrutiny today for their possibly oppressive implications. Sensibility, in particular, has been linked with idealizations of female debility and death and of a delicate, attenuated body type that strikes modern observers as more anorexic than spiritual.

This chapter examines the female body in Richardson's novels within three different contexts—the changing visions of maternity (with particular reference to breast-feeding), the contemporary attitudes toward sensibility, and the different possible meanings of anorexia—and touches upon a range of issues that succeeding chapters will explore further. The major point is the dazzling multiplicity of not only interpretations of the body but differing implications for apparently similar interpretations. The ambiguous interplay of the oppressive and the liberatory within a single schema, the relationship between socially imposed constraints and socially acceptable strategies for alleviating those constraints, even the sense of empowerment that can be attainable through apparently perverse modes of self-deprivation: all of these suggest the complexity of both social and physical experience. That complexity is my focus here.

MATERNITY AND BREAST-FEEDING

The idea of motherhood as spiritually exalted is perhaps the most important aspect of the eighteenth-century's intensified emphasis on maternity. Maternity, unlike sensibility, is a specifically female bodily capacity.[3] The glorification of maternity therefore appears to exalt the female body by privileging powers that are peculiarly its own. But while the idealization of maternity allows female physicality, this happens only in servitude: the healthy female body is desirable for what it can do for others, not for the pleasure and power it gives to its occupant. The maternal body, when used—as it often has been—to represent Charity allegorically, becomes the type of the self-sacrificing nurturer.[4]

The psychological dimensions that the eighteenth-century ideology of motherhood attributed to the physical experiences of maternity further intensified the preexistent sense of immutable psychological differences between men and women.[5] For example, the glorification of breast-feeding as one particularly piquant aspect of maternity accentuated the physical differences between male and female as an assumed basis for emotional differences. Women's powers of physical nurturance became a reason for attributing to women a "natural" capacity for psychological nurturance. The descriptive quickly can become prescriptive, however. The woman who fails to "nurture" is deemed unnatural as well as immoral.[6]

The idea that maternal feeling is an essential attribute of the female assumes a universal female nature engendered by the female body. As Elisabeth Badinter observes, "Because reproduction is a natural function, surely—or so it has been assumed—the biological and physiological fact of pregnancy must carry with it a corresponding battery of predetermined maternal attitudes and patterns of behavior" (xx). This concept of a universal female character concentrates attention on women's gender rather than their class or other variable social markers. The eighteenth-century debate on breast-feeding thus was part of the shift, traced by Nancy Armstrong, from privileging "the aristocratic woman" to exalting "the new [female] domestic ideal" (113). The shift, of course, was slow, gradual, and perhaps as much rhetorical as behavioral. In earlier centuries suckling was a class-specific activity: "throughout the period [1570–1720] and beyond it those rich women who breastfed their infants remained rare examples."[7] During Samuel Richardson's lifetime (1689–1761), notes Lawrence Stone, breast-feeding among the upper classes was rare.[8] To promote breast-feeding as a universal female activity helped remove women from the "political terms" within which "the male is . . . defined" (Armstrong 113). Indeed, Nancy Armstrong sees the conduct-book instructions to breast-feed as a way in which such books inculcated a new model of internalized "personal" morality.[9]

In addition to emphasizing women's private identity, however, the new domestic ideology merged two roles—those of wife and mother—that potentially could conflict. This perceived conflict, in fact, was responsible for many of the ambiguities in the contemporary debate over breast-feeding. Doctors and moralists insisted that the health and well-being of the child required maternal feeding. This concern went beyond medical advice into the realm of moral imperatives. The Anglican divine Jeremy Taylor argued that "to divorce the infant from the mother, the object from the affection, [is to] cut off the opportunities and occasions of [women's] charity or piety."[10] Archbishop of Canterbury John Tillotson included maternal suckling among those natural duties "of a more necessary and indispensable obligation than any positive precept of revealed religion."[11] Since breast-feeding mothers were expected to abstain from sexual activity, however, the practice went against the wishes of husbands who feared interference with their sexual interests (Lawrence Stone 270). In this conflict the needs of the child were pitted against the desires of the father and generally speaking, the father's wishes received first consideration. "[B]elieving . . . that the conjugal debt had priority above the welfare of the infant, the church had condoned wet-nursing" (McLaren 27). Even John Tillotson allowed that "the interposition of the father's authority" was sufficient "excuse" from what he elsewhere called women's "natural duty" (141).

As contradictory as these differing statements might appear, they consistently emphasize the importance of familial over class roles and posit a near antagonism between father and child. A woman should not worry about lowering her status by breast-feeding, but she could legitimately fear alienating her husband's affections. Of course, such alienation would arise in this situation only because the husband resents what he perceives as his wife favoring his children over him. Nowadays such resentment (even if it continues to be felt by some men) would be considered inappropriate at best. The idea that not only maternal love but maternal instinct are crucial components of feminine identity and indispensable attributes of a good wife has been widely held at least since the nineteenth century. In earlier centuries the assumption seems to have been that the duties of wife and mother are not always perfectly compatible, and in the ensuing conflict those of wife should predominate. Wife and mother can fully merge only when the husband and father perceives maternal devotion as an expression of spousal love. As a reminder that the two passions have not always appeared complementary, one might consider Chaucer's Griselda, whose submission to her husband extends to her acquiescing in his apparent slaughter of their children. Although Chaucer later shows Griselda to have mourned the children's supposed deaths in secret, her exemplary obedience precludes any attempt to thwart her husband's seemingly murderous intentions.[12] It is probably impossible to determine the reason for this historical shift, but Paula Marantz Cohen offers one intriguing hypothesis when she suggests that "the stabilization of the nuclear family, once romantic love had dissipated, could be effected by means of the couple's triangulation of their child."[13] Although Cohen uses "triangulation" to describe a specific process of concealing conflict between husband and wife by focusing their joint attention upon their child, her insight has broader applications. "Romantic love," as Cohen remarks, is a notably "tenuous tie" (19) and also a notoriously hard one to measure. Chaucer's Walter is content to monitor his wife's behavior; he exacts extravagant displays of obedience, but he ignores her inner life. Companionate marriage, however, differs from previous versions of matrimony precisely by highlighting the emotions of the spouses. An enlightened eighteenth-century husband at least theoretically would want his wife's affection as well as her obedience; villains from Fielding's Blifil to Richardson's Solmes show their baseness because they do not care whether the women they wish to marry love them or not. Yet no matter how strong the insistence on the desirability of marital love, commentators from the eighteenth through the twentieth centuries agree that the ardors of courtship cannot last. A wife must not expect her husband to remain her lover, and she certainly must not continue to play the sought-after mistress. Yet since marriage is more than ever the center of a woman's emotional as well as practical life, how can she demonstrate her continuing commitment to the amorphous, elusive yet crucial "love" that is supposed to inspire it? Maternal devotion allows a woman to remain an icon of love even as the glamour of romance steadily fades. By accepting this devotion as a result and a reflection of wifely love, both spouses—and society at large—can present the marriage as adhering to norms of marital as well as parental affection.[14] Parenthood comes to seem inevitable and necessary for not only the transmission of property and the preservation of bloodlines but the consummation of the personal relationship between spouses. One need only think of the couples who still have children in an effort to salvage a disintegrating marriage or of the incomprehension and occasional condemnation that greet couples who choose to remain childless in order to realize that the belief that marriage requires parenthood to be emotionally and even morally complete is very strong indeed.

The perception of breast-feeding, then, implies larger attitudes toward women's roles as mother and as wife and the way in which those roles fit into the overall family structure. The more strongly women are identified as not merely household managers and home economists but as the "hearts" of the homes over which they preside and the more their housekeeping functions are gauged in spiritual as well as practical terms, the more important it will be for them to display child- as well as mate-nurturing capacities. Motherhood comes to assume affective as well as practical responsibilities for women beyond those expected of men. As Toni Bowers tellingly points out, "From [Richard] Allestre on, conduct writers who treated motherhood started from the assumption that virtuous mothers naturally love their children more than do equally virtuous fathers."[15] This assumption illustrates women's new special status as the "carriers" of emotions and values that both men and women agree enrich life although men refuse responsibility for them. As the loci and embodiment of the softer affections, women have a sentimental stature that nonetheless does not extend to—and might even prohibit—political or economic power.[16] Samuel Richardson's novels are often cited as paradigms of the new perception of the "domestic woman" as sentimental icon,[17] and so to study the evolution of his treatment of breast-feeding from *Pamela II* to *Sir Charles Grandison*[18] is especially interesting. Richardson's glorification of female affective power remains consistent, but the terms and presentation of that glorification change subtly over the decades between the two books.[19]

We see the initial tension between the roles of wife and mother in the second volume of Samuel Richardson's *Pamela,* in which Mr. B refuses Pamela permission to breast-feed.[20] To Mr. B such an act is incompatible with "'personal graces.'"[21] He objects to "'the carelessness into which [he has] seen very nice ladies sink, when they became nurses'" (2:233). Here the physical processes of motherhood, not those of sexuality, become a degradation. They are a contamination, surprisingly enough in modern eyes, because they foreground a woman's role as mother rather than as wife. Mr. B's arguments make it abundantly clear that the devoted mother is perforce a negligent, even undutiful, wife. For Mr. B, his child is his rival, competing with him for Pamela's company and consideration. If Pamela breast-feeds, Mr. B says, she "'must take with her her infant and her nursery-maid wherever she goes; and I shall either have very fine company (shall I not?) or be obliged to deny myself yours'" (2:234–35). Thus, either the husband or the child, but not both, can take pleasure in the woman's presence. At night the suckling infant will invade the conjugal bed and demand an act that will disfigure Pamela's "'easy, genteel form,'" in which Mr. B takes "'laudable, and . . . honest pleasure'" (2:233). Yet the use to which Mr. B puts his undisturbed bed manifests itself in the perpetual distension of Pamela's form by pregnancy. The difference between Pamela's swelling belly and her swelling, milk-laden breasts is apparently that one implies the husband's use of the woman's body, the other the child's use. That pregnancy is perhaps the most obvious sign of sexual activity (so much so that even today some pregnant women report embarrassment over this evidence supplied by their gestating bodies)[22] is not a source of discomfort for either Pamela, modest though she is, or her husband. Marital sexuality apparently is an affirmation of proper role fulfillment for both husband and wife. A wife's subsequent physical involvement with her child, however, is not so clear-cut an affirmation. To be identified as a mother rather than as a wife is—paradoxically enough in modern terms—to reject ideal and ideally submissive femininity.

Mr. B's distaste for breast-feeding does not mean that he perceives it as *merely* physical, despite his expressions of disgust. Instead, conflating the physical with the psychological, Mr. B sees a threat to his emotional as well as physical primacy in his wife's life should she devote her body to anyone other than himself, even nonsexually. "'When I am at home,'" Mr. B pronounces, "'even a son and heir, so jealous am I of your affections, shall not be my rival'" in Pamela's "'sole attention'" (2:234). Mr. B here makes what is still a standard equation between a woman's bodily processes and her emotional life: the breast-feeding woman is ipso facto a woman attentive and devoted to her child. To Mr. B, however, this is an ominous rather than an idyllic thought. Maternal nursing of an infant is incompatible with wifely nurturing of a husband. Earlier, Mr. B praised the "'innocent pleasures that [he] now hourly taste[s]'" through contact with Pamela's virtue (2:2). Now, angry that Pamela persists in wanting to suckle her child, Mr. B warns her not to "'*wean* me from that love *to* you, and admiration *of* you, which hitherto has been rather increasing than otherwise as your merit, and regard for me have increased'" (2:235; Richardson's emphasis).

Pamela's role as mother gains steadily in importance and elevation through the remainder of the volume but does so partly by assuming a new form. From expressing the wish to provide her child's physical sustenance, Pamela voices suspicions about that sustenance itself. It is "the greatest mischief" when a nurse "cram[s] and stuff[s] [a baby's] little bowels, till ready to burst." This is antinourishment: the nurse wakes a child from "nourishing sleep" and forces upon it a "breast" that turns "its nutriment . . . to repletion, and bad humours!" (2:382). In its worst form such overly physical nursing is an actual threat. Pamela's last lament over Mr. B's veto of her suckling comes when her eldest son falls ill with smallpox. She suspects that "the nurse's constitution is too hale and rich for the dear baby" (2:340) and thus may have rendered him susceptible to disease. Far from being a nurturer, the suckling woman imposes her own gross physicality upon the infant in a potentially destructive manner. During her son's illness Pamela wishes to "nurse" the boy in another sense, but

Mr. B keeps her from prolonged contact with the child (2.340–42). As with Mr. B's earlier prohibition of her breast-feeding, Pamela mourns yet accepts her husband's dictates. This second removal of Pamela from physical contact with her children, however, does not slow the novel's increasing emphasis on her role as mother. Rather, Richardson exalts Pamela's maternity while suggesting that the true value of "mothering" lies in its nonphysical dimensions. Neither prenatal gestation nor physical caretaking matters compared to the mother's role in the child's socialization. This socialization, moreover, is a process in which the mother can engage without displeasing her husband and even with his active consent and endorsement. Whereas Pamela's physical involvement with her children had seemed a betrayal to Mr. B, her educational involvement with them strikes him as an expression of fealty. So it should, for her role as instructor derives from his authority and ideas.

Pamela's mentorship of her children and other young people is paradoxical, for it both establishes and limits her power. Pamela as mother becomes the supreme figure within the latter half of the novel, yet her authority as mother depends upon her fitting smoothly into place as an exemplary wife. Mr. B grants her maternal authority (and the conditions for that authority), even while her subsequent familial predominance gives her an emotional luster that he lacks. She is the focus of intense idealization and sentimental rhetoric as well as the guardian of social norms and standards, but only so long as she continually "earns" her stature by pleasing the husband who is both her worshiper and her monitor. Mr. B makes his own priorities for his wife clear: his "'chief delight in [Pamela] is for the beauties of [her] mind'" (2:233) and he expects her to be his "'instructress'" in "'virtue and piety'" just as she is his "'scholar'" in "'French and Latin'" (2:233–34). Likewise, even when denying Pamela the physical nurturance of her children, Mr. B wishes her to practice "'direction and superintendence'" of the nursery (2:234).[23] These more intellectual and abstract forms of mothering apparently are more dignified and therefore more appropriate forms of child care for his wife. Such mothering, however, leaves noticeable room for masculine intervention. After all, Mr. B instructs Pamela (2:235, 422), supplies her with her reading materials (2:378), and later directs her to record her own responses to one of these readings, Locke's *Treatise on Education*. She does so in a book with one blank page for each one she has written, the blanks being reserved for Mr. B's "alterations and corrections" of her tentative opinions (2:240).[24]

When she believes that Mr. B's involvement with another woman may threaten her marriage, Pamela pleads for the "'indulgence'" (2:320) of being allowed to keep Mr. B's children by vowing that she will "'digest'" "'all the books of education'" (2:320). The reader sees Mr. B's understanding of family roles shift as he now recognizes Pamela's desire for his children as an expression of her concern for him. Even more important, he recognizes her desire to pray for him and to cherish him although physically separated from him as an expression of utmost devotion. Paradoxically, this former rake, who seduced Sally Godfrey by insisting that only her sexual submission to him would prove her love, is deeply moved by his perception of Pamela's love for him as maternal-like in its nurturing—but nonphysically nurturing!—qualities. Pamela suggests that she will play for him in her anticipated role of cast-off wife the role he assigns her to play with his children: she will seek to safeguard his social and spiritual future through her own words (prayers) and example (2:319). Note the subtle change in power dynamics, however: although Pamela's efforts are on behalf of a marriage system oppressive to women, she earns stature by them. Once the marriage has been reestablished, Pamela's voice dominates. We are given her ruminations in a series of interpolated texts: the response to Locke that she writes at Mr. B's request, an exemplary story that she unfolds for an audience of young ladies, and two didactic "nursery tales" representative of those by which she teaches Mr. B's children.

Ironically in view of Mr. B's first strictures, Pamela increasingly emerges as a mother rather than a wife. She is instructor in virtue for her children, the role Mr. B originally had assigned her to play with him. Even Pamela's precepts for wifely duty highlight her maternal role, since they take the form of admonitions to young females over whom she presides as a mother figure. In a familiar irony, however, Pamela, although female, can speak authoritatively as long as she speaks of the need for general female submission. Earlier Mr. B had dictated a series of marital instructions designed to reinforce Pamela's "humility . . . [and] submission" as wife and his own "pride" as husband (2:44). Pamela continues the same gender division of attributes when she identifies her son's self-assertive "spirit" with his resemblance to "papa" and the child's tears of self-reproachful submission with his resemblance to "mamma" (2:412). Yet she is now the one decreeing the need for another's submission, which he (a male, albeit a young and relatively powerless one) must make to her. Declaring that only the father should order corporal punishment for his children, Pamela protests that no child could "dispute his authority to punish, from whom he receives and expects all the good things of his life" (2:410). But by making this matter the subject of her writing, Pamela neatly inserts herself into the topmost position of this punitive hierarchy: she judges who can judge the child's need for punishment. This is just one of the contradictions within the supposedly ideal family dynamic. The child, whether male or female, must display qualities of deference, humility, and submissiveness, which in adult life economically and socially privileged males at least are expected to shed. Thus Mr. B's sons must endure the subordination of childhood but can grow into the powerful role that their father models for them. Daughters, on the other hand, must move from the "true dignity" of maidenhood to the "state of humiliation" that is women's "married state" (2:476). Nonetheless the domestic power of the mother means that males and females alike begin their lives under a woman's authority, an authority that perhaps recompenses the mother for her subservience as a wife.

Although not a breast-feeding mother, Pamela is a powerful maternal figure nonetheless, one who legitimately focuses her attention upon the family's children. Her educational doctrines and moral nursery tales assume the textual importance that earlier had belonged to the premarital and marital negotiations between her and Mr. B. Her storytelling leads to her own apotheosis as Prudentia, the incarnation of feminine virtue. Miss Goodwin, Pamela's enthusiastic listener, identifies her with the heroine of the tale Pamela has just been telling, thus acknowledging not only her goodness but her authority to define and claim that goodness. Pamela's instructional role undercuts the humility that she posits as a prerequisite for the ideal feminine character.

As the maternal role allows Pamela a self-assertiveness that might seem at odds with sentimental femininity, her wifely role contains its own ambiguities. The very qualities—sweetness, complaisance, consideration—that elevate her as a wife to a place of moral authority cannot and should not be emulated by socially powerful males. She must represent certain qualities for her husband's admiration but plainly not for his imitation. Mr. B's instructions to Pamela rely on her virtues' actually indulging and facilitating his vices or—to be more precise—his displays of moodiness, irascibility, and petty injustice that would be vices if exhibited by a woman.

Where does one draw the line, however, between feminine meekness before masculine faultiness and feminine complicity in those faults? Richardson constantly struggles with the dilemma of the way his supremely virtuous heroines can properly subordinate themselves to men who are their moral inferiors. Under this weight the latter half of *Pamela* collapses: the novel's heroine must sink into adoration of the man she previously had despised and feared. Pamela excuses her devoutness before Mr. B on the grounds that his condescension in marrying a social inferior amply compensates for his earlier immorality. She thus endows him with moral as well as practical authority, but generations of critics and readers have been uneasy with this reversal of her original judgments. *Clarissa* avoids the difficulties posed by a union in which the wife overshadows the husband only by sidestepping the standard love plot: Clarissa can't get married because she must (according to gender hierarchy) marry her superior and no man in the book qualifies. In a similar context Henry Fielding has no special qualms about matching his angelic Amelia with the comparatively negligible Booth, but it is crucial for his purposes that Amelia never recognizes her own superiority and that Booth accepts a perfect wife as his due. Richardson, with a keener insight into human instincts toward self-torture, shows that even Lovelace, usually armored in arrogance, writhes at the thought of marrying a woman who would have the right to look down upon him (2:415–16). For Lovelace, that a virtuous woman would obey even a husband who is beneath her is not sufficient; she should be incapable of perceiving her husband as anything but a god. He wants not forbearance and duty but adoration.[25]

Throughout *Clarissa* Lovelace is at least as interested in controlling Clarissa's mind and emotions as he is in possessing her body. He drugs and rapes her not so much for orgasmic satisfaction but in the belief that physical subjugation will transform her into the creature of his sexual daydreams—erotic and thereby contaminated—but also nurturing in the fashion of the dawning maternal stereotype. This creature is doubly a source of nourishment, of milk for Lovelace's male children and of emotional fodder for his own voracious ego. Thus Lovelace imagines Clarissa with

> a twin Lovelace at each charming breast, drawing from it his first sustenance; the pious task, for physical reasons, continued for one month and no more!
>
> I now, methinks, behold this most charming of women in this sweet office: her conscious eye now dropped on one, now on the other, with a sigh of maternal tenderness; and then raised up to my delighted eye, full of wishes, for the sake of the pretty varlets, and for her own sake, that I would deign to legitimate; that I would condescend to put on the nuptial fetters. (2:477)

The same vision that had disgusted Mr. B delights Lovelace because the same bodily function that had signified Pamela's rebellion to Mr. B represents to Lovelace Clarissa's emotional dependence and sexual servitude. Lovelace's solipsism makes him unable to distinguish his imagined sons from himself, so that their suckling becomes his possession of Clarissa's body. This fantasy directly follows an encounter in which Lovelace, uncovering Clarissa's bosom, has attempted to "[press] with [his] burning lips the charmingest breast that ever [his] ravished eyes beheld" (2:476). The infantile feeding on Clarissa's milk represents another version of his own sexual appetite for Clarissa's body, and both types of feeding have as their ultimate target what Lovelace defines as Clarissa's culpable "pride."[26] Incensed that Clarissa has rebuffed his mouthing of her breasts, Lovelace asks, "[O]ught not that pride to be punished?" (2:477). His immediate reference is to his own plans to deflower her, but breast-feeding here also is punitive. This association of both sexual intercourse and suckling with women's degradation is inevitable since Lovelace treats sexual experience as a humiliation of women and yet believes that almost every physical experience they have is sexual in some way.[27] Most crucial of all, he believes that sufficient sexual humiliation will somehow bring out the submissiveness that to him should be the essence of womanhood.

In the framework of maternal ideology Lovelace's crime is not so much the oppressiveness as the salaciousness of his fantasy. Lovelace eroticizes rather than sentimentalizes the figure of the mother: he rejoices in the idea of feminine nurture while stripping it of its moral trappings. He would gladly see as mother a woman whose sexual fall has shown her unfit to mother in the monitory sense.

Nor is this the only way in which Lovelace twists the ideal of maternal nurture. In *Pamela* Mr. B's cast-off mistress, Sally Godfrey, renounces her child, leaving her for Mr. B's eventual wife to adopt and to raise. Pamela eagerly assumes this responsibility, and her exemplary fulfillment of it underscores the idea that readiness for maternity is a touchstone of female character. Sally's premarital pregnancy, although a sign of physical femaleness, proves her inferiority to purer women; she must therefore relinquish the full feminine role to another. The biological mother in this equation is inferior to the spiritual mother, whose words and example are responsible for the child's ultimate character. Cruel though this pattern might seem to those who sympathize with Sally Godfrey, it fits neatly into the familial standards that Richardson and others of his time struggle to consolidate.[28] Lovelace, on the other hand, obscenely parodies this ideal of spiritual nurture when he imagines Clarissa offering up her maidservants for his sexual satisfaction and then cherishing the resulting children as her own (2:416). In this scenario the ideal wife's complicity in her husband's philandering extends to procuring for him. Lovelace's feminine ideal is terrifyingly close to more conventional images of the unconditionally loving woman, but his version exists outside the elaborate rhetorical structures that sanctify such self-abnegation. In the hierarchical framework of the time the wife's devotion to her husband, like the child's obedience to a father, replicates the citizen's submission to the monarch and the Christian's surrender to God. The familial, social, and religious neatly coincide, so that the good wife will be good in all other ways as well.[29] Lovelace, however, imagines a feminine sexual subservience so total that it replaces both social norms and religious piety. His wife, he decrees, must violate the family sanctity by willingly turning the home into a harem and must "forgo even her *superior* [i.e. religious] *duties*" for him (2:416; Richardson's emphasis).

Richardson himself was distressed by the idea of a woman so loving that she ignores her mate's moral state, and his presentation of Lovelace's fantasy is clearly disapproving.[30] Yet Richardson's own subscription to a hierarchical ideology creates an impossible bind: marital norms decree that a wife must be inferior to her husband and therefore incapable of judging him. The idealization of women, on the other hand, makes them moral authorities who should be superior to their husbands. One way out is to imagine a woman so loving that she refuses to judge an erring husband even though she could. But anyone committed to extra- as well as intrafamilial moral standards (as Richardson surely was) cannot find this solution totally satisfying.[31] Indeed Richardson's willingness to imagine women judging the men in their lives may be one of his most radical qualities. It distinguishes him from, say, Dickens, who appears to cherish the unconditionally loving woman as Richardson does not. For Richardson the woman who is indifferent to her lover's or husband's moral standards ultimately will prove to have no moral standards of her own.

No one would argue that Richardson advocates full gender equality. Rather he seems to dissent from Lovelace's vision not from distaste for female submission but from fear that a sexually based submission cannot be as benign as Lovelace imagines. After all, the "fallen" woman theoretically at least is outside the realm of normal social duties and rights: having "given herself" presumably for the sake of love, she must now rely on love to support her. Lovelace imagines this economically, socially, and emotionally precarious position as a guarantee of feminine good behavior: he describes a mistress's "intermingled smiles, and tears, and caresses" as reinforcement of her entreaties for "consideration . . . and . . . *constancy*" as "all the favor she then has to ask" (2:246; Richardson's emphasis). Richardson shows us, however, that removing the social structure for sexual unions does not necessarily lead to such agreeable consequences for men. Among its many threads *Clarissa* contains the cautionary narrative of the rake Belton's humiliation by the woman he purposely chose to "keep" rather than to marry. Shrewish and faithless, Belton's mistress Thomasine has no familial interests or social expectations to keep her concerned with Belton's well-being—only sexual love, and that proves disastrously insufficient.[32] Far from exercising a triumphantly phallic sway over his mistress, Belton sees himself cuckolded by a burly hostler whose physical masculinity obviously dwarfs his own. Belton loses whatever shred of patriarchal stature he might retain with the realization that even his supposed sons are really the hostler's (3:480–81). Having chosen to base his authority on sexual rather than social grounds, Belton loses authority altogether (4:93). Meanwhile, Thomasine's indifference to Belton's concerns and even to his life, born of her awareness that her interests are distinct from his, is a far cry from the sweetly solicitous behavior Lovelace imagines in a woman whose dependence he believes will ensure her humility and gratitude.

One of Richardson's most telling criticisms of Lovelace's libertine philosophy is Lovelace's consistent miscalculation of the effect of sexual experience upon women. While he fantasizes about seduced women transfigured into humble, rapturously adoring handmaids, his actual victims subsequently become not merely profligate but cruel. The worst crimes of the whores who populate Mrs. Sinclair's brothel are not sexual but sadistic: Sally, Polly, Dorcas, and others gloat over Clarissa's doom and are eager to procure equal suffering for Anna Howe if possible. Although they (like Lovelace's ideal wife) are eager to facilitate Lovelace's sexual excursions, their viciousness bears no resemblance to the wifely demureness in Lovelace's fantasy. It is painfully obvious even to Lovelace himself that rage against other women, not devotion to himself, motivates their collusion in his schemes.[33] Despite his own sadism Lovelace is shocked by theirs. He pinpoints cruelty as women's worst flaw (2:242) and makes it the excuse for his own abusive behavior, as when he recounts his sexual punishment of a "charming little savage" who had enjoyed her cat's sporting with a mouse (2:248). There is no indication that punishment reformed his victim. The sweet complaisance that consistently characterizes Lovelace's fantasy women finds no echo in the fallen women Richardson presents to us.

The whores, especially Mrs. Sinclair, who as the brothel's madam is already in a quasi-maternal position, in many ways exemplify the "bad mother," in both the messy Kristevan abjection of their bodies and their dominating tendencies.[34] The fear of their ridicule drives Lovelace on to Clarissa's ruin even when he is least inclined to attempt the rape. Mocking, scolding, prodding, they collectively embody the mother who paradoxically emasculates her son not by denying his sexuality but by directing it.[35] This ferociousness helps explain why they are denied the pathos that Richardson grants the humbled and exiled Sally Godfrey and in *Sir Charles Grandison* the meek Mrs. Oldham. Though both are sexually fallen, and though Mrs. Oldham continues in her sexual misbehavior until the death of her lover, these two women remain "femininely" mild, thus retaining the possibility of redemption. The metamorphosis of *Clarissa's* fallen women into furies, on the other hand, helps make the dying Belton, and even Lovelace to some extent, victim rather than exploiter of seduced women. The onus once again falls on women, who are culpable not merely in their sexual indiscretion but in the cruelty that then taints them. Men, on the other hand, although recklessly irresponsible in their seductions, ultimately experience sexuality as a form of subjugation to the female— Lovelacian fantasies to the contrary.

This fear of female cruelty explains why female sexuality, in Richardson and others, undermines rather than demonstrates a woman's femininity. It is paradoxical that sexual activity—which surely proves at least anatomical femaleness—should often be construed as "desexing" its practitioners. Yet the most sexually experienced and desirous of Richardson's women are also the least feminine in conventional terms: the least sweet-tempered, the least gentle. Belford in *Clarissa* warns that male rakes cast off not only sexual morality in their pursuit of pleasure but *all* moral standards, including those that involve any consideration for others. Pope's famous dictum that "Ev'ry woman is at heart a rake" resonates with more than erotic implications when rakedom necessarily implies cruelty as well as sensuality.

If Lovelace's fantasies of sexually induced submissiveness are invalid, however, Richardson himself in his last novel hints that other physiological processes may tame and subdue unruly female spirits. In *Sir Charles Grandison* the issue of "natural" feminine mildness emerges most strongly through the figure of Charlotte Grandison, who, though sexually impeccable and altogether endearing, fails to meet the standards of sensibility and tenderness that now inform the female ideal.[36] Charlotte must become a "true woman" before the novel can reach its happy conclusion, and guiding her toward femininity is an unexpectedly lengthy and arduous process. Neither paternal nor fraternal authority is sufficient for that end, nor are marriage and sexual experience. Even on her way to the altar Charlotte tells her bridegroom, "'You don't know what you are about, man. I expect to have all my way: Remember that's one of my articles before marriage.'"[37] After marriage she is, if anything, more outrageously disrespectful of her mate. To soften Charlotte into a model wife and woman, motherhood is necessary.

Breast-feeding is the crucial factor here.[38] Charlotte, unlike Pamela, decides to nurse without even consulting her husband, thus continuing to bypass patriarchal authority. Lord G, having surprised Charlotte in the act (7:402), immediately announces his new sense that his wife is now as accessible to him as she is to their infant. No longer overawed by the woman who previously had repelled physical encroachments, he "devour[s] first one of [her] hands, then the other" (7:403) with kisses. Rather than Mr. B's disgusted jealousy or Lovelace's sadistic sense of mastery, this husband responds with delight. Yet he resembles the other men in interpreting the physical function as defining the woman's entire self in terms of his desire for her. To him the physical act of breast-feeding in itself means that Charlotte is a loving and feminine (i.e. submissive and domestic) woman. Like one modern writer on suckling, he sees "the flowing of the milk [as] a wholistic bodily metaphor for maternal caritas"[39] through which the female body demonstrates that "the feminine principle" is "the giving of love."[40] For Lord G, "understanding" that Charlotte is a nurturing woman means negating her intimidating qualities. Vowing his gratitude, Lord G declares, "'Never, never more shall it be in your *power* to make me so far forget myself, as to be angry!'" (7:403; Richardson's emphasis).

His declaration is ambiguous, since Charlotte's ability to provoke through her sauciness has always been an essential part of her identity. A Charlotte without this power is a different woman, proof indeed that once married there is "no such person as Charlotte Grandison" (4:391). She acquiesces in Lord G's reading of her identity when she accepts his assumption that breast-feeding of itself banishes her "roguery" and reveals how "dear" Lord G is to her (7:403–4). Her words will no longer matter: "'every thing [she] say[s] . . . will [Lord G] take for a favour'" (7:403), now that her body has shown her to be a true domestic woman.

We see a progression in Richardson's novels from Pamela's showing herself to be a good wife by proving herself a good monitor of children to Charlotte demonstrating her wifeliness by physical nurturance of children. Whereas Pamela's maternal role is as much socializer as caretaker, physical caretaking itself demonstrates Charlotte's essential goodness. In a sense Richardson's handling of Charlotte's motherhood elides and naturalizes the process of mothering: suckling comes to represent far more complex psychological matters than the simple physical act would necessarily suggest. Ironically the "easier" process of proving good mothering qualities by breast-feeding rather than by having to write all those tedious nursery tales is also potentially at least as constricting. Although breast-feeding appears to allow for unmediated contact between mother and child, Lord G's response to it exemplifies the interpretation and intervention to which it is subject no less than more obviously social forms of mothering. Indeed, whereas Pamela's voice (albeit conveying patriarchal messages) has dominated in motherhood, Charlotte's words will no longer matter: her body says everything that she is. Results of such embodiment are to de-emphasize a woman's moral agency and to highlight her state of psychological and physiological normalcy (or abnormalcy). Rather than having to make the morally fraught choice between chastity and illicit sexuality that faces Pamela and Sally Godfrey, Charlotte must learn to yield to what she "really" is: a woman and thereby "naturally" a nurturing mother and loving wife. For her to be anything else would be as unnatural as evil.

SENSIBILITY

The perspective of sensibility provides a different view of the female body. If the glorification of maternity directed attention to women's nurturant capabilities, the idealization of sensibility pinpointed women's bodies as virtual theaters of the extreme emotions in which sensitive souls rejoiced. Sensibility offered a new way to regard the female body: not as a maelstrom of sexuality but as a conveyer of fine feeling and lofty sentiments.[41] Like much "difference feminism" today, sensibility validated and valorized an affective sensitivity and expressiveness traditionally linked with femininity. Through its reinterpretation of these affects, it allowed reinterpreting the possibilities of female character. It removed much of the stigma from stereotypically "female" ways of being and relating to others. In something of a twentieth-century parallel, psychologist Carol Gilligan has argued that her female subjects' preference for the personal over the abstract could indicate as strong a moral development as Jean Piaget's male-based model of growth away from relationship-based judgments into "universal" rules. Likewise, in the eighteenth century, proponents of sensibility argued that strong feeling, rather than preventing principled behavior, could actually facilitate it. Women's assumed emotionalism therefore need not interfere with their capacity to be responsible moral agents. Men themselves might expand and enhance their moral understanding by opening themselves to the experience of sensibility.[42]

For believers in sensibility, moreover, "the body appears to be the only genuine and unmediated source for understanding psychological processes. The body itself speaks—and language is inadequate" (Van Sant 116). The perceived link between sensibility and bodily manifestations of feeling also undercuts gender hierarchies by allowing women a socially approved mode of expression. In a time of prohibitions upon forceful speech from women, sensibility suggested that women's bodies could legitimately communicate a host of feelings that otherwise had no vent. By treating women's bodies as powerfully expressive, the cult of sensibility allowed that women had serious feelings to communicate. Sensibility took seriously what women had to say even when their bodies, rather than their mouths, did the "talking." [43] Sensibility thus may have helped ease women's situation even though the situation itself, enforced silence that is, was oppressive.

Moreover, sensibility potentially could blur gender divisions. It is no accident that one of the classic texts of sensibility is Henry MacKenzie's *The Man of Feeling* [1771], whose title character expires at the novel's end of precisely the same vague debility that has perturbed some critics in heroines of sensibility.[44] Even more important, considering the limitations upon women's verbal expressiveness, sensibility stipulated—indeed demanded—respect for the nonverbal expression of emotion and endorsed empathetic understanding of such expressions as a form of moral behavior. Neither embracing stoicism himself nor forcing it upon others, the male proponent of sensibility bound himself to regard even "irrational" feminine eruptions as worthy of attention and consideration. Even if blushing, trembling, and fainting remained stereotypically female forms of behavior, they now became ways for women to communicate with men and to claim consideration from them.[45] Although male spectatorship of female pain could be one aspect of sensibility, it also offered the potential for empathetic understanding between men and women.

Some critics nonetheless remain suspicious of sensibility's effects upon women. When Claudia Johnson writes that "[s]ensibility is the affective arena of an ideology oppressive to women," she locates its power specifically in its relation with the body. "Through sensibility," she continues, "the injunctions and priorities which organize women's lives and structure their sense of possibility are written into their own bodies, and thus internalized, concealed, and executed from within." [46] Johnson's charge casts a sinister light on one of sensibility's trademarks: its treatment, as Janet Todd explains, of "[t]he female body [as] . . . an organism peculiarly susceptible to influence . . . [and] to express[ing] emotions more sincerely and spontaneously" than male bodies.[47] At the same time Johnson's condemnation fits into a tradition of feminist distrust for sensibility, a distrust whose origins Mary Poovey documents in her examination of Mary Wollstonecraft's writings.[48]

Janet Todd's study of sensibility as a literary and cultural movement points out the ambiguity of this bafflingly polymorphous phenomenon: while "the major English radical writers" criticized sensibility for "reinforc[ing] the legitimacy of the ruling classes," "conservative opinion" attacked it as a manifestation of "Radicalism." [49] Given this confusion of meaning, the conservative *Anti-Jacobin Review* could select as "one of its exemplars [of the excesses] synonymous [with] sensibility" (Todd 138) the radical and feminist Mary Wollstonecraft, who fiercely denounced sensibility as a trap for women. The sensibility that Wollstonecraft sees as contributing to women's enslavement the *Anti-Jacobin* fears as giving women a "licence" incompatible with domestic subordination (Todd 138). The conservative critics of sensibility commonly oppose their bête noire with the alternative ideal of manliness. Only masculine traditions of reason, they argue, could guarantee goodness; sensibility, while "emasculating . . . men," unjustifiably exalts feminine emotion as a form of insight rather than condemning it as evidence of "weak heads" (Todd 134). To reestablish unemotive masculinity as a criterion for the highest virtue, such critics attempt to rewrite sensibility's physical manifestations of emotion as signs of the worst aspects of stereotypical femininity: hysterical, hypocritical, and always implicitly sexual.

Sensibility as a phenomenon is multifaceted enough to lend itself to oppressive as well as liberatory uses. Such flexibility of purpose, however, is far removed from Johnson's view of sensibility as inevitably one part of an oppressive monolithic whole. As an example of the multivalence of sensibility, consider the way in which Richardson's novels employ sensibility's emphasis on the expressive female body to validate "injunctions and priorities" opposed to patriarchal authority.[50] Johnson accurately points out that "men of feeling" weep over "pitiable objects" while "women of feeling weep over their own troubles" (169). Yet there are two caveats to be stated about Johnson's criticism. First, it is something even for women to have "troubles" of their own, distinct from their caretaking responsibilities for others, and to feel justified in the self-absorption necessary for concern on their own behalf. The claim that "sensibility" distracted women from their socially prescribed selfless involvement with others constituted one of the strongest conservative arguments against it. Second, by positing, indeed relying upon a sympathetic audience of interpreters, the cult of sensibility implicitly denied the "naturalness" of masculine unconcern for women's feelings. By assuming that others—including men—would react compassionately and empathetically to the suffering they witness, believers in sensibility implicitly worked to establish such humane reactions as the norm. One might adapt Johnson's observation of the way in which ideologies can be internalized to suggest that female devotees of sensibility in particular had good reasons for wanting men to internalize higher standards of sensitivity, compassion, and gentleness. Unfortunately such internalization does not always "take," and if men or people in general did not accept its claims, there was no way to ensure merciful—or even just—behavior on their part. Sade's *Justine* is perhaps the most infamous example of a text that pinpoints this problem: his hapless heroine is a paragon of sensibility in a world that apparently exists only to gloat over, rather than to alleviate, her sufferings. Sade's highly sexualized version of sensibility, in which Justine's tormenters are rendered positively orgasmic by her distress, also gestures toward the way in which sexual feeling became imbricated in the disputes over sensibility. For more mainstream opponents of sensibility than de Sade, one way to impugn women's integrity of self was to reject sensibility's emphasis on bodily manifestations of feeling. At a time when women's limited opportunities for speaking out could make physical expressiveness potentially as important a means of communication as straightforward speech, conservative opponents of sensibility represented women's bodies as incapable of manifesting anything other than sexual arousal worth acknowledging. Another and subtler rejection of sensibility lay in the male spectator's refusal to accept the possibility of a virtuous embodiment by insisting that the virtuous woman was not really a bodily being. Richardson's novels show the potential oppressiveness of both forms of this antisensibility skepticism about the range of meanings available for female physicality.

In terms of sensibility Richardson's own treatment of women's bodies is notable not so much for the rejection of female sexuality that some critics attribute to him[51] but for his use of the body to reify the soul. Richardson "constructs a set of indubitable correspondences between internal and external" in which "the feminine body . . . is given us in the representation of gesture, convulsion, irresolution, and involuntary movement; these are the signs of sentiment's purity."[52] Samuel Johnson praised Richardson for making the emotions move "at the command of virtue,"[53] and we can expand that tribute to say that, in Richardson's virtuous characters, body and soul move together so that it is impossible to segregate the spiritual from the physiological response.[54] Thus Richardson illustrates the distinction that one eighteenth-century writer drew between "physical crying" and "moral weeping": the former is merely "the mechanism of the body" while the latter is the body's involvement in and expression of "such real sentiments of the mind, and feeling of the heart, as do honour to human nature."[55]

This distinction explains how the "trembling body" of a Richardson heroine can be as important a part of her "stubbornly virtuous" personhood (Mullan 223) as the extended verbal commentaries through which she asserts her self-definition. Those characters, from Mr. B to the Harlowes to Lovelace, who would degrade Richardson's heroines invariably deny this unity of flesh and spirit; they refuse to read the body as a source of spiritual expressiveness. Their reductionist view dismisses the physical code for fine feeling,[56] denying seriousness, sincerity, and significance to bodily responses. This aligns them with the "antisensibility" camp of eighteenth-century thought, but in this context to be "antisensibility" is to be profoundly antiwoman. The characters who disbelieve physical evidence of fine feeling believe instead that a woman's body can give proof only of what is ignoble and "low" about the woman—which, in their view, includes her sexuality. If female virtue can exist at all (something Lovelace, for instance, doubts), it can exist only in a mind disassociated from female flesh. Richardson, however, demonstrates that either type of denial of the body diminishes female authority. In Richardson's novels respect for the female body is a necessary part of acknowledging female dignity and integrity.

As an illustration of the importance of this respect, consider the climax of *Pamela*'s first volume, when Pamela's faintings, fits, and cold sweats effectively subdue Mr. B's last serious attempt at rape. Up until that point he has dismissed Pamela's fits as manipulative stratagems, exactly the view that Fielding was to employ in his vitriolically class- and gender-conservative *Shamela*. Only when convinced that these convulsions are the signs of a genuine moral protest does Mr. B begin to take seriously Pamela's claims to have some rights over her own body.[57] "[C]hanged" by having witnessed Pamela's "paroxysm," "B. will never again attempt the worst" (Erickson 97). Pamela's reactions are intensely physical; as she herself points out, it is not her eloquence in moral argument that saved her in this "most dreadful trial" (1:183–84). Literally her body saves her or, more precisely, the indivisibility of her body and spirit, as Mr. B is forced to acknowledge that her corpselike condition shows even her physiology to be indicative of her moral attitudes.

Pamela's temporary unconsciousness, therefore, is actually the sign of the highest sensibility, in which even the body's involuntary responses (like sweat, fits, and fainting) are in tune with deeply held principles. On such ingrained principles Pamela bases her resolute defiance of one who is both her economic "master" and "a powerfully seductive father figure."[58] Proclaiming her personal lowliness time and again, Pamela nonetheless asserts her right and obligation to follow a duty that clearly is as intensely felt as it is ethically principled.

Marriage and motherhood deprive Pamela of the self-definition that had been her source of power, however, eventually leading to a changed interpretation of her body's responses. Pamela's "healthy candid pride" diminishes as "conventional social relationship" (Erickson 93, 101) asserts itself over the power of the expressive female body. As discussed above in the section on maternity, Mr. B forbids Pamela to nurse, although she wishes to breast-feed her children and believes that she is morally obliged to do so (2:233). When Mr. B definitively rejects Pamela's pleas to be allowed to do what she considers her duty, she acquiesces in the veto but weeps at the disappointment. She assents to a view of her own physiological and moral responses as alike marked by gendered fallibility. The shower of tears with which she renounces what she believes to be a religious injunction are merely what Mr. B calls a "sacrifice [. . .] to

[her] sex," which demonstrates only her gender's weakness (2:240). To use the distinction given above, Pamela's tears are no longer perceived as "moral weeping" but simply as "physical crying," a bodily reaction not even capable of moving a bystander, much less of representing a significant emotion and attitude in the one who cries.

In the prolonged episode of Mr. B's flirtation with a widowed countess, this distrust of feminine physical responsiveness brings obvious results. Intellectually Pamela resigns herself to patient long-suffering, while her body registers an emphatic protest through pallor, vapors, and involuntary tears.[59] But far from winning Mr. B's reformation, as fits had helped to do earlier, Pamela's bodily responses only provoke and exasperate him: they are a sign of female perversity and low sexual jealousy, not justifiable moral reproach (2:303).[60] Pamela wins back Mr. B only after she puts herself on trial in a highly stylized version of the abstract rhetoric used in courts of law (2:312–20). At this time she removes the body from discussion by declaring her only concern to be Mr. B's soul (not his assumed physical adultery) and proposing to facilitate his new love through removing her own body from his house while continuing to love and to pray for him. Mr. B is moved and impressed, but he shows his softened feelings by withdrawing immediately: her physical presence is incompatible with the lofty emotions she has revealed and roused in him.

After Pamela's "trial" Mr. B declares that he will be directed only by his "tutelary angel" (2:320). By locating virtue only in the mind, however, he conceals that he continues to control Pamela's disposal of her body, most seriously during their eldest son's almost fatal illness. Pamela now wishes to "nurse" her son in another sense, but her contact with the child is erratic and entirely at Mr. B's discretion (2:340–42). Accepting the "cruel kindness" of being kept from her child at the climax of his illness, Pamela displays again a widening gap between her spirit and body when she notes that her "strange hardness of heart would not give up one tear, for the passage from that to [her] eyes seemed quite choked up" (2:342).

This alienation of Pamela from her own body runs parallel with the redefinition of her authority. What stature she retains is contingent upon her separation from the idea of "woman" as both body and group (as one speaks of a "body of women" as a gathering of females). Whereas Pamela in the first volume had opposed Mr. B's patriarchal power with a claim for her autonomous worth that relied on the dissolution of gender and class hierarchies, she now draws her authority from him. His stature as a model husband proves her excellence as a wife and thus her expertise as an advisor in domestic matters (2:215–16, 2:252). Even more strikingly, Pamela contributes to a rewriting of her own earlier story. The "brilliant insubordination" that Pamela shows in the first volume of her story illuminates the "disadvantages" for all women of "belonging to the weaker sex"[61] and legitimates protest against those disadvantages. Now Mr. B justifies his own misalliance by claiming that it is a special case rather than a precedent (2:172–75). Pamela's story does not open up possibilities of strength and self-determination for other women; if anything, her tale is more likely to induce feminine despair and self-contempt, for who could match her? Pamela is a freak of virtue, an "angel, dropped from down heaven, and received into bodily organs" (2:255). This bizarre description indicates how entirely Pamela's actions have become proof of her own unbodied merit rather than of any general female capacity for independent moral action.

The subsequent subplot involving Pamela's maid, Polly Barlow, provides an example of what to expect from ordinary female bodies: a shameless posturing under the direction of a calculating mind. Like Fielding's Shamela, Polly is a potential Pamela "force[d] into the more easily acceptable mould of the feminine fortune hunter."[62] Pamela's condemnation of this "intriguing slut" (2:353) "almost beneath pity" (2:198) relies on a stereotypical suspicion of feminine demeanor. The maid's "tears" and the "grief [she] carries in her looks" after the discovery of her flirtation with a young nobleman, like her "simpers" when hoping to attract a proposal from a clergyman, are the signs not of a moral nature that demands respect but of a sly shallowness (2:351–52) that removes her from the realm of moral beings. Polly represents the negation of Richardson's usual assumption that "[s]ince women are so much associated with sensibility, the female body is sincere" (Todd 79). As Tassie Gwilliam puts it, "Polly's hypocrisy . . . softens the novel's revolutionary edge and placates the forces of conservatism" (40). Unfortunately that conservatism evinces a deep contempt for the emotional and spiritual possibilities of the average woman, who is directly opposed to the now disembodied Pamela.

That women's bodies cannot provide a morally significant statement of internal states is an assumption shared by the many characters in *Clarissa* who persecute the heroine. The Harlowes initiate and justify their ill-treatment of Clarissa through their refusal to believe that her physical aversion to Solmes is the sign of an intellectual and spiritual as well as sexual incompatibility. By interpreting Clarissa's disgust as one sign of a materialism that also manifests itself in lust for the handsome Lovelace, the Harlowes deny the weight and even the honesty of Clarissa's pleas to be allowed to live single.

Clarissa, however, can justly claim that she is a dutiful family member even as she resists her family's pressure to marry Solmes because her distaste for her suitor is part of a principled stand: she does not want to be and she "ought not" be "Mrs. Solmes" (1:93). Clarissa freely admits that her "eye [is] disgusted" by Solmes (1:75); her "heart is shocked" by his "first appearance" as well as by "every conversation afterwards" (1:75). Yet her horror at Solmes's physical presence is more than mere squeamishness: the man's repulsive "person [is] the true representative of his mind" (1:73). Marriage to him would only serve her brother's "ambition" while "depriving Mr. Solmes's relations of their natural rights" (1:93–94) and forcing Clarissa herself into inevitable "breach[es] of an altar-vowed duty" (1:287). Such a prospect makes marriage to Solmes a violation of human and sacred duties and possibly even a threat to Clarissa's own salvation. Her protestations of obedience even as she formally disobeys her family's expressed commands make sense, therefore, because she recognizes that the truth of the loathing revealed by her body has its ultimate source in the divine revelation that underlies all true obedience. The same religious traditions that support parental rights "would . . . permi[t]—nay, enjoi[n]—[Clarissa to refuse to marry Solmes] in order to protect herself from a moral injustice." Solmes preeminently qualifies as a "proposed husband . . . [whose] nature . . . would prevent the wife from doing her duty,"[63] so Clarissa's disgust, from which springs her technical disobedience, is one with her conscience.

The Harlowes, on the other hand, refusing to admit that Clarissa's body can prompt her to morally correct action, refuse also to acknowledge the genuineness of the obedience she offers. To them the physical expressions of her dutifulness—the curtsies, kneelings, and other deferential bodily attitudes—are proof only of a contemptibly transparent dishonesty. This interpretation splits the body and soul: Clarissa has "limbs so supple; will so stubborn," while her "outward gestures of respect" only "mock" those who want the "heart" (1:90). Yet this easy equation of the physical with the superficial is really a rejection of Clarissa's heart, for it leaves no possibility for the heart to show itself—except through the total loss of selfhood implied in slavish acquiescence to the projected marriage. The Harlowes criticize Clarissa in terms familiar to critics of sensibility: they charge her with making an exhibition of fine feelings but refusing to live up to ordinary obligations. The problem is that their definition of her duties differs radically from her own since theirs allows no room for her feelings whatsoever. In rejecting such a definition Clarissa is not dismissing the idea of duty altogether, a common charge against the proponents of sensibility. She insists upon retaining the right to judge her duty for herself, thus demonstrating exactly the independence of thought that Claudia Johnson accuses sensibility of blocking.[64]

Lovelace pushes contempt for the female body even further. His attitude modifies as well as extends that of the Harlowes and Mr. B, however. The latter at least grants the possibility of a virtuous female mind distinct from the body, although that possibility cannot secure female power. Lovelace argues that the female mind and body are one but that this union has only one meaning: sexual neediness. Every aspect of women's bodies reveals the same eagerness for masculine favor that occupies their minds. Lovelace joins conservative critics in reading the effusiveness supposedly induced by sensibility as actually a damning sign of sexual susceptibility.[65] Thus Lovelace, like the Harlowes or Mr. B, can dismiss the expressiveness of feminine physiology or reduce it to the meaning he desires. Lovelace echoes Mr. B's claim that women's tears allow women to escape the emotion that tears supposedly express (3:29). As a result Lovelace "view[s] Clarissa's pathos aesthetically rather than morally or emotionally."[66] In a subtly disturbing scene he even relishes Sally's sexualized parody of Clarissa's anguish: Sally's "well-aped" "crying, sobbing, praying, begging, exclaiming, fainting" are proof that "there's no minding" this "artful sex" or their "grief and their concern" (4:134).

In part Lovelace's "detachment" (Golden 121) seems a logical result of the disjuncture between his own mind and body. As Clarissa remarks, Lovelace is a "perfect Proteus" (2:82) in his transformations, whose bodily motions, whether voluntary or involuntary, are never an accurate image of his inner self. Even on the rare occasions when Lovelace sheds spontaneous tears at Clarissa's grief, his weeping is not in accord with his moral consciousness and therefore is "mere feeling . . . [with] no reform of the will or transformation of the spirit" (Hagstrum 197). In his resolution to live by his rake's code despite the momentarily disorienting influences of compassion, Lovelace perverts antisensibility arguments "divorcing . . . emotion from morality." While many opponents of sensibility equated its "self-indulgent feeling" with "effeminacy and emasculation" and urged a reliance on "reason" as the means to a broader "benevolence and humanitarianism" (Todd 140), Lovelace uses his reason to justify precisely those "violent and vicious appetites" supposedly linked with sensibility (Todd 141). Seeing all sympathy as emasculation, Lovelace is able to preen himself simultaneously on his ability to counterfeit tender sentiments and his inability actually to feel, or at least to sustain, them.

Despite his claims to understand the female sex, Lovelace feels free to victimize women because of his underlying sense that they are creatures radically different from and inferior to himself. He bases this proud alienation from women not on obvious anatomical difference alone but on the difference he perceives between women's hopeless, hapless embodiment and his sense of the separation of his own physical presence from his conscious self. This division is a great source of pride: his ability to manipulate his own body is one aspect of the more general ability to gain and use power that fuels his self-esteem. This power he explicitly pits against what he perceives to be women's domination by sexual feeling, which limits female bodies to a single, transparent meaning. Women may attempt duplicity, such as Sally Martin with her aping of outraged virtue and her carefully prepared fits (2:209), but all their stratagems spring from one easily discerned motive: their craving for male attention. Thus women's manipulations of their bodies and their involuntary responses alike reveal abjection, not power.

With typical self-contradiction Lovelace at times assumes that women control all their physiological responses, at other times that female nature forces women into self-exposure. He coaches the prostitutes with whom he surrounds Clarissa in recapturing "the innocent appearance" he had thought "born with . . . all [women]" (3:187). Yet he is dismayed at the ease with which "so young a creature can forget" the demeanor "she first charmed by" (2:187). The "difficult[y]" of "regain[ing]" a modest appearance proves how unnatural it is; the "natural . . . lesson" is one that destroys female innocence and results in the "significantly arch" "leer" of the prostitute (2:186–87).

At the same time Lovelace is unwilling to credit that even an innocent appearance signifies innocence itself. He would rather attribute "modest" responses to calculation: perhaps "the sex have as a great a command over their blushes as they are said to have over their tears" (2:456). Whether controlled or not blushing, intended by women to "be a sign of grace and modesty," is to Lovelace one more sign of sexual susceptibility (2:188). A "blus[h]" at a "bad book, a light quotation, or an indecent picture" is only one category below a "lee[r] and smil[e]" in stamping a woman as Lovelace's, and "Satan['s]," own (2:188). A blush ultimately becomes a sign of sexual excitement: after bestowing a kiss on a young dairymaid, Lovelace records that she "blushed, and seemed sensible all over" (2:22). Another blush, this time at the appearance of her elder sister, signals the "conscious girl"'s awareness of impropriety but does not imply regret: by sharing his kisses between both girls, Lovelace secures their gratitude and assures himself either would fall during "a trial" (2:22).

Lovelace's use of the word "conscious" to describe sexually aroused shame is important for the twist it gives to a term that throughout *Clarissa* is most often applied to the heroine's recognition of her own merit (2:389, 3:171, 3:187). Clarissa amply displays what many critics of sensibility deplored as its worst trait: a keen awareness of the value of one's own fine feelings. Yet in the context of constant emotional and physical assaults Clarissa's self-scrutiny becomes self-affirmation and a dismissal of patriarchal urgings toward feminine self-effacement. That consciousness of virtue, however, even of superiority over Lovelace himself, becomes in his fantasies an awareness of subservience only. He imagines Clarissa's "conscious eye" moving from her illegitimate children to their father, her mind "full of wishes . . . that [he] would condescend to put on the nuptial fetters" (2:477). This inversion of meaning is typical also of Lovelace's treatment of the blushes, the trembling, and the accelerated respiration that signal the strength of Clarissa's resistance and outrage (2:141). During Lovelace's approaches to Clarissa after the fire alarm, Clarissa's "every . . . glowing feature," "eyes running over," "bosom . . . heaving with sighs," and "quivering lips" (2:502–3) show "how much in earnest she was in her resentment" (2:503). Ironically, Lovelace had earlier envisioned the same repertoire of physical responses in one of his many fantasies of a subdued Clarissa. Lovelace imagines himself "rejoicing in [Clarissa's] every mantling feature; . . . heaving sighs" and tears as signs that she is "wholly in [his] power" (2:251). For Lovelace these physiological reactions signal a submissiveness that is the woman. The only Clarissa Lovelace can accept is one void of all consciousness except of adoration for him: she must make him "the subject of her dreams, as well as of her waking thoughts" and "think every moment lost, that is not passed with [him]" (2:416).

Thus Lovelace rapes Clarissa at a time when she is "in a manner dead" (4:416), an apparently unsouled body in which Lovelace wishes to place not only sperm but a new set of impulses to replace those animating principles, "implanted . . . by the first gracious Planter," by which Clarissa has hitherto lived (2:306). Lovelace first recognizes the failure of his plot when the violated Clarissa, even though mute and temporarily deprived of her "head," signals her profound grief and repulsion by her alternate "stupefaction" (3:201) and "hurry" (3:204).

Yet one need not be a Lovelace—or a man—to accept the narrow view of women that a dismissal of sensibility entails. Even Richardson's two delightful antisensibility heroines, Anna Howe and Charlotte Grandison, are guilty of that view. Although Anna and Charlotte proclaim themselves bolder spirits than their tremulous counterparts, Clarissa and Harriet, both evince a comparatively constricted conception of the possibilities for women's sense of self.

Anna Howe shows her essential inferiority to Clarissa primarily by her occasional willingness to read the female body as reductively as the Harlowes or as Lovelace. Anna's initial willingness to assume that a "glow" and "throb" must signal "LOVE" and not "generosity" (1:46) presages the rapidity with which she accepts Lovelace's substitution of a corrupt body for Clarissa's pure one. At the height of his attempts to divide the two women, in addition to intercepting their correspondence Lovelace persuades a lewd widow to impersonate Clarissa and so deceive Anna's messenger. Quickly losing faith in the "angelic" qualities that once she found apparent in her friend's "shape and mien" (3:376), Anna accepts the image of the false Clarissa's "bloated, and flush-coloured" body "lying upon a couch" (3:348) as substantiation of her suspicions. The severity of Anna's tone at this point clearly shows that "disgust" has already superseded her "love of mind," which she now celebrates only as an abstract concept (3:350). As Janet Todd remarks, in the best moments of their friendship, Anna may find both Clarissa's spirit and her body "precious," but she "approache[s] Lovelace in attitude" when the rake is able to make her think of her friend's body as "degenerate" and "shocking."[67]

Anna's easy suspicions are a sign of the conventionality that Keiko Izubuchi finds predominant in her character despite her apparently subversive rhetoric. The same conventional attitudes toward the female body condemn the witty Charlotte Grandison to acquiescence in the male superiority against which she ostensibly rebels. Charlotte proclaims her contempt for almost all men except her brother, but she, unlike Richardson's major heroines, cannot contemplate

a single life. To Charlotte, spinsterhood, even when filled with family responsibilities, condemns women to life as "a kind of dream" in which they are "dead
to the Present" in body and spirit: their vacant minds filling with "resveries"
because the "realities" of female experience have passed them by (5:655). The
result is a transparency of meaning in which amused observers can perceive
sexual deprivation as the only significance of the spinster's body. Possessed by
a lascivious "prudery . . . [that] ma[k]e[s] out the rest [i.e. imagines the details
of sexual misconduct], and, perhaps, a great deal more than the rest" in the
slightest hint of sexual impropriety, the spinster betrays her heated imagination with her intended gestures of modesty: a downward glance, an attempted
blush, a shudder (5:500). By her inability to imagine women's bodies as expressive of anything other than sexual need, Charlotte shows she is unable to
imagine other possibilities for women than what Izubuchi terms the "usual"
dependence on men.[68]

One empowering potential that sensibility had for women was to offer
them an alternative "voice" through the expressive body at a time of severe
constraints upon female speech. At the same time this "voice" could of course
experience silencing of its own: either by being denied to all but the most exceptional women (such as Pamela) or by being subjected to a reductive interpretation with only one possible meaning (Clarissa's case). Moreover, as the reactions to Richardson's heroines indicate, the more that sensibility appears
uniquely female, the more likely it is to become an instrument of oppression
rather than liberation. When the novelists' men perceive both a woman's
virtues and her pain as something fundamentally separate from their own potential qualities and experiences, the result is alienation rather than empathy—
even if the alienation expresses itself through a dehumanizing idealization.
Thus the reformed Belford moves from seeing all women as sexual prey to believing, as Gwilliam explains, "that there are two species of women: those who
are all body, and those who, like Clarissa, are all mind." Belford announces his
reformation by renouncing sexual interest in the former "species," but subsequently he can recognize the virtue of a Clarissa only by "her difference from
other women," which necessitates "her eventual departure from the body that
threatens to deny her difference" (Gwilliam 83, 82). To him "a neat and clean
woman must be an angel of a creature, [while] a sluttish one is the impurest
animal in nature" (4:381). But one collorary appears to be that an angelic
woman must distance herself from female physiological processes: he is reluctant not only to imagine Clarissa's marrying and therefore becoming sexually
active but even to think of her becoming a mother (2:243–44). Indeed his new
faith in *disembodied* female merit renders him passive throughout the lengthy
period of Lovelace's assaults on Clarissa's freedom and person. He too easily assumes that a noble mind—to him Clarissa is "all mind" (2:243)—will induce

total forgetfulness of the body even in such a body-obsessed man as Lovelace (3:466). But what Belford himself obviously cannot imagine is a good woman who remains indisputably embodied even to those who admire her most.

EATING AND ANOREXIA

While I argue that Belford too easily dismisses the body, some other readers have argued that Clarissa is equally dismissive of the flesh—including her own. Certainly her death appears to be the result of self-inflicted starvation, which diminishes the body before ending life itself. A recurring criticism of Richardson has been that his greatest heroine dies as a result of denying her own appetites—both sexual and nutritive—and therefore lacks the "insight" that Nancy K. Miller finds granted even to Lovelace (95). The eighteenth century, however, whatever its incidence of actual eating disorders may have been, did not categorize them in the ways to which we are now accustomed. Eighteenth-century conceptions of consumption might have been at least as much influenced by earlier idealization of asceticism (especially religious asceticism) as by later concerns about abstention as an expression of self-hatred. The suffering that anorexia inflicts upon its real-life victims demands alleviation no matter what value the anorexic might find in her situation. In literary terms, however, there might be more than one symbolic meaning even for that pain. Margaret R. Miles has argued that anorexia might best be understood as resistance to "an unwanted socialization." [69] This resistance, she continues, offers its own pleasure, particularly through "the development of a centered, chosen self, built up gradually from the many decisions, the many choices, the many disciplines occurring over a period of time" (62). Although Miles notes the dangers of extreme fasting, she points out that in the eyes of its practitioners, it can seem a positive choice: a decision to pursue a desired selfhood rather than a rejection of adulthood and/or of adult sexuality. Rather than simply dwindling—"becoming thin, small, childlike again," as one commentator describes it (Cohen, *Daughter's Dilemma* 1)—the anorexic might be seen as constructing herself. The problem is that the individual's desired self may have no acceptable place within the surrounding society. What then does an individual gain or lose in the process of accepting nourishment from that society?

Before examining Clarissa's self-starvation, let us look first at the relations Richardson's other major heroine has with food and with the more general forms of nourishment that food often represents. Pamela has seemed an "anti-Clarissa" to many critics precisely because she lives and thrives under conditions reminiscent of those that Clarissa rejects at the cost of her life. [70] Like Clarissa, she is the victim of sexual persecution, but, unlike the later heroine, she eventually accepts and submits (albeit in marriage) to the man who has harassed her. Certainly she begins with a feistiness at least equal to Clarissa's, especially considering that her would-be seducer is the male head of the household in which she is a servant.[71] Mr. B, however, perceives Pamela not merely as an employee, but as an edible object of consumption; since the first moment of his attraction to her, he has been waiting for her to "'ripen'" for him like a fruit (2:110). Pamela refuses to become the sexual equivalent of food, a dish, like his "'boiled chicken with butter and parsley'" (1:163), to be ordered and consumed. Pamela's rebellion shows in her having "'little stomach'" (1:112). During her imprisonment, when all her actions are subject to Mrs. Jewkes's lewd misreadings, Pamela's reluctance to eat demonstrates that she will not participate in the cycle of consumption her captors want to establish.

Pamela finally does eat when she accepts her wooer as her husband and acquiesces in his attempts to feed her (1:305). But Mr. B, who signals his affection by his new concern with Pamela's food and drink (1:305, 370), thereby internalizes within Pamela the control she previously has resisted. By taking her as his domestic rather than merely his sexual partner, Mr. B gains the power to determine when she should eat and drink, sleep and rise (1:338), and how she should array and compose herself (1:337–38, 341–42). That well-arranged body is to be at his domestic service in a submission as complete and unilateral as Pamela had perceived a mistress's sexual submission to be.

Mr. B likewise triumphs over his headstrong sister, Lady Davers, when she finally gives in to his urging that she eat, a request that she initially perceives as an "'insult'" (1:396). Mr. B insists he must "'prevail on [her] to drink this glass of wine'" (1:397) so that having drunk, she will "perhaps eat something" (1:396). But Mr. B expects to prevail in forcing his sister also to accept his new marriage and to renounce her own "'passion'" against him (1:397). Although Lady Davers insists she has good reason for her fury, Mr. B treats it as a physical disorder that nourishment will cure (1:396). Only by submitting her body to his direction will she regain the decorum that befits a woman. Lady Davers accepts this diagnosis and his authority by calming down as she begins to "[help] herself with some little freedom" to food and to call for "a glass of the same wine she drank before" at Mr. B's behest. She declares that she is "'soothed'" by her brother's gentle force-feeding; having taken in what he gave her, she cannot immediately let out words like "'wench'" or "'creature'" against his wife (1:397). The meal that Mr. B forces Lady Davers to share with her new sister-in-law is the beginning of her communion with Pamela as women jointly submissive to their male head.[72]

Lovelace, typically, replays Mr. B's tactics in cruder form. Like Mr. B he wants to feed the women he wishes to subjugate, but for him the process is less nurturant and more sexual. For Lovelace, women's appetite for food is important because it represents the process of sexual appetite. A "captivated lady . . . will even refuse her sustenance for some time, *especially if . . . she thinks she gives you concern by her refusal.* But then the stomach of the dear sullen one will soon return" (2:246; emphasis added). She "comes to eat and drink, *to oblige you*: . . . her exclamations will, in the next place, be turned into blandishments. . . . She will draw you to her, instead of pushing you from her" (2:246; emphasis added). Accepting nourishment here becomes an acquiescence in sexual violation, with the woman who admits to an appetite for food all too soon revealing her appetite for the very man who has abused her.

Understanding this metaphor helps to explain the self-starvation with which Clarissa responds to Lovelace's violence. After all, the rape whereby Lovelace hopes to establish Clarissa's sexual desire is facilitated by an earlier appeal to a more basic physical urge: thirst. The decisive moment in Clarissa's violation comes when she is "made to drink two dishes [of tea] with milk" (3:368). The supposed "London milk" (3:368) that gives Mrs. Sinclair's tea its suspicious flavor is actually the soporific that leaves Clarissa "in a manner dead" (4:416), a suitable piece of meat for the "hungry maw" of the tigerish Lovelace (3:206). Later, Clarissa "refuses to repeat that physical act which . . . led to violation"[73] and hence starves herself to death in paradoxical self-defense. Whereas Lovelace had denied autonomy to women on the grounds of their supposed domination by bodily appetites, Clarissa uses her dying body to signal her transcendence of appetite and achieve unprecedented self-definition. The problem remains, however, that she cannot imagine a way to incorporate natural functions into this self-definition.

Surviving rape only subjects Clarissa to concerted pressure to marry her rapist, pressure that she rejects as misplaced because her certainty of her impending death makes any thought of marriage, much less marriage to Lovelace, inappropriate. Yet although "emaciated" (4:332) and, according to the doctor, needing nourishment more than medicine, Clarissa denies the guilt of suicide (4:13). Her behavior, she claims, is inevitable in a world that cannot sustain her: "'Nothing you call nourishing will stay on my stomach'" (4:13). Her refusal to feed herself counters Lovelace's belief that even the worst-treated women always eventually will eat in order that they themselves may serve as sexual "food." Clarissa will not be food in any sense. This is true even literally, since during starvation breast milk dries up. (If one accepts Linda Kauffman's surmise that Clarissa may be pregnant at the time of her death [150], the ironic disjuncture from Lovelace's vision intensifies.)[74]

The self-destructive element in Clarissa's abstinence is easy to see: indeed it is overwhelmingly important. But it need not necessarily lead us to interpret Clarissa's death as simple victimization. Raymond Hilliard, for one, provides such an interpretation when he argues that Clarissa's anorexic death is a socially sanctioned sacrifice, in which Clarissa shows "avid complicity" (1092) in patriarchal repression and female self-sacrifice. "In starving herself," Hilliard explains, "Clarissa is identifying both with the patriarchal aggressors and with her mother" (1093), the downtrodden servant of masculine authority. Yet there are other ways to read Clarissa's final days than as a case study of brainwashing. During the long process of dying Clarissa turns away from various roles that a male-dominated society attempts to prescribe for her. Although "'an angel'" (4:138), she rejects the ministering role by refusing to marry Lovelace even after he appeals to her charity (4:90–91). She refuses to marry at all, even when an unexceptional suitor offers himself (4:204–5), and postpones—thereby, as she well knows, refusing—an exile as a penitent Magdalene, the role that her family wishes to impose on her (4:190). "I am nobody's," she writes in her will (4:416). While the statement is partially an admission of tragic isolation (nobody is obligated to provide for her), it is also a declaration of radical independence (there is nobody whose claims upon her she is undeniably obligated to fulfill). Clarissa's declaration defies Lovelace's earlier assertion that independence is an impossibility for women (3:24). In her self-declared freedom Clarissa rejects even the claims of affection that are supposed to be paramount with domestic women. When friends, from Belford to Anna Howe, plead with Clarissa to live for *their* sakes (4:287), Clarissa warns that she must now be loved "with a weaning love" (3:479). She can urge this only because she has achieved detachment herself. One of the funerary symbols with which she decorates her coffin illustrates this detachment in its self-sufficiency and its connection with mortality. The decoration is that of a serpent with its tail in its mouth: an emblem of the self-consuming—but therefore also the self-nourishing—individual (4:257).

Clarissa will not seek her satisfaction through others nor will she be the source of others' satisfaction; rather she will generate a book to establish the reality of her personhood against Lovelace's reductionist distortions. William Beatty Warner does not read Clarissa's "clarity of meaning" as positively as I do, but he nonetheless justly emphasizes the importance of Clarissa's originating "the book that will guarantee her triumph" (76). That triumph encompasses not only Lovelace's greed for her flesh, but all attempts to seize her spirit. Her "dying words," as Margaret Doody reminds us, are "a declaration of independence from society."[75] For Clarissa breaking free from social definitions of womanhood means insisting that she is what she says she is, not what people believe to be inherent in the female body. In a sense this is a triumph over Lovelace's attempt to naturalize women's contingency. Yet Clarissa recognizes the artifice behind Lovelace's "nature" only to realize that his conception of the natural is shared in less flamboyant fashion by the entire culture. Well before falling into Lovelace's hands, Clarissa had declared her preference for the single life, perhaps the closest that a woman of that time could come to living for herself. As Ellen Pollak points out, the eighteenth century condemned spinsterhood as it "represented the antithesis of both perfection and virtue." Even physically, the spinster "was an embodiment of deformity and decay."[76] No longer virginal, determined not to marry, deprived of the financial and emotional supports that might have made a single life viable, Clarissa cannot successfully oppose society as a whole. She dies, one might say, not as a warning against female sexuality, but as an example that her society will not tolerate a woman who rejects sexuality as femininity's defining characteristic.

Whereas Lovelace perceives sexuality—which he interprets as inevitably entailing encroachments upon others—as empowering him, Clarissa locates the source of her power in an almost fanatic bodily self-control. While in happier days she had monitored her own sleep in order not to spend more time than necessary unconscious and thus not an active agent, now she exercises agency by making her own death an active process. As part of this, she is determined to retain control not only of her body but of the symbolism—the layers of meaning—that will surround it throughout her last days and beyond into death.[77] Her eagerness to design, handle, and make herself familiar (to paraphrase Margaret Anne Doody) with her own funeral paraphernalia may seem morbid to modern readers, but it exemplifies Clarissa's mastery of "all aspects, physical and spiritual" of her body's final experience: death. As Doody points out, "Clarissa considers death not only with her intellect but also with her senses and imagination" (175). Her *ars moriendi* is not so much a rejection of the body as that full and, to most of us, terrifying acceptance of it that entails accepting even its mortality.[78]

Clarissa's death, while tragic, is therefore far from the simple capitulation to patriarchy that Claudia Johnson envisions as the true story of the sentimental heroine's demise ("Sweet Face" 167–70). While dying, Clarissa responds only to the "authority" of her own bodily and spiritual consciousness: her certainty of her own death and her confidence in her own salvation (4:301).[79] Drawing her strength from this union of body and mind, Clarissa can live her final days as an autonomous individual. Even in the care with which she attends the iconographic implications of her material presence, particularly in her command that her body remain inviolate after death, she demonstrates a concern for her body as the emblem of her inner self rather than as the property or instrument of others. "[F]iercely independent, Clarissa jealously guards control over her death," taking full responsibility for the final decisions about her body.[80] During the last days of her life her person is no more at the disposal of others than she will allow it to be after death. She justifies her disregard for others' wishes and commands by her intuitive knowledge of her impending dissolution, a knowledge that cannot be disputed because its source is internal, within the body whose dissolution gives firmness to her will (4:190, 204–5). Her nearness to "that great and awful moment in which, and even in the ardent preparation to which, every sense of indignity or injury that concerns not the immortal soul ought to be absorbed in higher and more important contemplations" even emboldens her to reject the advice of her "spiritual guide and director" Dr. Lewen (4:186) to persecute Lovelace for his attack. By living as though she were in a sense already dead, Clarissa—ironically—is able to live life on her own terms.

Clarissa thus is able to escape her family's and Lovelace's restrictive views of her personhood, but only through an interpretation of the body that shifts its locus from sexuality to mortality—a Pyrrhic victory, to be sure. Mortality, in the terms used by Clarissa and by standard Christian theology, erases sexual difference and the power inequities typically enacted through sexuality. She dies, but that death, in her terms, is a happy cooperation between flesh and spirit devoted to her own ultimate good. The body embraces mortality in order to serve the soul's immortality. This particular form of self-care is not likely to inspire enthusiasm in an age that has largely lost faith in the promise of an afterlife. Yet Clarissa's death differs from the "sentimental scenes" of feminine mortality that cater to masculine "self-gratification" by supplying evidence that a "still passionately loved" man is the focus of the dying woman's thoughts.[81] Clarissa spends the long period of her dying unashamedly thinking of herself.

If Richardson limits Clarissa's authority, perhaps it is not because of the fears of female sexuality that critics from Dorothy Van Ghent to Judith Wilt have ascribed to him but because the embodiment of autonomous feminine virtue is too threatening for him *or* the majority of his readers to accept. After all, Clarissa's death leaves her survivors free to "go on being themselves," not "radically changed" by having "known, admired and wept for" the woman they claim to honor.[82] Thus Clarissa becomes perhaps the most extreme example of the phenomenon noted above for Pamela: the good woman's virtues may command masculine admiration but never male emulation.

Richardson's emphasis on the unmatchable (and unmatched) woman could account for some of the troubling ambiguities in his novels. He seems consistently and sincerely attracted to the idea of assertive female virtue, but at the same time he can never forget that his magnificent heroines—*as women*—should be subordinate to men. The problem is that masculine virtue is obviously less compelling to him and therefore harder to dramatize. At times Richardson seems as disdainful of the "good man" as he is enamored of the "good woman." In *Pamela* Mr. Williams, who struggles to aid the heroine, is a dupe and a laughingstock, while Mr. B, after bouts of kidnapping, abuse, and attempted rape, emerges as the hero. Belford and Hickman in *Clarissa* and Lord G in *Sir Charles Grandison* amply suggest Richardson's concern that honest, decent men may lack the erotic power and effortless authority of a monster like Lovelace. Sir Charles Grandison is Richardson's one self-conscious attempt to provide a masculine parallel to his heroic women, an effort made only in response to requests from female readers. Even while acquiescing with those requests, he asks plaintively, "How can we hope that ladies will not think a good man a tame man?"[83] Regardless of whether they find him "tame," many readers do find Sir Charles problematic as a paragon. Whatever his virtues, he suffers from an almost parodically exaggerated version of the predicament facing Pamela after her marriage to Mr. B: he is blessed with every social, financial, and material advantage and is the cynosure of admiration from everybody else in the book and subject to wearying litanies of praise that rouse most readers' resistance. Perhaps Sir Charles's hyperbolic perfection—though chaste, he is irresistible to women; though opposed to duels on principle, he is triumphant in every conflict—stems from Richardson's desperation to prove that a virtuous man can still be heroic. That possibility, unfortunately, is not supported in the rest of his fiction.

Perhaps Sir Charles's most notable difference from Richardson's heroines is that he does not suffer the way the women do. Pain seems inseparable from Richardson's conception of female virtue while Sir Charles's virtue actually renders him impervious to the torments of fallible humanity. Female suffering brings out some of Richardson's most inspired writing, and the very vividness with which he imagines scenes of feminine misery has led some readers to see him as Lovelacian in his enjoyment of them. Richardson applauds female virtue, but especially when it is virtue "in distress," and this brings us back to the issue of the ultimate ends of that virtue. In Richardson's world, female virtue exists only in order to be victimized—as happens initially with Pamela and throughout with Clarissa—or to be subordinated to male authority—as happens eventually with Pamela and immediately with every woman who enters Sir Charles's ken. The one possibility Richardson does not entertain is that of a woman whose autonomous virtue enables her power on the material as well as spiritual plane. The obvious conclusion to draw from Sir Charles Grandison's successes is that high morality is a leadership quality. But women's moral stature consists partly in submission: no matter how good, women cannot lead. At the same time, though, what is one to do with the woman who is obviously superior—better and more virtuous—than those around her? Richardson makes that woman an "angel." That transfiguration, however, eliminates any need for men to change their own standards and behavior: since they cannot hope to reach the same heights, they need not try; and since angels are few and far between, they need not rethink their treatment of ordinary women (except insofar as they might shun whores).

Thus Richardson and his readers get to imagine women who are as heroic, as tantalizing, and perhaps in some ways as discomfiting, as mythical Amazons were to the ancient Greeks, but who are equally far removed from any impact on the social relations around them. It seems crucial to Richardson to maintain this separation between the heroic female and the "real life" she might invade. Perhaps the final irony of Richardson's fascinatingly ambiguous fictions is that female sexuality, the focus of so many power struggles in his novels, is not as threatening to him as the power of female virtue.

2 Frances Burney and the Embodiment of Delicacy

ONE STRAND IN THE PRECEDING CHAPTER was the idea that physical expressiveness enabled women to communicate their inner states in a world that allowed them little open speech. Such physical expressiveness remains a crucial element in the novels of Frances Burney, the heroines of which almost always labor under exceptional verbal constraints as well as those deemed "normal" by their society. If Samuel Richardson uses the conventions that sensibility attached to the female body to illustrate shifting power dynamics within families and between spouses as well as between sexual prey and predator, Burney uses them largely to expose the terrifying vulnerability of women in a world that seems based upon sexual aggression. Her heroines' almost morbid sensitivity—a quality that makes them conduct-book exemplars—emerges as a panicked response to the threats latent in their world: an exploitative male sexuality and an even more ominous male violence. In the face of these menaces, hope lies with the possibility of accurate and therefore respectful male interpreters of women's bodies. Through the mutual understanding that this possibility admits, harsh gender divisions blur, and Burney's beleaguered heroines reach the security they crave.

The past two decades have seen an increasing interest in Frances Burney, whose works explore female pain in a patriarchal society as much as offer the light comedy initially perceived as their main attraction. Critics from Susan Staves to Judith Newton to Kristina Straub and Julia Epstein have focused on the perpetual dangers Burney's heroines face from men who are as predatory toward young women as they are hostile toward elderly ones.[1] And, despite the resolutely happy heterosexual unions that end her novels, Burney amply illustrates "[t]he assumption in many eighteenth-century and early nineteenth-century novels . . . that men are predators. All but the worthiest of them are liable to take advantage of women at the slightest opportunity."[2] Yet despite the inner rebelliousness some critics find in them and in their creator, Burney rarely allows these heroines to speak out against the conditions and the men that constrain them. Regardless of how Burney's heroines articulate their discontents to themselves or to intimate (usually female) friends, in public scenes they generally maintain the reticence advocated by eighteenth-century moralists as an attribute of the virtuous woman.

Burney's apparent homage to the ideal of female reserve makes it all the more interesting that her novels consistently place her heroines in situations necessitating some kind of defense or explanation—a need that usually would require verbal self-exculpation.[3] At the same time, however, Burney inveterately invents reasons even beyond decorum why her heroines must remain silent on subjects that urgently involve them. Evelina cannot invoke the name of the father whose identity would protect her from harassment because he has apparently refused to acknowledge her. Camilla cannot explain her financial woes and consequent troubles without incriminating her brother Lionel, whose ruthless exploitation has created her debts. Cecilia, whose lover wishes to persuade her into a secret marriage, has as potential confidantes only that lover's mother and her own unwitting rival for her lover's affections. Most striking of all, Juliet spends almost the whole of the lengthy novel *The Wanderer* unable even to reveal her name, much less her honorable birth, lest such revelations lead to her guardian's execution by French revolutionaries. This pattern for the major framework of the novel repeats itself in minor incidents as well: over and again, Burney's heroines suffer excruciating embarrassment because they must endure in silence egregious misrepresentations of their characters and motivations. If the modest woman speaks little, then Burney's heroines exemplify modesty pushed to an extreme—and all too often into dire straits.

Burney routinely provides a context in which female outspokenness is both impolitic and impractical. When her heroines do seize the opportunity to voice their own preferences and decisions, they usually find no listeners. Instead, those whom they most wish to persuade either ignore every word or interpret it to mean its exact opposite. Thus all Evelina's entreaties cannot dissuade the Branghtons from "borrowing" Lord Orville's coach,[4] nor can Camilla's positive assertions prevent her brother Lionel from assuming that she will become Lady Sedley Clarendel.[5] This deafness to women's words, like the injunctions for women to be silent, seems rooted in the belief that women cannot use language in a way worthy of attention. Language itself emerges as a medium in which women cannot convey their true intentions: Burney's books are full of charac-

ters who resemble Jane Austen's Mr. Collins in not heeding the declarations of
"elegant females."[6] This refusal is also a refusal to empathize with women's feelings and to respect their thoughts. "'What can I ever say, to make you hear me,
or feel for me?'" Camilla cries to her brother Lionel at one point (*Camilla* 523),
her plea amply establishing that Lionel's willful deafness allows him to disregard Camilla's suffering as well as her language. Even when Lionel has driven
Camilla half-frantic with worry, he will not believe in her pain.

Yet interpretation is so multifaceted a process that a sympathetic critic may
feel that the empathetic understanding of women's pain is a reason for dis-
carding the surface meaning of women's language. In an unusually arresting
and suggestive reading of *Evelina*, Julia Epstein argues that "[w]e cannot expect
. . . that [Evelina's] letters to this guardian [Villars] to whom she writes most
regularly and frequently, will be straightforward. . . . The covert distortions
that her self-editing necessarily prompts control the narrative Evelina's letters
ultimately produce" (98–99). In Epstein's argument Evelina "divulges her real
thoughts and feelings only to [her friend] Maria" (101), while her letters to
Villars move from "fawning and cunning cultivation" to "calculated silence"
(102–3). Epstein is interested in exploring, rather than ignoring, Evelina's psychology and circumstances, yet she relies upon a dismissal as sweeping as Mr.
Collins's of the possibility that women's words—in this case Evelina's words to
Villars—might really mean what they ostensibly do.

For that matter, Burney's exposure of language's untrustworthiness as a
means for women to communicate their situations and feelings in some ways
parallels recent criticism's attention to the fissures and divisions in her own
texts. Specifically, Kristina Straub points out that feminist criticism has argued
against the idea of "unity" as a supreme literary value and has privileged "frag-
mentary" texts in which "textual disruptions" and "contradictions . . . tend to
leave disturbing rifts in the fabric of words" (2–3). Certainly Burney's novels,
in which women tend to alternate between enforced silence and frenzied eruptions of misunderstood language, might function as critiques of "an already
established symbolic order" with "a conventional conceptual framework,
[which] furnish[es a woman] with a language that has already determined who
she is."[7] Joanne Cutting-Gray continues with perhaps the bleakest assessment
when she observes that "[t]o enter into the social order that normally prohibits
a woman from speaking her desires, her feelings, and her sense of who she is—
she must either adopt the prevailing discourse as her own, thereby disobeying
the prohibition against woman's speaking, or she must speak in a manner that
is unintelligible to the public world and interpretable only as madness" (47).

If eighteenth-century social norms constrained women's verbal expression,
they endorsed another form of "speech": the language of the body. The most
important of women's various nonverbal communications perhaps was the
blush, an involuntary rush of blood to the skin (particularly the cheek) that

attains an importance in eighteenth- and nineteenth-century literature far beyond its transient physiological effect.[8] In addition, sighs, tremblings, carriage, the direction and the luster of the eyes—all that could be comprised in the words "air," "appearance," "manner"—could, theoretically at least, display virtue and convey or even enforce the proper will of a modest woman. No less an authority on female conduct than Dr. Fordyce, whose *Sermons to Young Women* were widely read, could claim "this breach of her most sacred law [that of female delicacy], the justice of Nature has generally branded with a look and manner peculiarly characteristic and significant; as, on the other side, she has always (I think always) marked the genuine feelings of modesty with a look and manner no less correspondent and expressive."[9]

Regardless of how Burney herself regarded the preachings of the conduct books, she could hardly help but be aware of their counsel. Joyce Hemlow, for one, has demonstrated Burney's personal and literary familiarity with conduct books and their authors.[10] A chapter of Burney's novel *Camilla* fits the conduct-book pattern neatly enough to have been excerpted and abridged for inclusion in one.[11] While urging women to be quiet, these books nonetheless praise the worth that a woman can portray through the dignity of her physical presence alone. For all that a delicate woman is supposed to be unaware of the body, authorities other than Dr. Fordyce also embody delicacy in its unmistakable physical manifestations.[12] "The first of all virtues is innocence," declares a 1786 essay in *The New Lady's Magazine,* "and her companion is shamefacedness."[13] This virtuous shamefacedness turns out to be virtually identical with the capacity for blushing, since "[s]hamefacedness carries the very colour of virtue, and that blush which spreads itself over her face, is a mark of her abhorrence of vice." Women who have lost this precious capacity are "ready to clothe themselves with an infinity of vice" (27). One can hardly imagine a stricter correlation between body and mind.

At the same time, while limiting the range of what a good woman can communicate (mostly virtuous love for a good man and virtuous indignation toward a bad one), the enthusiasts of female delicacy see these messages as conveyed by an even more limited range of bodily signs. As Ruth Bernard Yeazell points out, a blush can be a sign of ardent response to a beloved person as well as one of shame at the licentious behavior of a reprobate. One can tremble with excitement as well as outrage and sigh for either pleasure or pain. All these meanings could be appropriate depending upon the circumstances and individuals who evoke the physical disturbances, but interpreting the body's language would be difficult when its vocabulary was so sparse. As we have seen in the preceding chapter, an unscrupulous interpreter such as Lovelace could exploit that sparseness by choosing to "read" all bodily signs lewdly.

To conduct-book authors, however, bodily signs should have a dual effect: the signs of feminine humility also are signs of dignified pride. According to

"On Shamefacedness" modesty conveys "severity" as well as "sweetness"; "female weakness" necessitates modesty, yet it is women's "strongest armour." A virtuous woman's appearance thus both repels and attracts, depending upon the merits of her observers. By itself it cannot merely silence but even prevent improper language, much less improper actions, from men, for it "keeps insolence itself at bay" (27). Yet while awing and distancing the rakish, it inspires good men with possessive and protective love.

At the same time a timid shrinking from notice can indicate consciousness of guilt as much as of innocence, and a blush can betoken shame or anger as much as any nobler and softer emotion. Somehow, the conduct books imply, all these contradictory meanings become (or *should* become) clear in the presence of the body that carries them. What the conduct books do not acknowledge, and what both Richardson and Burney dramatize in their different ways, is that some men may be either blind or indifferent to the subtle distinctions of women's nonverbal gestures. Only by optimistically assuming that all men read and respect these signs can moralists claim that a woman need not forego feminine gentleness in self-defense against masculine predation. Once made, however, this assumption points toward the conclusion that forthrightness and boldness, no matter how employed, are the worst ways to meet unwelcome advances. Those qualities lower a woman's worth and thus make her more rather than less likely to suffer insolence.

There emerges in contemporary authorities a picture of women whose bodies convey meanings that words must not reveal. Burney employs this convention throughout her fiction. In *Camilla* Mrs. Tyrold realizes her daughter's passionate love for Edgar Mandlebert because of Camilla's tremulousness and tears, not because Camilla verbally confesses her attraction to him (220). Even the family maid can see that Camilla is "mortal fond" of Edgar because at the mention of his name "one may almost see one self in her eyes, it makes them shine so" (350). Likewise, the eponymous heroine of *Cecilia* betrays her love for Mortimer Delville because "at the sound of [his] name, she blushes; at the mention of [his] illness, she turns pale."[14] Conversely, *The Wanderer*'s Juliet, barred from clearing her character through explanations of her circumstances, can defend herself from presumptuous advances by turning "pale and cold" and by "an air of dignity the most impressive"—this being sufficient to send her essentially virtuous would-be seducer "grovelling upon the earth."[15] This method of communication shifts attention from hearing to seeing, from sifting of words to scrutinizing of bodies.

To a modern reader the result seems to anticipate recent speculations about women's supposed estrangement from "phallocentric" language. Whether one subscribes to Jacques Lacan's identification of "la langue" with the Name-of-the-Father and thus with the patriarchal order that excludes femaleness, or to Hélène Cixous's desire for a new language in which linguistic polysemy mirrors the diffuseness with which women's bodies experience sexual pleasure, the result is the same. Women, theoretically at least, are pronounced alien to the world of logical, syntactic speech and writing. Their communicative abilities apparently reside largely in the realm of the preverbal (exemplified to Lacan by the mother/infant symbiosis) and what one might term the "differently-verbal": the outpouring that Cixous compares to the flow of maternal milk.[16] Far removed as the jouissance that Cixous celebrates is from the moralistic tenets of eighteenth-century writings on women, nonetheless those earlier writings also emphasize the extent to which women's bodies speak. They privilege the communicative body, since they consistently show women to be most persuasive through physical presence, not through command of logic.

Obviously the renunciation of straightforward statement and linear argument carries dangers as well as possibilities. As noted above, already a potential polysemy exists in the traits of sensibility, which can convey passion, shame, innocence, love, and anger. When the vocabulary is thus restricted, any meaning that emerges in the public masculine world with its theoretically unambiguous language must depend at least partly upon the skills of the interpreter. Just how the authority with which this invests the interpreter might serve masculine interests rather than feminine needs is best illustrated by a striking passage in Jean-Jacques Rousseau's "Letter to M. d'Alembert on the Theatre." In the midst of a fiery declaration that women should use chaste "fears, . . . tricks, . . . reserves, . . . timid avowals, . . . tender and naive delicacy" as ways to inflame love while they should abstain strictly from open declarations of passion, Rousseau pauses to explain the interpretative powers that women's nonverbal language requires from men. Only a "satyr," Rousseau claims, would "wish to satisfy his desires insolently, without the consent of the one who gave rise to them."[17] Yet this consent need not, indeed should not, necessarily be verbal. Far more often it is "silent," and

> to read [this silent consent] in the eyes, to see it in the ways in spite of the mouth's denial, that is the art of he who knows how to love. If he then completes his happiness, he is not brutal, he is decent. He does not insult chasteness; he respects it; he serves it. He leaves it the honor of still defending what it would have perhaps abandoned. (85)

Burney, however, does not share Rousseau's cheerful confidence in men's intuitive powers. One problem that most often afflicts Burney's heroines, like Richardson's, is the persecution of a man who insists on believing that a woman's verbal negative means nothing. Like Rousseau's ideal man these gallants read in women's faces and bodies the "silent consent" they want to hear. Burney, if anything, is more pessimistic than Richardson about the obduracy of men's misreadings: there is no parallel in her novels for Mr. B's transformation from persecutor to protector. Burney's closest approach to showing such a change of heart is her depiction of Lord Melbury's brief descent into improper advances toward Juliet in *The Wanderer*, speedily followed by his repentance and expiation. Juliet is exceptionally lucky in being approached by a basically noble though momentarily misguided man, for a true rake is not easy to quell. Thus Sir Clement cannot believe it "possible" for Evelina to be "cruel" (i.e. to reject his advances), when "the sweet bloom upon those charming cheeks . . . appears as much the result of good humour as of beauty" (*Evelina* 97). *Camilla's* Sir Sedley likewise regards Camilla's "blushes" and her attempted "look of haughtiness" as only "coquetry, or bashful embarrassment." His "conception of her meaning," far "different" from her intended message, only adds to his "self-complacency" and sense of "secret triumph" (*Camilla* 507). So pervasive is this misapprehension of women's meaning that women themselves come to fear the binding force of misinterpretation. Thus Camilla's sisters think that her conduct has committed her to Sir Sedley, and Camilla herself is tormented by the thought that honor bids her accept the proposal of the unwelcome suitor who has read her smiles and soft looks as encouragement (526, 528, 530).

The language of the body can entrap women precisely because of its open-endedness, its susceptibility to varying interpretations. In exposing this weakness Burney dares to question the confidence of the conduct books that women *can* avoid insult if they are sufficiently pure. For every rake who finds "the garb of virtue" a "formidable" and "primeval power" (*Camilla* 614), Burney shows us three or four who see in a woman's "modest mien, and evident embarrassment" the signs of a "peculiarly attractive" prey, a purity that they will "adore but to demolish" (*The Wanderer* 242). Nevertheless, the delicate woman's repertoire of bodily signs remains the primary language available to Burney's heroines, replacing both speech and writing. Even Evelina, who *must* write in order to maintain the framework of the epistolary novel, narrates mostly the scenes of her own silence.[18] The body perforce is the vehicle of meaning, as Burney consistently tries to allow her women through their bodies the expressive possibilities that she denies them in speech.

Burney's handling of the expressive body, however, subtly controverts the conduct-book theory that differently gendered bodies give rise to differently gendered virtues. In the minds of its theorists the psychological and moral attribute of delicacy that could also be called modesty was closely allied with the physical delicacy that could more bluntly be termed weakness. Dr. Fordyce imagines a personified Nature imploring men to protect "yet uncorrupted" women because "[t]hey are timid, and want to be defended. They are frail; so do not take advantage of their weakness. Let their fears and blushes endear them" (99–100). Fordyce's circumlocution leaves it unclear whether his maternally anxious Nature fears the rape or the seduction of her charges. Are the frailty and the weakness that she commits to men's protective custody an emotional susceptibility to a lover's wiles or a physical vulnerability to assault? In either case women are defined both bodily and psychologically by their fragility. Men's only proper response, Fordyce emphasizes, is chivalrous guardianship, but that in itself presupposes the superiority of strength that will enable men to defend their wards. Women, meanwhile, whose physical delicacy urgently needs masculine protection, can successfully appeal for it only when they are equally delicate psychologically. Fordyce is at pains to insist that no man will feel called upon to protect a bold-faced woman. In a painfully Lovelacian image he declares that men will regard an apparently immodest (even if technically virtuous) woman "as lawful game, to be hunted down without hesitation" (108). Unless a correlative timidity accompanies women's muscular inferiority, then their feeble bodies become the mere badge of an inferior species, the fitting targets of a huntsman's aggression.[19]

Rousseau, typically more interested than Fordyce in the erotic possibilities of women's weakness, argues that women's physical expressiveness is inseparable from their physical frailty, which in turn is inseparable from their chastity. All three of these female attributes, he claims, come directly from nature.

> Is it not nature which adorns young women with those features so sweet and which a little shame renders even more touching? Is it not nature which puts that timid and tender glance in their eyes which is resisted with such difficulty? Is it not nature which gives their complexion more lustre and their skin more delicacy so that a modest blush can be better perceived? Is it not nature which renders them apprehensive so that they flee, and feeble so that they succumb? To what end are they given a heart more sensitive to pity, in running less speed, a body less robust, a shorter stature, more delicate muscles, if nature had not destined them to let themselves be vanquished? (86)

The combined physical and psychological characteristics upon which Rousseau draws form an interlocking pattern. Women's physical weakness makes it incongruous for them, rather than men, to make the first advances—because not only is physical weakness accompanied by psychological timidity, this combination, expressed through women's soft bodies and delicate, easily blushing skin, is what makes them alluring to men in the first place. The right to speak out that Rousseau would deny to women with one hand, he claims to grant with the other when he suggests that women's modest airs actually have the "seductive" effect that words would fail to possess (84). Rousseau leaves final responsibility to women when he writes that they are "strong enough to succumb only when they want to and feeble enough always to have a pretext for submitting" (86). In short, according to Rousseau, women's inferior strength actually facilitates their desires: though able to avoid unwanted encroachments (by means Rousseau never specifies), they can enjoy romantic intimacies without forfeiting their modesty. Only the sharp division of their bodies from men's enables this enjoyment, however; the assumption that men are naturally stronger and more aggressive justifies women's "submitting" to them.

The corollary to this association of women's physical fragility with their psychological modesty is the supposed connection between men's physical strength and their psychological assertiveness. These physical distinctions, no less than men's supposedly superior intellectual powers, become a way to secure men a greater voice in the world. As Burney's Elinor points out, however, this exclusively gendered distinction ignores variation among men as opposed to that between men and women. Elinor exclaims against the injustice of being

> condemned, as weaker vessels in intellect, because, inferiour in bodily strength and stature, we cannot cope with them as boxers and wrestlers! They appreciate not the understanding of each other by such manual and muscular criterions. They assert not that one man has more brains than another, because he is taller; that he is endowed with more illustrious virtues, because he is stouter. They judge him not to be less ably formed for haranguing in the senate; for administering justice in the courts of law; for teaching science at the university, because he could ill resist a bully, or conquer a footpad! (*The Wanderer* 399)

Regardless of this inconsistency, however, the theory of immutable differences in size and strength between men and women provides the foundation on which to build the whole superstructure of patriarchy. Women's weakness requires male protection, but men will protect only what belongs to them exclusively. Hence arises the urgent need for female chastity, which in turn requires more male protectiveness in order to guard women from both physical injury and the scandal that would deprive them of all protection.

For all the familiarity of the values summarized above, Burney reminds us of their power by the relentless intensity with which her novels illustrate their operation. Few authors can match her in conveying the helplessness (even if socially acquired) of young women trying to ward off a world that regards them as prey. Repeated scenes of casual insult and appropriation[20] both justify and exacerbate the fearful concern with securing escorts, chaperones, and—above all—others' good opinions, which alone can ensure continued protection. Perhaps the violence, latent and otherwise, that Margaret Anne Doody sees lurking everywhere in Burney's fiction (3) is most fully felt in the sense of a constantly impending attack that female circumspection must prevent rather than fight.

This circumspection catches women in a further double bind, however. Feminine decorum ideally should preserve them even from a knowledge of what they must avoid. Evelina, tricked into entering Sir Clement's coach and realizing too late that he does not intend to take her home, cries out in poignant confusion, "If you do not intend to murder me, for mercy's, for pity's sake, let me get out!" (99). As Susan Staves points out, it is improbable that Evelina actually fears designs on her life from Sir Clement, but modesty forbids her the use of "terms directly descriptive of sexual assault and rape" (371). Yet Burney shows masculine aggression as so pervasive that women have knowledge of the perils thrust upon them: knowledge that they nonetheless still have no words to articulate.

In this quandary, denied language for both self-defense and accusation, women must manifest their continued innocence and hence their continued worthiness for protection, through delicate, trembling, blushing bodies. The positive side of this imperative in Burney's novels is that women's bodies are amply adequate for communicative responsibilities. Evelina sets the pattern for subsequent Burney heroines: her "silence does not prevent her self-revelation when she admits that behavior, mood, and other non-verbal gestures create a horizon of possible meaning for Orville to interpret."[21] Evelina's physicality, indeed, ultimately supersedes all speech—whether hers or others'—in advocating for her with her hitherto-unknown father. "It is Evelina's resemblance to her mother" that "convinces Sir John Belmont that Evelina is his daughter" (ibid. 29). The physical replication of the injured, innocent mother in the innocent, injured daughter is thus the broadest example of a motif running through Burney's fiction: that the female body is a means of communication as much as anything else. One of the few genuinely optimistic—indeed, utopian—elements in Burney's fiction is that she consistently provides her heroines with heroes whose interpretative powers, though not infallible, nonetheless ultimately enable them to decipher the meaning of bodily signs.

Thus a recurring scene in Burney's fiction shows misunderstanding between hero and heroine resolved through the woman's physical display of the worth that the man has been disposed to doubt. The plots of her novels commonly revolve around such scenes. In *Evelina* Lord Orville is constantly watching the young girl to whom he is attracted in order to solve the mystery of her name and of her vulgar relations. *Camilla*'s Edgar Mandlebert consciously sets himself the task of observing his beloved in order to ascertain her fitness to be his bride. In *Cecilia* Mortimer Delville, initially believing the heroine all but engaged to another man, feels free to enjoy her company without concern that he might engage her affections. Harleigh in *The Wanderer* is little more than a witness to Juliet's tribulations, even while he remains haplessly ignorant of their cause.[22]

Cunningly as Burney plots to pit appearances against her heroines, however, she no less carefully uses the heroine's appearance to restore her to the hero's favor. Even Edgar, although warned by his mentor to be on his guard against female wiles, consistently accepts Camilla's blushes, soft glances, and tears as reassurance that his various condemnations of her have been unjust.[23] Harleigh, as well as the secondary hero of *The Wanderer*, Lord Melbury, is no less susceptible to persuasion by Juliet's eyes, cheeks, and posture. He can tell that "the blush upon her cheeks shewed her wholly unaccustomed even to the mention of any personal liberty" (90). Embarrassment itself, which might seem evidence of guilt, only testifies to Juliet's worth: when Harleigh "perceived, in her blushes, the force which she had put upon her modesty; and read, in the expression of her glistening eyes, that an innate sense of delicacy was still more wounded," his "respect, therefore, [was] redoubled" and "his interest beyond all calculation increased" (159). Juliet's steadfast refusal to reveal so much as her name cannot shake the faith that the men found on the integrity of her body. The heroes' consistently benign and sensitive interpretations of women's physical signs even allow the heroines to disclose their partiality without fear either of compromising their modesty or of laying themselves open to exploitation. Unlike Sir Clement, Orville can justifiably be "'[his] own interpreter'" in judging that "Miss Anville's countenance pronounces [his] pardon'" (*Evelina* 304) because, unlike the self-absorbed Sir Clement, Lord Orville, "profoundly attentive" to Evelina (305), does not make such a judgment only to further his own desires.

This very attentiveness, however—Burney's heroes functioning primarily as readers of female signs—may explain the colorlessness in them of which many critics have complained.[24] They have no real stories of their own: they exist only to bring forth the heroine's story. For other critics their ceaseless watching seems an act of aggression in itself: an invasive appraisal as sinister as the panoptic surveillance that Jeremy Bentham planned and as selfish—though not as salacious—as Lovelace's voyeuristic prying into Clarissa's privacy. Although the male "gaze" has been the target of much disapprobation, there is another way to construe the act of watching. After all, to be beneath notice, socially invisible, is potentially as damaging and demeaning as to be the object of scrutiny. Evelina, ignored by the fashionable folk around her, bitterly realizes that she is "'*Nobody*'" to them, yet her feeling "extremely uncomfortable" is "changed" when Orville appears and gives her "his entire attention" (289).[25] While a hostile gaze can be oppressive, a merely attentive—and much more a friendly and admiring—gaze can be affirming.

Most striking of all, perhaps, Burney's male watchers ultimately learn that trust must be the precondition, not the result, of their observation. At a moment when Evelina seems seriously compromised, Orville declares, "I seek no explanation, for I have no doubt" (240), and he must later confirm and reconfirm the same sentiment. Orville must be one of the few heroes in literature to arrange a rendezvous between the woman he loves and his apparent rival at the woman's request, despite her refusal to give an explanation. Edgar likewise learns to replace the distrust Dr. Marchmont sought to inculcate in him with a "generous confidence" that is the precondition for Camilla's making him the "repository of her every thought" (913). Here Edgar, in a strikingly female image, is merely the receptacle for the thoughts of another and that Camilla's—a woman's—thoughts are the crucial subject.

Burney's heroes are thus important primarily for recognizing and appreciating women's characters, not for traditional virility: rarely have ideal heroes been so physically ineffectual. Edgar, who while he submits to the directives of his tutor Dr. Marchmont, is a "piece of congelation that nothing seems to thaw" (*Camilla* 460), later becomes the receptive vessel for his wife's musings. Lord Orville resembles Mr. Villars, an old man, in character and temperament; even more striking, the rakes who pride themselves on their masculinity dismiss him as an "old woman" (288). Critics have remarked on Evelina's surprising willingness to imagine Lord Orville (during the first dawn of her love) in decrepit old age, but here again Burney breaks down any associations between the strong male body and masculine protectiveness. The strong male body in Burney's fiction is almost exclusively a menace, precisely because its power is based on the opposition of masculine strength to female weakness. Rather she predicates genuine helpfulness to women upon an ability to perceive personality and emotion, not merely enticing susceptibility, in the female body. A Burney heroine does not need musculature to safeguard her: she needs a regard that encompasses more than her youthful beauty. As Kristina Straub points out, "Villars and Orville are the only two men who seem likely to extend Evelina's personal consequence beyond the courtship stage of her worth as a sexual commodity; if Villars gives comfort and order to Evelina's youth, Lord Orville holds out the hope that a man exists who can do the same for her maturity and old age" (75). In possibly the most extreme case of Burney's quiescent men, *The Wanderer's* Harleigh, who cannot act on his interest in Juliet, is the passive target of another woman's "masculine" love. He does not even have the authority to secure Juliet a place on the boat she seeks to board to escape from France. Although his intercession on her behalf wins her gratitude, she owes her physical safety to the commands of an admiral (11–12). Yet it is Harleigh, as noted above, who consistently maintains faith in Juliet through all the circumstances that conspire to blight her reputation.

This faith is perhaps the crucial offering that a man can make to a woman in a Burney novel, yet the delicacy that enables that faith also places men at some of the psychological disadvantages that afflict females. It is easiest to see this in those men who are relatively low in social authority. Thus Villars, Evelina's guardian, is humble enough in rank and fortune to be ill equipped for a legal struggle with her powerful father. Even more than his practical disadvantages, however, Villars clearly shares the internal hesitations and timidities of his ward, which for both of them are moral as much as psychological factors. Like Evelina, Villars is and should remain unworldly, even when unworldliness entails inhibitions.

Yet one need not be an obscure clergyman to suffer inhibitions similar to

Villars's. No matter how superior to the heroines in affluence and in social status, Burney's heroes are no less susceptible to embarrassment and silence.
Again, she insists here on commonalities rather than differences as the basis for
positive interaction between male and female. While Fordyce and Rousseau
insist that men's immunity to women's fears enables their protectiveness,
Burney suggests that only the empathetic understanding born of psychological similarities allows men a positive influence upon women's lives.

Thus even Orville, privileged alike by rank and by wealth, fears being
"impertinent" (239) in showing his interest in Evelina. Uncertain even how to
acknowledge that he has seen her in the company of prostitutes, yet aware that
such company could endanger her, Orville's own manner is "femininely" indirect and fearful (as femininity is constructed by society). "[W]ithout looking
at [her], in a low voice and hesitating manner," he can only ask Evelina "'Were
those ladies with whom I saw you last night, ever in your company before?'"
(240). As much as Evelina herself, when she is trapped in the carriage with Sir
Clement, he cannot name directly what is to be feared. "[S]o *feminine* [is] his
delicacy" (261) that he cannot use a word such as "prostitute" or "whore."
Indeed, the one instance in which this paragon appears "to forfeit his character" (260)—a term that again reminds us of a fate usually destined for
women—occurs when Willoughby forges a letter in Orville's name.
Significantly, this letter, which contains "expressions of his own regard," at first
gives Evelina "no sensation but of delight" (257). Evelina wishes for a declaration of love from Orville, so her first rapture is understandable, but the speed
with which that rapture turns to resentment and even to a "contempt" equal
to that which she imagines him to feel for her (257) reminds us that men, no
less than women, must be delicate in their avowals. Orville, in a stunning
irony, is unknowingly the victim of the very bind that constrains women:
although he has long been the object of Evelina's ardent desire, he disgusts her
the moment that he supposedly announces his own.

In *Camilla* Edgar's "manly honour" is as "scrupulous" as "[t]he most timid
female delicacy" to avoid giving the appearance of romantic interest, a precau-
tion that is all the more important because, like a woman, he cannot correct a
mistaken impression through "any declaration by words." Fearful that the
beautiful Indiana has credited "the false report" of his devotion to her, he has
"[o]ne only line of conduct" open to him: "wholly to avoid her, till the rumour
sunk into its own nothingness" (207). Edgar's only "unexceptionable" action
is feminine inaction (207): avoidance rather than aggression, silence rather
than declaration.

No wonder then that Burney's heroes communicate through many of the
same indirect means as her heroines. In a bitter moment Camilla exclaims to
her sister about men, "They are not like us, Lavinia. They think themselves
free if they have made no verbal profession; though they may have pledged

themselves by looks, by actions, by attentions, and by manners, a thousand, and a thousand times!" (538). Camilla's anger is understandable since she believes that Edgar is retreating from the commitment he has made nonverbally. But Edgar could never deserve his role as Camilla's future husband were he capable of such a retreat: here we see the parallel between the lovers in their mutual observation of each other and in their gradual movement toward more accurate judgment of what they see. At this moment neither can interpret correctly what they observe, but both—not simply Camilla—are subject to adverse readings.

The strongest instance of a man's nonverbal gestures outweighing his language occurs when Evelina renounces her anger against Lord Orville. Although justly indignant over the letter he supposedly has sent her, Evelina is "struck . . . with his manner," "with a countenance open, manly, and charming!—with a smile that indicated pleasure, and eyes that sparkled with delight!" "[W]ith what sweetness did he look at me!" Evelina marvels (281), and the continuance of just such looks and manners, not a formal explanation, will melt away her resentment. As damning as the letter appears, Evelina refuses to accept its words as the ultimate revelation of Orville's personality. "In rejecting the false letter as a misrepresentation of Orville, Evelina acts from the stronger conviction that she knows him through a broader context of experience—character, regard, comportment."[26] Evelina's increasing confidence in her own interpretative abilities and Orville's extensive use of nonverbal signals account for the depth and seriousness of a relationship that superficially is little more than an acquaintance.[27] Even glances exchanged across a dinner table become a form of communion. Evelina, put off by the combined epicurism and gluttony of the fops, remarks, "I should have been quite sick of their remarks, had I not been entertained by seeing that Lord Orville, who, I am sure, was equally disgusted, not only read my sentiments, but, by his countenance, communicated to me his own" (288). More personally, Evelina feels reassured of Orville's high opinion of her by "his looks, his attentions, his desire of drawing me into conversation, and his solicitude to oblige me" (296–97). Here the indirect messages of demeanor and expression are as crucial for men as for women in conveying thoughts and feelings.

Insofar as virtuous male and female discourse differs in Burney, it differs in men's greater freedom to speak on women's behalf. Having understood the meaning of female signs, good men can articulate their knowledge by using their own voices to defend slandered women and to enforce respect for them. Thus through their own speech can men turn female silence into positive declarations. Lord Orville, for example, marks his growing appreciation of Evelina by moving from public disparagement to public praise of her. Having first dismissed her silence as proof of imbecility (35), he gradually realizes that the reserve that impedes speedy intimacy shows the depth and richness of her character (347).

Even Orville's initial dismissal is an indirect tribute to female potential. His disappointment at Evelina's apparent inability to converse and her seeming rudeness to Lovel indicates that he expects and values female intelligence and sensitivity. Sir Clement, on the other hand, is willing to dispense with everything except beauty, and his low standards are far more insulting than Orville's initial misjudgment. The rakes in Burney's novels do not care about women's behavior because any beautiful young body or face is sufficient for them: it is a blank on which they can inscribe whatever meaning they want. In a reverse parallel *Camilla's* Melmond incorrectly assumes that Indiana's beauty must prove her sensitivity: he does care for female character but is inept at deciphering it. Burney exposes Melmond's folly most decisively by rewarding him ultimately with the scarred and deformed Eugenia, whose inner worth makes her his true soul mate.

The fops' simplistic equation of female beauty with female worth is a grotesque perversion of the good man's sensitive reading of female signs. Burney shows that this equation also leads to the perversion of the chivalric code predicated upon male strength and "beauty's weakness and debility."[28] A protective urge based upon beauty dissolves into nothing when beauty is absent; therefore the truly noble and innocent Eugenia, because she is ugly, must endure "gleeful, unrelenting cruelty." A system of opposition that assumes men are strong while women are beautiful "comprehends the bodies of only certain females, virtually unsexing all the rest" (Johnson 152, 28). Again, a system emphasizing the differences between gendered bodies ends by facilitating antagonism between the sexes. At its most extreme it leads to egregious brutality. Thus the fops in *Evelina*, who believe themselves to be gallant, are ready to wager on a footrace between two old women because the women's age and decrepitude, like their low social standing, mean that they are not fitting objects of gallantry.

Consistently then, Burney challenges the tenet that gender differentiation fosters men's good treatment of women. Even the men who put their physical strength at women's service may fail them in more important ways. Sir Sedley, not Edgar, saves Camilla from runaway horses (*Camilla* 404); he negates all the good of that action, however, by the insolently presumptuous language with which he addresses her when he believes her ready to be his. By contrast the admirable Orville merely *threatens* Lovel with a duel in an attempt to save Evelina from his slights; he represses others' contempt through speaking, not fighting, for her.

When Burney does show a heroic act of physical rescue, the rescuer is female and the heroism accompanied by trembling, tears, and not one but two fainting fits (182–84). Evelina wrests two pistols from the apparently suicidal MacCartney in a scene that invests "strength and courage" (182) with all the physical signs of the most abundant female delicacy. The result is to dismiss totally the traditional coupling of physical courage with masculine prowess. The conservative Villars himself declares that "the right line of conduct is the same for both sexes," and thus Evelina's "gentleness and modesty" join easily and naturally with "fortitude and firmness" (217). The delicate, tremulous female body, it turns out, is at least as well fitted for heroism as sturdier male physiques—and the psychological attributes of compassion and humanitarian concern are more powerful incentives for rescue than is a mere erotic interest in the victim.

Burney's willingness to discard the idea of masculine violence as a protective device for women is only one of the ways in which she undercuts the mystique of male aggressiveness. As we have seen, conduct-book divisions of male and female set up masculine hardiness and feminine vulnerability as two mutually exclusive qualities. Burney, however, construes masculine boldness as, paradoxically, a source of male weakness. The rakes who are ready to violate women's physical and psychological integrity obviously feel invulnerable, and their swagger contrasts strongly with the timidity of most women. But Burney shows that male training in aggressiveness results in violence against the self as well as against others. Just like macho hot-rodders and helmetless motorcyclists of today, the fops of *Evelina* delight in dangerous driving although they equally run the risk of being "incapacitated for any better employment." One has already "overturned his phaeton, and broke it all to pieces" in driving that clearly is "dangerous" to himself as well as to his vehicle (287). Much stronger examples are the self-inflicted deaths of Harrell in *Cecilia* (403–7) and of Bellamy in *Camilla* (886–87). Both ruthless men eager to exploit women, they are potentially or actually violent, but their targets ultimately are themselves. Both end up as suicides, one through premeditation, the other through a horribly botched attempt at intimidation and threatened murder. Even the generally sympathetic MacCartney in *Evelina* must expiate the violent tendencies he shows first by attacking his own—although unknown—father and then by planning a highwayman's career. MacCartney's plans show the conflation of aggression and self-destruction: he hopes to threaten others into giving him their valuables with the intention of killing himself should his threats not work. There has been much discussion recently of the extent to which women, trained to suppress anger, turn it inward and express their rage through psychological and physical suffering. Burney's characterizations persuasively suggest that men's socialization into choleric displays can be equally self-destructive. Violence comes so easily to these men that they use it against themselves as well as against others.

Burney forcibly reminds us that men, no matter how socially licensed their aggression, share the fragility of all flesh. The bloody ending of *Evelina,* which leaves the fop Lovel disfigured and agonized, is a forcible reminder that male bodies can be as easily torn open by outside forces as women's. The division between hardy male physiques and delicate female ones breaks down because the male body also is subject to pain.

Burney's interest in blurring gender divisions does not mean that all indistinction is benign. Although she obviously approves of men being gentle, her meaning becomes more ambiguous when she shows women being fierce. Her novels invariably contain at least one woman whose verbal. aggressiveness counterbalances the extreme reticence of the heroine. Critics are divided on Burney's own attitude toward these characters,[29] but few can dispute that whatever personal attraction Burney may feel toward them, she nonetheless abundantly describes the social disapproval they face. To complicate the matter, however, the terms of society's disapproval clearly differ from any Burney might use. Mrs. Selwyn in *Evelina,* for example, alienates the rakes because of her "unmerciful propensity to satire" (269), but they are equally willing to condemn her because she is over thirty, and they "don't know what the devil a woman lives for after thirty; she is only in other folks way" (275).

Insofar as Burney has qualms of her own about these women's tart articulateness, her hesitations again are reminiscent of recent concerns that women cannot break free from patriarchal patterns of thinking as long as they continue to use "phallocentric" language. The worst quality these women share is their inherent privileging of men over women even when—or perhaps especially when—they most assert their own freedom from restrictions on their sex. Mrs. Selwyn, for instance, is bolder than Mr. Villars in her willingness to confront Sir John Belmont on Evelina's behalf. Yet the same "masculine" spirit (268–69) makes her treat Evelina herself as a foolish coquette whose own statement of her intentions cannot outweigh imputations of feminine caprice (325–26). She implicitly condones the bad manners Evelina must endure at Clifton (294), and echoes the vulgar misogyny of Mr. Smith when, like him, she facetiously warns Evelina to beware lest less attractive women poison her food and drink (328). Above all, like other outspoken women in Burney's fiction, she willingly aligns herself with a woman-hating fop. Sir Clement Willoughby, one of Evelina's tormenters, is a "favorite" of Mrs. Selwyn's (328), just as Sir Sedley Clarendel, Camilla's insolent pursuer, is Mrs. Arlbery's. Thus, as Kristina Straub points out, "[Mrs. Selwyn's] apparent freedom from male control is, however, actually an unconscious, left-handed deference to masculine authority: her desire to entertain, impress, and dominate the male wits of the novel consumes her energies and condemns her to labor for the male approval she can never command" (27). Straub emphasizes that Burney's verbally aggressive women are only fitful allies of other women; even when more interested in competing with men than in charming them, they subscribe to the notion that women's standing with men supersedes women's relationships with one another.

The fullest illustration of a woman whose verbal facility does not lead to

her freedom or to real bonding with other women is Elinor in *The Wanderer.*
Explicitly feminist, Elinor's political opinions justify her decision to declare
her love for Harleigh to him directly. Yet Elinor's willingness to initiate love
talk traps her into a constricting dependence on love. As Margaret Doody
points out, Elinor's passionate declarations align her as much with male fantasies of abject female submission as with utopian goals of women's emancipation (345). Even Elinor's theoretical feminism alienates her from other
women, as she disparages Juliet's soft-spoken endurance of severe material
hardship (349–50), and attempts to interpret her less-dramatic personality as
proof of an absence of "generous feeling . . . [and] liberal impulse" (*The
Wanderer* 585).

Burney's outspoken women thus represent a limited ideal, even if they
remind us of alternatives to eloquent blushes. They are unable to adopt the
language of male wit without also adopting a male wit's derogatory attitude
toward women. They do not so much break the divisions of male and female
language as switch sides themselves. The satire Burney brings to bear on them,
however, is mild compared to her exposure of the cruelty and folly that too
strict an adherence to those divisions fosters.

As discussed above, the violence of the fops ultimately points up their own
vulnerability. In parallel fashion the exaggerated vulnerability of fine ladies can
become a subtle form of psychological violence. From Lady Louisa in *Evelina,*
her first novel, to Mrs. Ireton in *The Wanderer,* her last, Burney shows how self-
indulgent delicacy can allow women to exercise the self-centeredness and
aggressiveness that feminine norms tell women to suppress. Lady Louisa, who
claims to be "*nerve* all over," shows her delicacy by "dying with the headache"
(286) and brandishing smelling salts (287), but differentiates herself from her
truly delicate brother Orville by her "contemptuous failure" of the "politeness"
he invariably shows (286). Lady Louisa's rudeness, however, is only a pale fore-
shadowing of Mrs. Ireton's viciousness, which is directly predicated upon her
assumption that she alone has the sensibility to suffer. Selfish in her supposed
invalidism, Mrs. Ireton makes the truly suffering Juliet "the repository of all
her complaints, whether against nature, for constructing her frame with such
exquisite daintiness, or against fate, for it's total insensibility to the tenderness
which that frame required" (*The Wanderer* 42). Once Juliet has the misfortune
to become her paid companion, Mrs. Ireton inflicts upon her the full force of
her sadism, harassing and humiliating her dependent at every turn. At the
peak of one tantrum, Mrs. Ireton exclaims, "'How unfortunate it is to have
such nerves, such sensations, when one lives with such mere speaking
machines!'" (*The Wanderer* 481). Again, one is reminded that for Burney's finer
characters "nerves" and "sensations" enable empathy: they understand that the
feelings they experience are also shared with others. Mrs. Ireton, however, perceives her feelings as invalidating those of the people around her. Priding her-

self on a stereotypically female sensibility, she shows that this supposedly gendered attribute can lead to "masculine" aggression as easily as to "feminine" tenderness.

Probably Burney's most nightmarish vision of extreme and yet inevitably ambiguous gender differentiation emerges through the prolonged miscommunication practiced between Captain Mirvan and Madame Duval in *Evelina*. Both function as near-burlesque representatives of their respective genders. Both insist on gender differentiation, but only in order to claim their sex's privileges without any attention to the supposedly accompanying virtues. Madame Duval feels free to appeal for protection without showing any feminine modesty. Captain Mirvan, even more egregiously, claims masculine authority without offering masculine chivalry.

Each relies on his or her body rather than on speech to get his or her own way. Captain Mirvan, despising French as effeminate, persists in using his own crude and blasphemous English to address even those who do not know the language. Madame Duval, although English-born, prefers French as a way both to disguise her imperfect command of her native language and to speak the politest of tongues. She grants French this distinction because she believes it to be the language of "more politer" people, who would never "talk to ladies in such a rude, old-fashion way" as Captain Mirvan does (61). Yet Evelina observes that she perverts the very reason for her preference by praising "politeness . . . in language . . . repugnant to it" (67). Mirvan and Duval's mutual unwillingness to consider their listeners goes beyond their choice of speech forms, however. It is indicative of their general misuse of all possibilities for communication, including those inherent in the body.

Certainly Duval's willingness to decorate and dress her body with unbecoming finery and to display it in spectacularly inappropriate dancing constitutes more than easy satire on the vanity of an old woman. Her problem is not so much that she is too old to pass for a beauty, but that she mistakenly attributes the power of a woman's body to its sexual attractiveness alone, not to its potential to convey intelligence, gentleness, and dignity. Her rouge captures the outward appearance of a blush, but a true blush does more than provide a rosy hue: it proclaims the delicacy of a woman's soul. Madame Duval all too obviously has no delicacy, a flaw that her considerable attention to feminine embellishments cannot disguise.

Bad as she is, however, Madame Duval is far less pernicious than Captain Mirvan because, as Burney realistically shows, she is far less powerful. Even her reluctant bilingualism—her ability to understand and to speak (though she wishes not to) the captain's "masculine" English—attests that he is better able to force concessions from her than she from him. Madame Duval's physical refinements excite Mirvan only to ridicule and abuse, not to the courtesy she is trying to inspire. By contrast he is able to impose his own "speech" upon her when, in the guise of a highwayman, he beats her. Silent throughout the incident lest Duval recognize his voice, Mirvan lets his body speak for him, and it expresses everything he wants to convey. He can impose his own meaning on her; although she is vociferous in her exhortations and outcries, she is nonetheless silenced—which, of course, is exactly what Mirvan intends. As this encounter illustrates, Mirvan, who defines himself as a "*man*!" (81), coarsens the idea that male physiology imbues men with more energy than women into the notion that male strength is inseparable from and justifies brutality. He breaks the implicit contract of gender division by refusing to devote any of his energy to protecting female delicacy.

He abdicates his proper protective role in part because he refuses to acknowledge the language of the female body. To him the "white and red" of Evelina's cheeks is not eloquence; it is physical matter that will "moulder away" (112). Denying women the expressive powers of their bodies leads him to deny them verbal expressiveness as well. During the same conversation in which he dismisses the possibility for female bodily communication, he becomes outraged at the suggestion that his female companions have enjoyed the opera, an art uncongenial to him. "I desire I may hear no more of their liking such nonsense," he declares, charging his daughter in particular "never again [to] be so impertinent as to have a taste of your own before my face" (109).

In Mirvan and Duval, Burney shows her readers the most extreme proponents of gender differentiation. Both stake their own powers on the divisions between male or female bodies, and both trust to their bodies the communicative and persuasive functions normally entrusted to language. Yet Burney undermines their stances by making them repulsive characters as well as showing that even these two extremists cannot avoid the blurring of bodily differences. Their emotional similarities dissolve the meaning of the traditional signs whereby a gendered body indicates a gendered sensibility. Madame Duval shows "masculine" aggression even—or perhaps most—when her body displays the signs of "feminine" delicacy. She trembles, but with anger, not with Rousseau's eroticized timidity (57). She sobs with rage rather than with tender susceptibility (66); and "fury," not affection, sends blood to her face and makes her eyes "sparkl[e]" (85).

Even her physical qualities are not clearly gendered. Among the many humiliations that Madame Duval undergoes at Captain Mirvan's hands is the exposure of her baldness, a condition normally associated with men rather than with women. Tellingly enough, Mirvan's references to Duval as a "Turkey Cock" (85) and an "old buck" (147), although crudely cruel, capture the sexual ambiguity that baldness implies. Duval's own body seems less exclusively female than she wishes.

Mirvan, meanwhile, has earlier acknowledged his own tendency to redden under the stress of emotion. He privileges his anger, the precipitant for his changed complexion, over the "bedaub[ing]" that he assumes is responsible for the "high colour" of the "painted Jezabel[s]" around him (79). Then too, his willingness to act on the anger that inflames his face shows his confidence that he may express emotion however he pleases, a confidence that women cannot share. Mirvan forces Madame Duval to suppress a temper tantrum when he tells her that "you must know I never suffer any body to be in a passion in my house, but myself" (85). Yet despite Mirvan's contempt for women's emotions, he has already unwittingly declared his commonality with the female bodies that he also despises.

Burney undercuts Mirvan's masculinity even more decisively during his final appearance. Eager to torment the fop Lovel, Mirvan introduces a richly dressed monkey into the same room as his target. Mirvan has prepared Lovel to meet his own image, so the use of the animal is an extension of Mirvan's earlier comparison of effeminate men (a category in which he includes Lovel) to monkeys (113). Yet Mirvan's intended meaning clouds as the monkey increasingly becomes a stand-in for the captain himself. When venting his rage at the joke, Lovel uses the beast as a surrogate for the beast's master; the monkey then responds with the ferocity of Mirvan himself. Lovel's companions urge him to confront the captain in a duel, but the only "duel" is between the man and the monkey: Lovel fights for himself, and the animal for Captain Mirvan. The latter's own association of monkeys with effeminacy now returns to let readers see this exchange as the substitution of the animal's stunted yet foppishly (i.e. womanishly) dressed body for the captain's would-be virile one. In relying on brutality to establish his unambiguous maleness Mirvan only exposes it to doubt.

Thus while eighteenth-century theories typically assigned gender division as the cause and necessary precondition for expressive and communicative functions that then facilitated relations between men and women, Burney shows gender commonality as more genuinely conducive to both those functions and relations. Bodily ambiguity she shows to be unavoidable; but only those willing to accept it can profit by it. At the same time, that profit is subject to social limitations on even the most heroic individuals, and especially on the most heroic women—because women must rely on sympathetic interpreters in order to get their message across. Unscrupulous men, however, can impose unmistakable messages of power and cruelty whether women want to listen or not.

The issue of power most clearly differentiates Burney's fictions of female virtue from Richardson's. Richardson imagines women whose virtue imbues them with power even as it subjects them to victimization. Their supreme value drives men of superior wealth and social standing, such as Mr. B and Lovelace, to extraordinary, obsessive lengths and finally to either marriage (Mr. B) or death (Lovelace). Burney is under no such illusions about the power of even the most upstanding woman. Her heroines are pure, modest, and "good" by all the standards of their time, but the most their virtue can win them is the sympathetic understanding and appreciation of a few honorable men. Their combination of moral probity and youthful beauty—although reminiscent of Richardson's heroines—carries them no further. They do not even inspire obsession among their victimizers; Burney's rakes are notable for the casualness with which they pursue women and the carelessness with which they blight reputations. One result of the more realistic scale of Burney's heroines is that she does not differentiate them from all other women as fastidiously as Richardson does. When Pamela is described as an angel, the tone is disconcertingly sincere; when Lady Howard exclaims that Evelina is "a little angel!" (21), she is recognizably indulging in conventional rhetoric. Evelina's distaste for the overblown and hence inevitably insincere compliments of flattering men is predicated upon the impossibility of any woman living up to such hyperbole. Burney's heroines are admirable but not so exceptional that no other women could match them. Even more crucial, perhaps, Burney consistently suggests that men too can match the standards of delicacy and tact set by sensitive women. Burney's admirable men and admirable women—unlike Richardson's—have much in common, and this commonality is the basis for whatever hope Burney offers for relations between the sexes.

3 | "The Feeders of Men"
Food and the Nurturing Woman in
Dickens and Thackeray

IN DISCUSSING THE PHYSICAL MANIFESTATIONS
of sensibility, the previous two chapters have examined how Samuel
Richardson constructed an impossibly heroic femininity that nonetheless must
bow to mundane masculinity while Frances Burney revised the code of feminine virtue into standards applicable to both sexes. The next two chapters continue this comparison of the differing treatments male and female authors give
a central bodily trope. This time, however, the physical function in question is
eating. Ever since Gilbert and Gubar's groundbreaking work in *The
Madwoman in the Attic* on anorexia nervosa as one of the characteristic diseases
of the Victorian heroine, critics have stressed that unlike her epicurean male
counterparts the Victorian heroine "laughs, flirts, and presides over presumably
empty plates."[1] Many have argued that an "unconscious equation of food and
sex"[2] means that the suppression of women's gustatory appetites coincides with
the repression of their sexual urges. Clearly this linkage of sexual with nutritive
hungers works well with theories that postulate the anorexic female as attempting to deny her own sexuality. Applying such a theory to Victorian literature
(and possibly to life as well) suggests that the characters (and women) who
refuse to eat have accepted the view that they should be without sexual desire,
indeed, without desire at all. Thus the anorexic's "emaciated physique literally
represent[s] the diminished and narrow existence of women as well as the
extinction of desire."[3] Raymond Hilliard's comments about Richardson's
Clarissa apply equally well to this model of the unappetitive Victorian female.

Hilliard argues that Clarissa is complicitous in her own oppression as well as her own death because her self-starvation signals her acquiescence to society's misogynistic denial of the female body and will.[4] His interpretation suggests that the compulsively achievement-oriented, perfectionist personality that some psychiatrists have discerned in modern anorexics appears in Victorian anorexia interlocked with the domestic ideology that defines female worth and achievement as self-suppression. In that context the anorexic's astonishing control over her own body is a paradoxically willful means to renounce self-will.

Yet perceptions of female relations with food are as multiplicitous as these relations. Anorexia itself, as Gail Houston points out, is fraught with ambiguity: "though the anorexic voluntarily starves, nevertheless, she is profoundly and obsessively interested in food, often cooking for family and friends without indulging herself"(16). More crucially, not all documentation supports Houston's unambiguous claim that "the delicate—and anorexic—young woman was the ideal heroine in the Victorian novel" and—presumably—"in real life" (16). On the contrary, Lilian R. Furst describes regulation rather than admiration of nineteenth-century anorexic girls: "a strong-minded nurse was to be hired to take charge of nutritional management and to govern the patient's regimen without heed either to the subject's inclinations or to the parents' misguided solicitude. It is quite evident that a grim power struggle for the right to control oneself formed the implicit agenda behind this scenario."[5] This drive to force the anorexic into acceptable eating habits illustrates Furst's contention that "eating, like noneating, is a tool for power both over oneself and over one's surroundings. The individual, especially when forced into a coercive situation of any sort, can exercise control and a measure of choice by the mode and amount of food ingested. The order of eating thus becomes a very fundamental vehicle for self-expression, and simultaneously for manipulation" (4).

It is worth questioning, therefore, whether Victorians idealized female abstinence as unequivocally as some critics claim[6]—especially since contemporary writings about women and food devote far more praise to the woman who feeds others than to the one who deprives herself. Insofar as female abstinence receives praise at all, that praise goes toward abstinence that is a concomitant of self-sacrificing nurture rather than a display of bodily control or inappetence. "[T]hroughout history, women's feeding others has been coupled with the necessity of self-denial"[7] and at least in Victorian times the feeding of others seems to have been the real cause for idealizing the woman of modest appetite. The suspicion of self-denial for its own sake suggests that at least some Victorians shared the modern perception that "denying self" may replace, rather than facilitate, "nurturing others" and that "female fasting" may be a "self-absorbed and narcissistic" activity (Counihan 362, 369). To take matters one step further, there is positive horror at the woman who deprives others, neglecting or punishing appetites rather than satisfying them. While some sexual significance may well adhere to females' provision and males' consumption of food, perhaps even greater significance resides in the conception of female nature on which the above division rests. "[T]he always slight, self-denying, seemingly never hungry, but obsessively nourishing Dickensian [or Victorian] heroine" (Houston 16) is remarkable not because she is scanty in body and in appetite, but because she is replete with psychic and spiritual riches. Thus Harvey Peter Sucksmith can plausibly identify Amy Dorrit (for Houston, one of the Dickens heroines closest to a "clinical exampl[e] of anorexia," 16) with "an *anima*-like redeemer of man" and the mediator between man and "the healing voice of Nature."[8] Sucksmith's Jungian terminology, although anachronistic for a Victorian heroine, is nonetheless appropriate, since the Victorian idealization of a hypothetical female nature anticipates Jung's optimistic female archetyping. The idea of women (or perhaps "Woman") as an ever abundant source of physical and spiritual nourishment for needy men presupposes an inexhaustible feminine love. Even the common perception of "women as gatekeepers of food consumption" is simply the recognition that physical consumption is one aspect of women's "role to produce a happy, emotionally stable home."[9] To threaten the presupposition that women *can* single-handedly produce happiness and emotional stability for others—and that they are eager to do so—is potentially far more terrifying than to imagine a more energetic female sexuality than Victorian literature usually acknowledges openly.[10] Thus the true monster of Victorian literature emerges not as the passionately sexual woman but as the one whose passion is to deny and castigate others' various appetites.

Abstinence itself, unless directly in the service of others, appears suspicious, since it might reflect a detachment that extends to others. When denouncing the laissez-faire assumption that self-interest was the primary human motivation, Ruskin used the example of a mother and children with only a crust of bread among them in order to imply that the mother's "natural" reaction would be to feed her children rather than herself.[11] Such self-sacrifice would indeed be typical of the idealized Victorian notion of maternal love—of women's love generally. But the idea of fasting on principle, rather than of fasting in response to another's immediate need, evokes a far more negative response. Accordingly, opponents of religious sisterhoods, both Roman Catholic and Anglican, included ordained fasts among the institutional abuses of these hapless women. Symbolic of the "sisters'" extravagant folly as well as of their suffering, such fasts were denied any spiritual worth. The antisisterhood denunciations clearly assumed that women should and must eat normally in order to function properly. One could hardly get further from the idea of the disembodied Victorian woman too ethereal for food!

Frances Power Cobbe's stinging comments are typical. Condemning asceticism in general, she declares that there is an "error . . . in imagining that that rightful sacrifice [of body and soul to God] *can* be paid in any other way than the 'reasonable, holy, and acceptable sacrifice' of a life of love to Him and to our neighbor."[12] For Cobbe, gratuitous self-mortification generally and fasting particularly are morally degrading rather than exalting. "[A]bstinence from natural food," she observes, ". . . is always, by some fatality, made the first merit of asceticism, as if the Gnostic blasphemy were true, and the Creator of the world were an evil being whose bounteous gifts we should please the true God by rejecting with disdain." An insult to God, abstinence also weakens, even "'pollute[s],'" the human soul (781, 782). Thus Cobbe quotes a friend's description of her own fasting experiments: "I think the chief results were that I thought only of myself, and that I grew very hard-hearted toward my fellow-creatures. Instead of feeling for the poor and suffering as I used to do, I came to think, 'Well, after all, they are not more uncomfortable than I am'" (782). There could hardly be a stronger condemnation of abstention as part of a deliberate strategy for spiritual self-improvement rather than as a self-sacrifice in response to others' needs.

In sisterhoods, of course, asceticism included celibacy as well as fasting, thus purging the female body of two putatively contaminating forces. Nonetheless, the strong Victorian feeling against sisterhoods does little to support Helena Michie's contention that the age unequivocally glorified the combination of "delicate appetites" with "virginity" (16). Medically, as well, the inability to eat could be linked with hysteria,[13] a disease that, as Elaine Showalter has illustrated in *The Female Malady,* drew moral reproof as well as medical treatment. This contemporary picture of the fasting Victorian female as irrational and morally corrupt does little to support modern claims that the Victorians "equat[ed] . . . starvation and feminine spirituality" and that the "aesthetics of deprivation forced eating to become a private activity and abstemiousness a public avowal of femininity" (Michie 17, 20). Admittedly the response to sisterhoods was complicated by anti-Catholicism. Nonetheless, fasting as a form of self-discipline or as simple revulsion from food, although exactly what one would have expected an anorexia-loving age to endorse, was frowned upon.

Class feeling further complicated women's involvement with food. The bland assumption that women are the providers of food, or at least that "the nature and object of food . . . [is] a subject . . . fit only for the occupation of women,"[14] did not necessarily translate into making all women cooks, far less all cooks female. It is a "brotherhood" of cooks that the *Cornhill Magazine* hailed in its 1861 article on the subject, for instance.[15] While most household domestics, including cooks, were female, the best-paid and most prestigious chefs, such as Alexis Soyer, were male. These professionals, often catering to such masculine institutions as the armed services or men's clubs, represented the scientific or even the artistic approach to food preparation, approaches that English periodicals tend to link with the French.[16] At another extreme female domestics who produced a household's daily meals suffered from the same class stigma as other servants: their labors might have been necessary, but they ranked low in the Victorian hierarchy.

Meanwhile, the precise degree of involvement that a "lady" might have in household chores was a vexed issue before and throughout the nineteenth century. As early as *Pride and Prejudice* (1813), Mrs. Bennet resentfully assures Mr. Collins that neither she nor her daughters had any share in producing the evening meal. Then, throughout the century, the more affluent the household, the less likely that its female head actually cooked. Yet her dealings with the domestics who did cook rendered her responsible for the success or failure of the meals that underlings actually prepared. In other words, regardless of how much time she actually spent in the kitchen, the ideal woman assumed responsibility for what emerged from it.[17] Although class feeling might provoke distaste at the thought of ladies in the kitchen, most Victorian gender ideology stressed domestic nurture as one primary marker of femininity. Throughout the nineteenth century women of all ranks thus faced some pressure to demonstrate their competence in providing nourishment—no matter how indirectly—for others.

Whether practically involved in preparing meals or not, the middle- or upper-class woman who presided over them had an entirely different position to food than did either the professional or the domestic. Her task, in literature at any rate, was to introduce what one writer calls "the poetry of diet," to etherealize the "commonplace, . . . ordinary, . . . low and vulgar . . . gratification of our alimentiveness"[18] into emotional as well as physical nourishment. Periodical articles show an acute awareness of both the nutritive and sensual qualities of food,[19] and an equal willingness to assign responsibility for both to women. This responsibility could extend literally to matters of life and death. An 1863 *Cornhill Magazine* article, for instance, blames "the extraordinary and disproportionate fatality of disease in the very young" on "defective nutrition."[20] The cause of this malnutrition, in turn, is the "sheer ignorance or prejudice" common among both working- and leisure-class women, the "extraordinary perversity and stupidity of nurses and mothers in their ideas of what forms a proper artificial food for a young infant" (37). Thus, although women might not be supposed to eat heartily themselves, they are held responsible for knowing and administering to the nutritional and gastronomic needs of others. Ideally their duty will constitute their pleasure as well. If a woman's relationship with food is primarily to feed others, then her primary pleasure occurs vicariously through their eating, not through her own.

Women therefore did not—or should not—have the kind of choice that men faced between the homely domestic meal and the luxurious club dinner. The contrast between club dining as a sign of the single man's self-indulgence and a household meal as the symbol of familial bliss was one common way for

Victorians to invest food with symbolic value. Yet club dinners did not simply emerge as the inferior portion of this comparison. It was cause for shame among Englishwomen if they did not at least attempt to provide their husbands with culinary pleasures equal to those of a club. "[A] class to be sincerely pitied is that composed of men cursed with a moderate competency, and who have married under the delusion that they are going to be comfortable and enjoy at home their club messes," one 1856 article intoned. "Poor fellows! how soon and how bitterly they are disappointed!"[21] Nor is this simply a matter of unsatisfied palates: female ignorance about food has disastrous social consequences. The "English artisan . . . through his wife's ignorance of the first principles of cookery, seeks refuge in the gin palace, and deadens his appetite at the same time that he is destroying his constitution" (167). Reverting to the middle-class concerns that are his main topic, the writer insists that, unless husbands can "shame our wives into attending to our comforts" (171), men cannot be sure of good health or good temper.

The 1865 *Good Words* article "On the Nature and Composition of Food" eloquently encapsulates the importance of women's relations with food. Neatly blending the appeals of science and religion, the author writes:

> Women are the feeders as well as the mothers of men, and if our ladies would but devote a small fraction of the time, which they expend in exercising their fingers by playing scales on the piano, in cultivating a knowledge of the science of life, it would serve them well when they experience their "joy that a man is born into the world;" they would then more seriously fulfill the solemn duties which they have to perform, would largely diminish the amount of infantile mortality, and would give to the world successive generations more fitted to accomplish the purposes of the great God who created them. As part of this rational education an acquaintance both with the science and art of cookery should rank high in importance.[22]

Here one finds culinary expertise touted not merely as desirable skill but well-nigh as religious duty, particularly crucial to the maternal role. Although the author praises as "a benefactor to his country, [the man] who makes two blades of grass grow where one grew before" (162), it is nonetheless women whom he singles out as the "feeders . . . of men."

Ultimately even the male-only dinners of the club or the pub became part of the purview and the duties of the perfect domestic woman. In accordance with the indulgent aspects of the nurturing woman, the ideal wife does not deny her husband his "male-bonding dinners." Instead, she domesticates them by her approval. If her husband ventures to the club or off with friends, he does so knowing that he can return to the security of a family meal whenever he wishes. Thus a nurturance that includes acceptance of all her husband's appetites, including those for masculine dinners, alcohol, and tobacco, seems to encompass the whole of a woman's ideal relations to food. She should be neither self-indulgent nor squeamish.

Whatever negative associations remain about women and food have little to do with women's sexuality and far more to do with women's potential for cruelty. One might argue that the "secret" behind women's uneasy relationship with food in Victorian novels has to do with the fear not of the sexual woman but of the punitive woman, the woman who destroys rather than nourishes. Thus the casually popular belief that women were not naturally as much meat eaters as men[23] draws its currency from the idea of not only women's delicacy but also their gentleness. An anonymous writer in *Bentley's Miscellany*, writing on food in general [1856], offers his readers an exuberant passage from Jules Michelet describing the ideal woman:

> She has no great appetite; a few vegetables, some fruit, and milk, are most pleasing to her. Your carnivorous regime is very far from attracting her. She has a horror of death, a horror of blood; a thing that is very natural, for she is, herself, the flower of life. It is for that reason she requires the country girl, of whom I have already spoken. She would gladly prepare your food, but how? a kitchen stained with blood would be repugnant to her feelings.[24]

Clearly, neither Michelet nor the author who quotes him is propagandizing for vegetarianism, which supposedly brings with it "pale faces and small forms."[25] But the minority position that links vegetarianism with "the gentleness of the turtle dove" and a carnivorous diet with "the rapacity of the vulture" (ibid.) forms one end of a far-extending continuum.[26] The 1865 *Good Words* article, for example, moves from observing, "In Africa, the flesh-eaters conquer and subdue the miserable tribes who subsist on vegetable products" to gravely declaring that "England would never dare to trust her defence to an army of vegetarians." Quoting Prior's association of meat-eating with "'rage'" and "'force,'" this writer defends an omnivorous diet in terms geared specifically for men (Playfair 164). "Rage" and "force" do not fit into rhetoric about feminine gentleness and tenderheartedness. Even though meat eating was a fact of life for the vast majority of Victorians, the sentimentality about "ladies" (not, one notes, about Michelet's "country girl" servant!) makes it impossible to imagine the ideal woman in a blood-stained apron, far less with bloody hands or mouth.[27]

In literary contexts the emphasis on feminine nurturing qualities actually works to associate women with food. The love of the nurturing wife/mother, however angelically pure she may be, inevitably commits her to gratifying the appetites of her charges. This gratification, in turn, associates the pure woman with a joyful sensuality, even if not ostensibly a sexual one. Perhaps two of the best paradigms of this association are that "nice, soft, fat, smooth, pussy, cuddly, delicious creature," Mrs. Doasyouwouldbedoneby in Charles Kingsley's *The Water Babies* (1863), who nurses and cuddles thumb-sucking children, and her sister, Mrs. Bedonebyasyoudid, who distributes sweets to those same children.[28] Mrs. Bedonebyasyoudid and Mrs. Doasyouwouldbedoneby, as their names suggest, are simply different facets of the same "beautiful and good spirit" (188) that Kingsley ostensibly links with Christianity but more immediately connects with an embracing maternity that directs the universe. The two sisters' generosity with candy and encouragement of thumb-sucking orality make them not merely nursemaids but archetypes of Divine Love.

On the other hand, near the end of the century Thomas Hardy provides a paradigmatic figure for the punitively nonnurturing woman. Arabella in *Jude the Obscure* (1895) is condemned partly for her gross sexuality, but far more for her cruelty. It is not the gradual revelation of her sexual cunning that precipitates the end of her first marriage with Jude, for example, but rather her willingness to butcher the pig he would rather spare. Arabella's inability to see the animal as anything but a source of food and her consequent indifference to its suffering expose the emotional gulf between her and her husband.[29] What to him is "a dismal, sordid, ugly spectacle" is to her nothing "other than an ordinary obtaining of meat," in which any awareness of pain or pity is out of place.[30] Arabella's callousness here foreshadows the greater callousness that she shows toward the dying Jude himself, thus fulfilling his bitter wish that "something should serve me as I served that animal" (305). Abandoning her husband on his deathbed without appeasing his thirst, Arabella despite her apparent sensuality denies as many appetites as does the sexually frigid Sue Bridehead.

Hardy, like Kingsley, paints more graphically a vision that also runs through the works of other artists. Like Mrs. Doasyouwouldbedoneby, for example, the ideal woman in both Dickens's and Thackeray's novels devotes herself to satisfying others' appetites. Arabella, meanwhile, might be seen as a fin-de-siècle version of another character common in Dickens and Thackeray: the woman who punishes those who rely on her for sustenance. In Dickens's and Thackeray's handling of this subject we see terror of and outrage against such a punitive woman. Both novelists portray fears and longings that go beyond the sexual to the sources of vulnerability and comfort that begin with infancy and never end.

In Dickens's and Thackeray's novels, then, the ideal wife is essentially maternal in her care of her husband, so that, although she might not eat noticeably herself, she must be a figure of food's bounty. Those women who fail to provide solid physical pleasures for their menfolk have therefore betrayed a fundamental lack of femininity, no matter how superficially charming and suitably dainty they may appear. They have assumed the role of the "bad breast," which fails to gratify the voracious hungers—both physical and psychic—of the would-be feeder.[31] Thus Dora's fairylike delicacy in *David Copperfield* is no indication of nobility. Rather, her inability to provide satisfactory meals represents her manifold failures as a wife.[32] Even the oysters that she purchases for a dinner party with David's friend Traddles are unopened and therefore inaccessible. The mouths that she makes at David to signal this fact lead him to think she wants to kiss him, but his delight at this possibility quickly evaporates when he realizes her household ineptitude (524–25). Dora can offer kisses, but she can't offer anything more substantial: her sexual attractiveness is insufficient because she has no food to give, and that inability to nourish through food is symbolic of her general failure to sustain David.[33]

By contrast, the ideal Mrs. Bagnet in *Bleak House,* although initially appearing almost a desexed "good sort of fellow,"[34] shows her true womanliness by cooking for her family as part of her general beneficence. The reader is first introduced to her through another character's comment, "She's, as usual, washing greens. I never saw her, except upon a baggage-waggon, when she wasn't washing greens!" (438). Mrs. Bagnet's kitchen skills become a synecdoche for her general indispensability, while her husband's inability to cook reflects his general reliance upon her. Her birthday "celebration," during which Mr. Bagnet assumes responsibility for the dinner, becomes a comic means to signal that Mrs. Bagnet alone is suited to domestic duties and that they are her joy. She is uncomfortable throughout her birthday because she wants to be cooking. To serve is her pleasure as it is her proficiency.

Mrs. Bagnet's housekeeping abilities are the outward sign of her ability to be a counselor as well as cook. The negative side of this equation, however, is that women who unlike Mrs. Bagnet ignore their family's nourishment needs thereby also reveal themselves as unfit for the spiritual and emotional aspects of mothering. In *Bleak House* Mrs. Jellyby serves forth filthy, inedible meals and never notices the unappetizing nature of the food or her family's and guests' distress at their fare. Consequently, before marrying, her daughter must learn to cook from that domestic paragon, Esther. Mrs. Pardiggle, meanwhile, deprives her children of sweets, thereby signaling her indifference to their youthful urges and to everything that might make their childhood pleasant.

Mrs. Pardiggle's resolute denial of her offspring's childhood exemplifies a central issue that Dickens dramatizes through food: the innocent who is made to feel ashamed of natural appetites and the callous or sadistic exploiter who induces that shame. The undertaker's wife in *Oliver Twist* who begrudges Oliver every scrap of food and regards his hunger as proof of depravity is comic but malign. Sally Brass in *The Old Curiosity Shop* provides a more sinister example of the appetite-denying female. Apparently mother as well as employer of the downtrodden maid whom Dick Swiveller christens "The Marchioness," Sally acknowledges the child only as a servant and treats her with a savagery that seems to have its roots in Sally's discomfort with her own maternity. Forcing the girl to acquiesce in her meager portions and to disclaim her own appetite, Sally, one of many shame-inducing and abusive Dickensian mothers, suffers an appropriate punishment at novel's end, when she and her brother must eat offal in order to continue a miserable existence. The degradation as well as the physical misery of this subsistence make it an apt retribution for Sally.

Mrs. Joe Gargery in *Great Expectations,* however, is perhaps Dickens's most sustained example of a nonnurturing maternal figure. Literally nonmaternal in that she is Pip's older sister rather than his parent, Mrs. Joe has nonetheless functioned as his mother, notably by having carried him through what should have been a period of breast-feeding.[35] Continually reminding Pip that she has brought him up "by hand," Mrs. Joe makes her cold-spirited and artificial nursing of the infant Pip an excuse for bringing him up "by jerks" in a long series of "punishments, disgraces, fasts and vigils, and other penitential performances."[36] The result is to cripple the growing child psychologically and emotionally as much as prolonged malnutrition would physically cripple a developing body. Even the bread and butter over which Pip communes with Joe carries the hidden threat of the pins from Mrs. Joe's apron. An apron—one symbol of domestic femininity—thus becomes emblematic of Mrs. Joe's unwomanly nature: her sharp temper, aggression, and manifold hostilities.[37] Presiding over a horrific Christmas Day "feast," Mrs. Joe ensures that Pip receives only "the scaly tips of the drumsticks of the fowls, and . . . those obscure corners of pork of which the pig, when living, had had the least reason to be vain" (22). Denied any gustatory pleasure, Pip himself is symbolically devoured by the rest of the company (save for Joe). The others play with the idea that Pip was "born a Squeaker [pig]," as his sister insists he "*was,* if ever child was," and imagine butchery as his only alternative to his sister's merciless bringing-up (24). Clearly Pip's desire for nourishment, whether for himself or the convict he aids, is not bestial, but it is treated as such by Mrs. Joe and her cohorts. Pip's public humiliation at the Christmas dinner is a natural extension of the many smaller humiliations his sister continually inflicts upon him. Mrs. Joe—whose own marriage is childless—parodies the maternal ideal through both her artificial nursing and her emotional impact on the child she supposedly is rearing: her attentions make the youthful Pip only wish for oblivion rather than life.

In this book where men often are far more nurturing and "feminine" than women, Joe takes the position with food that his wife should occupy. Joe and his wife neatly exemplify Dickens's paradigmatic contrast of "fathers who nurture with mothers who devour."[38] Joe transforms his and Pip's nightly bread and butter from mere food into an instance of their "free-masonry" and "good-natured companionship" (8). He comforts Pip with gravy during Pip's Christmas feast ordeal (23). Pip himself is at his most sympathetic when feeding the escaped convict and accompanying that food with words affirming Magwitch's humanity (16–17). Joe with Pip, and to a lesser extent Pip with Magwitch, preempts "the ideal of omnicompetent motherhood" in order to "interven[e as] the male nurturer" in a dynamic that Mary Burgan considers typical of Dickens's fiction (87).

By contrast even loving women can love the wrong way. Flora Finching's love in *Little Dorrit,* for example, is inappropriate and distasteful because it is designed to feed her own appetite for romance (as strong as her appetite for brandy) rather than Arthur's hunger for a self-forgetfully devoted woman. Obese and brandy-scented, Flora is desexualized by her greed, since her excessive orality suggests that her pleasures in flirtatiousness and at the table are equivalent as ultimately self-serving satisfactions. In this context Robert Polhemus points out the assertion of self in a mouth "which [is] open to ingest external nature and to emit personal voice,"[39] an observation the implications of which Sarah Gilead logically draws out: "oral excessiveness is aggressive; gustatory or verbal, open mouths strive to ingest the external world or to impose self on the world."[40] It is this aggressiveness that appears to pain Dickens: indeed, he separates Flora's genuine good nature and kindliness from her self-aggrandizing romantic pretensions. Sympathetic though she is, her zest for food and her nonstop talking—so different from the deferential, attentive silence of Amy Dorrit—reflect her absorption in her own pleasures. Yet this self-absorption emerges through Flora's eagerness to employ a romantic model of feminine vulnerability rather than the maternal model of indefatigable strength through which Amy expresses her own love. While the robust Flora constantly threatens to swoon, requires Arthur's assisting arm whenever possible, and claims to resort to brandy as a restorative, the frail-looking Amy effectively "mothers" both her own father and her lover. The frequent allusions to Amy's diminutive stature and delicate features should not obscure that she shatters every convention of Victorian feminine dependence. Her femininity is exemplary precisely because it is *not* dependence but (to use Burgan's term) omnicompetence. Her competence serves as an implicit reproach to such women as Flora who demand special care rather than providing that care to others.

Charlotte in *Oliver Twist* is eager to serve but is devoid of the grace that makes female servitude attractively "feminine." In the context of Victorian social hierarchies her lower-class status undercuts her femininity from the beginning, but in her unstinting devotion to, and trust in, the callow Noah Claypole, Charlotte fulfills the expectations for women's self-sacrificial love. Shelling oysters and hand-feeding them to her recumbent swain as though he were an infant and she his mother, she assures him, "I like to see you eat 'em, Noah dear, better than eating 'em myself."[41] Those words encapsulate the ideal relations that a Victorian woman could have to food, yet the narrative treats Charlotte with a contempt that apparently includes even her unselfish love.

Laboring after Noah like a pack animal on their journey to London, accepting "homoeopathic doses" of food and drink from Noah and "eating and drinking at his pleasure" (270), Charlotte is reminiscent of nothing so much as a farm animal. Admittedly Charlotte's reward for her sacrifices is Noah's casually expressed affection: by denying herself gustatory pleasures, Charlotte plainly seeks sexual ones. Yet not merely Charlotte's possible desires but her passivity and patience themselves are subject to suspicion. When Fagin admires Noah for knowing "'how to train the girl already'" (270) or when Noah, "in the tone of a keeper who has tamed some wild animal," boasts of having "'kept [Charlotte] tolerably well under'" (272), perhaps the two reveal only their own insensitivity. Yet the narrator as well dismisses Charlotte as a "female" rather than a "woman," whose "robust and hardy make" fits her for the burden she (not the spindly Noah) carries (267). Charlotte's suppression of her nutritive appetites and her laboriousness on behalf of an admittedly unworthy object win her no moral credit, despite her appearance in the same book that makes a virtue of Nancy's devotion to the murderous Bill Sikes. This slighting of Charlotte's submission betrays a suspicion of the moral stature that such displays of deference are supposed to confer—ironically enough—on the women who make them.[42] Dickens's treatment of Charlotte thus complicates his already tension-filled idealization of improbably selfless heroines. Dickens's heroines are isolated in their moral splendor because they contrast with the selfish and ill-tempered members of their sex as well as with the women whose meekness, unlike theirs, is not granted celestial status.

If the deferentially nurturing woman from one angle can be contemptible, the woman who pretends a deferential nurturance she does not feel is actually threatening. In *Hard Times* Mrs. Sparsit ostentatiously refuses to "lunch" and insists on her reluctance to eat after she has been taken into Mr. Bounderby's house. Mrs. Sparsit, however, is demonic precisely because she apes the self-sacrifice of an Esther Summerson without possessing her truly nurturing qualities. With hypocritical tenderness Mrs. Sparsit insists upon making Mr. Bounderby's tea and serving his food, tributes that his wife does not pay him. Mrs. Sparsit schemes to present her abstinence as proof of her gentility, yet her dietary habits merely show her appetite for power. Despite her flaunted moderation the private meals that she allows herself feature bloody organ meats in a genteel tea-table setting: an apt representation of her outward airs and inner vindictiveness. Critic Diane Belcher notes "that Mrs. Sparsit most often appears either presiding over meals or consuming them" and that "[t]he cumulative effect of all this dining and food imagery is our eventual sense of Mrs. Sparsit not as a gracious lady but as a predatory bird."[43] Not only through consumption, however, does Mrs. Sparsit reveal her predatory nature. She manifests the same will for power whether declining or devouring food. Initially she abstains in order to demonstrate superiority: "[s]he supervised [lunch] officially, but implied that in her own stately person she considered lunch a weakness."[44] Later, and even more dangerously, she abstains as part of her mock humility toward Mr. Bounderby: a "[h]ermetical state of mind led to her renunciation of made dishes and wines at dinner, until fairly commanded by Mr. Bounderby to take them" and made her "deeply apologetic for wanting the salt" (213). Mrs. Sparsit's selfish cruelty intensifies along with her affectation of not eating. By having her manipulate images of feminine abstemiousness, Dickens reveals their inappropriateness for a representation of true womanly goodness.

The truly good woman is too serviceable to be overly delicate. As Ian Watt points out, Dickens condemns "genteel female indifference" to, and "disgust" at, masculine appetites, while he applauds "proper feminine concern for the creature comforts of . . . males."[45] The Marchioness in *The Old Curiosity Shop,* for example, establishes herself as a redemptive angel by feeding Dick; his casual nourishment of her with beer and hot potatoes inspires her much more serious and sustained salvation of him. Significantly, even her own hunger becomes a means for serving him: while searching for the key to the meat safe she overhears the secrets that enable her to assist others. After her marriage, part of her virtue as a wife is that she humors her husband's desire for "bachelor" dinners: by recognizing and fulfilling masculine appetites, even rakish ones, the Marchioness proves her own goodness.

Dickens's ideal women not only feed their charges, they do so with an epicure's attention to appetite and taste. As a child Esther Summerson politely declines a piece of cake as too rich for her to digest, but she grows into a housekeeper notable for making sweet jellies and jams. Amy Dorrit brings home to her father the meat that she has received as part of her midday meal at work, and while preparing it for her father's delectation she does not neglect the condiments, including "[s]uch zests as his particular little phial of cayenne pepper and his pennyworth of pickles in a saucer," which might enhance it.[46] Amy Dorrit's relationship with appetite then, like Esther Summerson's, is double-sided. Not merely ascetic, she combines self-denial with a sensual awareness that manifests itself in her attentiveness to the piquancy of pepper and pickles and her willingness to tempt and gratify her father's palate as well as to provide his nutritional needs.

The same need for feminine endorsement of masculine appetites appears in Thackeray's novels. The Little Sister in *The Adventures of Philip* encourages her protégés to smoke, hosts convivial evenings for them, and mixes a tidy little drink in off-hours. She is an all-nurturing, all-giving figure, the real heroine of the novel, but because she is from the working class, she can never assume the superiority that would enable her to induce shame in others—even were she willing to be so harsh. Even children recognize her errors in speech, but these make her only the more satisfying as a figure of abundance whose innate inferiority allows others to take her gifts as their due. She resembles the other vulgar and beneficently maternal woman of the novel, Mrs. Mugford, whose array of country goodies revives the delicate Charlotte from postpartum languor.[47] Charlotte herself as a model wife encourages Philip's all-male dinners with his friends, while also asking for his favorite recipes to prepare for him at home.

On the other hand, Thackeray savagely satirizes the gentility of ladies who reveal their coldness in their aversion to precisely those hearty pleasures to which good women cater. Agnes Twysden, Philip's first love, comes from a family whose culinary stinginess is a byword. The Twysdens' unnourishing, unappetizing dinners symbolize their heartless respectability and Pharisaical hypocrisy. Their "sham bounties" are cause for anger at a "hospitality" in which "dinner, and guest, and host are humbugs together" (33). Agnes herself presides at fastidiously meager teas with her gentleman callers, both Philip and his rival, during which she "served the teapot with the smallest and least frequent spoon" (110). She scolds Philip for preferring heartier fare with his male comrades, but her excruciatingly "lady-like" afternoons are as unsatisfying physically as they are empty emotionally. Agnes's tea-table "bounty"—such as it is—no more indicates a fine spirit than it constitutes a real meal. When faced with a rich wooer, Agnes jilts Philip and marries Woolcomb in a virtual act of prostitution. Yet neither Agnes's mercenary marriage nor her later series of illicit affairs signal strong sexual appetites. Agnes actually is condemned not for too *much* sexual feeling but for too little. Insufficiently warmhearted and abnormally cold-blooded, Agnes forgoes Philip's brawny charms in favor of a puny and effeminate fop. A better woman, Thackeray implies, would have been incapable of resisting Philip's wholesome masculinity. A "cold wife," Agnes "never cared for parents, sister, or brother; or for baby; or for man (except once for Philip a little, little bit, when her pulse would sometimes go up two beats in a minute at his appearance)" (598). Despite her tarnished reputation Agnes's true flaw is not sexual impropriety but asexuality: she too easily rejects normal sexual feeling and turns instead to the comforts of a financially advantageous marriage with an unmanly suitor.

This willingness to forego the sexual for the financial is one of Thackeray's most frequent charges against female characters and is a corruption that he signals partially by their relations to food. In *Pendennis,* for example, Emily Fotheringay's hearty appetite is a sign not of her sexuality but of her stolidity. She can eat well because she has no other appetites to stir, not even when young Pen is pursuing her with breathless devotion. As with Agnes, moreover, faulty domesticity signals erotic insensitivity. Emily and her father consistently send out for food and drink from a neighboring dining establishment,[48] a sign that their life is transitory and rootless and also that she lacks the domestic virtues Pen ascribes to her. By not "busying herself with the humble offices of domestic life, cooking dishes to make her old father comfortable," as Pen dotingly imagines (86), she fails to fill the role of sacrificial daughter into which Pen tries to fit her. Kindly but dispassionate toward her father, Emily is likewise benevolent toward but emotionally detached from Pen himself. Her dominant characteristics are "a healthy dullness and cheerful insensibility" that enable her to eat and drink whatever her circumstances (175) and to ponder "how they should dress the cold mutton" while Pen "spout[s] . . . passion and poetry" (91). Although able as an actress to achieve "heart-rending pathos" and to "come out trembling with emotion before the audience, and looking so exhausted and tearful that you fancied she would faint with sensibility," Emily goes "home to a mutton chop and a glass of brown stout," before retiring to a bed where she "snore[s] as resolutely and as regularly as a porter" (93). Her unfailing appetite and excellent digestion are the physical manifestations of her imperturbable indifference, which precludes ill will as well as sexual attraction. She is one of the many women through whom this book debunks the myth of feminine sensibility.

In some ways Emily's stolidity is more deflating to her pursuers than any form of passion would be. Thackeray's frequent references to seductive females as mermaids devouring sailors are easy to interpret as references to an ominous female sexuality, but strong counterbalancing motifs in his fiction suggest that female impenetrability is at least as threatening as female sexual rapacity, perhaps even more so. Thackeray exposes the emotional shallowness of his ostensibly seductive women even more damningly than he undercuts their physical allure. The worst flaw in many of Thackeray's femmes fatales then is not excessive sexual feeling but a lack of any feeling whatsoever, a numbness that enables cruelty because it prevents empathy.

Blanche Amory in *Pendennis,* perhaps Thackeray's supreme example of the literally unfeeling predator, likewise manifests her shallow and hypocritical character through her relation with food. Blanche has a hearty appetite and conceals it; under no circumstances is she interested in helping others to food or to anything else. Blanche's unwillingness to eat publicly is a way for her to exploit the public association of female abstinence with female spirituality; she claims identification with images of female delicacy and daintiness. Yet her secret eating does not reveal a more material, more sexual presence, because Blanche has no sexuality, any more than she has any genuine emotions. Rather her selfish vapidity arises from a hollowness that also manifests itself in her indifference and consequent cruelty to others. For all her near-hysteria, Blanche "was not able to carry out any emotion to the full; but had a sham enthusiasm, a sham hatred, a sham love, a shame [*sic*] taste, a sham grief, each of which flared and shone very vehemently for an instant, but subsided and gave place to the next sham emotion" (757). Hence the Blanche who composes lachrymose poems about her younger brother is also capable of boxing his ears. The Blanche who goes into high-flown effusions upon any pretext also makes those around her miserable (251).

Her sentimental hypocrisy parallels her gastronomic falsity: "When nobody was near, our little sylphide, who scarcely ate at dinner more than the six grains of rice of Amina, the friend of the Ghouls in the Arabian Nights, was most active with her knife and fork, and consumed a very substantial portion of mutton cutlets" (398). The allusion here to the Amina story in *The Thousand and One Nights* puts Blanche's private eating in context: Amina is a ghoul who, after eating a few grains of rice for dinner with her new husband, descends upon a graveyard to feast upon corpses. Amina's secret, like Blanche's, is cruelty rather than sexuality; she leaves her marital bed not to pursue erotic delights but to desecrate the dead.[49] Thackeray's satire thus is against more than the "affected excesses of young girls" (ibid. 185). Similarly in *The Fitz-Boodle Papers* the narrator declares that "a woman who eats a grain of rice, like Amina in the 'Arabian Nights,' is absurd and unnatural; but there is a *modus in rebus*: there is no reason why she should be a ghoul, a monster, an ogress, a horrid gourmandiseress—faugh!"[50] The apparent opposition actually does not exist: Amina *is* literally a ghoul and a monster, although she employs absurd affectations to disguise her vicious tastes. Thus the unnaturally abstemious woman, like the gourmandizing woman, is suspect in far more serious sins than gluttony. Thackeray uses the Amina parallel in both *Pendennis* and *The Fitz-Boodle Papers* to attack female selfishness and cruelty, not sexuality. Ottilia, the "cannibal" and "butcher's shop" of *The Fitz-Boodle Papers* (313), is like Blanche in overeating and malice, even toward her supposedly best friend Dolly (304–5). Worst of all, she is like Blanche in employing the rhetoric of feminine sentimentality (and sentimentality over females) to disguise her heartlessness. Both Ottilia and Blanche engage in pathetic versifying, exploitation of stereotypes about female virtue, and parading of themselves as poetic objects *and* subjects. As a result they are dangerous to any male (such as Blanche's Harry Foker) foolish enough to accept stock notions about the superior virtue of feminine sensibility. The "pale and delicate" (305) appearance that Ottilia and Blanche share misrepresents not only their eating habits but their inner selves. Significantly, the *Fitz-Boodle* narrator learns to prefer "Dolly," a woman who *shows* the signs of gustatory self-indulgence by growing stout. Dolly's plumpness comes from being a good wife and mother who "has children, and makes puddings" (305), attributes that connect her fleshiness with her nurturance of others. Ottilia, on the other hand, remains "as thin as ever" (313) despite her gorging, but lives only to consume, indifferent to others' appetites except as she can make them serve her own. Indeed she destroys the last vestiges of her suitor's devotion when she appropriates oysters from him (314).

Blanche, of course, is a fuller study of the female poseur than Ottilia,[51] and Thackeray clearly enjoys puncturing her pretensions. The farcically pompous chef Mirobolant is one pin with which Thackeray deflates her. Mirobolant is Blanche's admirer and in at least one way her double: like her he is an artist manqué. While Blanche pens patently insincere and inappropriately elevated verse, Mirobolant treats his culinary labors as aesthetic endeavors that entitle him with artistic status. Like Blanche, Mirobolant fully subscribes to the false pathos of the Romantic artist. "It was a grand sight," the novel's narrator intones, "to behold him in his dressing-gown composing a menu. He always sate down and played the piano for some time before. If interrupted, he remonstrated pathetically. Every great artist, he said, had need of solitude to perfectionate his works" (244–45). Moreover, just as Blanche consciously sets out to be a femme fatale, so Mirobolant declares himself to be "a fatal man. . . . To inspire hopeless passion is my destiny" (259). As self-romanticizing and self-deluded as Blanche, Mirobolant nonetheless is superior to her because of his good nature and condescendingly gracious bonhomie. Yet the irony to which the narrator subjects the hapless cook's pretensions foreshadows the far more devastating irony of which Blanche will be the target. One initial means of deflating Blanche's puffed-up conceit is giving her a cook as an admirer; since the narrator clearly does not share Mirobolant's illusions about a cook's status and sensibility, such infatuation only indicates Blanche's actual vulgarity. Mirobolant unwittingly exposes the hypocrisy of her attempts to "etherealize" her personality at the very moments when he caters to those attempts. He expresses his devotion to her by the food he serves, most notably by a lavish array of delicacies he prepares for her and a group of female friends. His description of that feast, though lengthy, is worth quoting in full:

> . . . the charming Miss entertained some comrades of the pension; and I advised myself to send up a little repast suitable to so delicate young palates. Her lovely name is Blanche. The veil of the maiden is white; the wreath of roses which she wears is white. I determined that my dinner should be as spotless as the snow. At her accustomed hour, and instead of the rude *gigot à l'eau* which was ordinarily served at her too simple table, I sent her up a little *potage à la Reine—à la Reine Blanche* I called it,—as white as her own tint—and confectioned with the most fragrant cream and almonds. I then offered up at her shrine a *filet de merlan à l'Agnès*, and a delicate *plat*, which I have designated as *Eperlan à la Sainte Thérèse*, and of which my charming Miss partook with pleasure. I followed this by two little *entrées* of sweetbread and chicken; and the only brown thing which I permitted myself in the entertainment was a little roast of lamb, which I laid in a meadow of spinaches, surrounded with croustillons, representing sheep, and ornamented with daisies and other savage flowers. After this came my second service: a pudding *à la Reine Elizabeth* (who . . . was a maiden princess); a dish of opal-coloured plovers' eggs, which I called *Nid de tourtereaux à la Roucoule*: placing in the midst of them two of those tender volatiles, billing each other, and confectioned with butter; a basket containing little *gâteaux* of apricots, which, I

know, all young ladies adore; and a jelly of marasquin, bland, insinuating, intox-
icating as the glance of beauty. This I designated *Ambroisie de Calypso à la
Souveraine de mon Coeur.* And when the ice was brought in—an ice of *plombière*
and cherries—how do you think I had shaped them . . . ? In the form of two
hearts united with an arrow, on which I had laid, before it entered, a bridal veil
in cut-paper, surmounted by a wreath of virginal orange-flowers. (258)

Mirobolant claims that his cooking enables soul to speak to soul: "I corre-
spond with her by means of my art. She partakes of dishes which I make
expressly for her. I insinuate to her thus a thousand hints, which, as she is perfectly spiritual, she receives" (259). But Mirobolant is as deceived in Blanche's
spirituality as he is in the artistry of his own profession. Blanche is no more
"spiritual" in her hypocritical eating than she is in her versification or her flir-
tations. Mistaking his food for art rather than nutriment, he similarly misper-
ceives her grossness as delicacy. No wonder then that he ends the book as
Blanche's lover: his tributes to her have always accommodated her perception
of herself as ethereal while catering to her materiality.

Mirobolant's comic and not altogether masculine personality makes him an
apt partner for this hollow woman who seeks only to feed herself, with flattery
as well as with food. A true woman, on the other hand, not only feeds her man
but would feed him with herself if need be. Thus in *The Adventures of Philip*
both Mrs. Pendennis and Charlotte are described at various points as willingly
making themselves food for their son and husband respectively. Mrs.
Pendennis, "if [her] child were hungry, . . . would chop off [her] head to make
him broth" (2) while Charlotte, if her husband's favorite dish "consisted of
minced Charlotte, . . . would cheerfully chop herself up, and have herself
served with a little cream-sauce and snippets of toast for [his] dinner" (510).
Yet this metaphor, which insists upon the women's transcendent love also
depends upon their actual materiality. They must have bodies in order to sacrifice those bodies to their menfolk's hypothetically cannibalistic urges. The
effect of this figure is therefore reminiscent of Thackeray's reference in *The
History of Pendennis* to the women who "licked [Pendennis's] hand and shoe"
just as his dog Ponto does (297–98). Sublime female love, which perhaps
could link women to the divine presence of Christ in communion bread and
wine, could also connect women to the purely animal. Is such love divine self-
sacrifice or merely the inevitable fate of inferior creatures?

After all, Helen, Laura, and Charlotte love, but Thackeray sadly concludes
that love itself is selfish. "If you have reduced your mistress to a crust,"
Pendennis's narrator warns men, "depend upon it that she won't repine, and
only take a very little bit of it for herself provided you will eat the remainder
in her company." This self-sacrifice is possible, however, only because "calami-
ty is welcome to women if they think it will bring truant affection home again"

(230). But the love that rejoices in the loved one's suffering clearly differs from the entirely selfless devotion extolled in conventional rhetoric about women's love. The narrator asks, "Do you suppose it is all for the man's sake that you [women] love, and not a bit for your own? Do you suppose you would drink if you were not thirsty, or eat if you were not hungry?" (553). Women's love, even when chaste, is not an ethereal effusion but an emotional hunger that demands its own gratification. Even maternal love is capable of "selfish ambition" comparable to Caesar's (696).

A wistful disillusionment therefore undercuts claims in Thackeray's novels that "a good woman is the loveliest flower that blooms under heaven, made up of nothing but "silent grace, . . . pure fragrance, . . . [and] delicate bloom of beauty" (527). Helen's love for her son, for instance, makes her unjust toward Laura and then, with Laura's support, even crueler and more unjust to Fanny Bolton. Exhibiting nothing but "[h]ard-heartedness and gloom," without "the faintest gleam of mercy or sympathy" (538), the two women justify Pendennis's later outburst calling them "'cruel'" (593). A purity—or prudery—that protects itself by unchristian and unforgiving wrath against an offender is hypocritical, Thackeray suggests. Such censoriousness mistakes cruelty and injustice for virtues while distrusting every kindly and natural instinct. Thus even a "good" woman shares with a "fallen" one an essential cruelty, however differently it may manifest itself. "[P]rudery in our females is such," Pendennis's narrator comments drily, "that before all expression of feeling, or natural kindness and regard, a woman is taught to think of herself and the proprieties" and to disown "kindly friendship" as shameful (596). Thackeray's femmes fatales, including Becky Sharp, show few signs of sexual responsiveness, however much they may exploit their charms for their own advantage. Marketing themselves as morsels for male consumption, these women consume the men whose own appetites render them helpless. Cold-bloodedness, however, not heated passion, enables the women to perpetuate their sadistic misdeeds. Typically, Becky reduces Jo Sedley to abject terror long before she murders him as the culmination of a long series of injuries she has inflicted upon others.

Thackeray's "good" women, likewise, while not objects of sexual scandal, betray a cruelty as deeply rooted as Becky's own.[52] Even their love carries with it the potential for harm: Helen can sincerely wish that her son "had died almost" or (perhaps worse) that he marry Fanny Bolton rather than that he live on as Fanny's seducer (561–63). Smotheringly devoted, Helen nonetheless can envision for her son only a life as repressed as her own. "'She persecutes me,'" Pendennis thinks in a rare moment of rebelliousness, "'and she comes to me with the air of a martyr'" (593). Laura, Pen's eventual wife, whom George Orwell damns as an even worse example of Victorian sentimentality about women than Dickens's Agnes Wickfield,[53] assumes Helen's mantle of female sanctity in later books narrated by Pendennis. Yet her conventional piety and obtrusive moralizing are at such odds with the narrator's subtle observation and wry world-weariness that his commentary makes a mockery of hers. However much Laura and her kind may believe in the sanctity of "bourgeois institutions," the book's total vision insists that "they are merely cultural fictions masking a much more anarchic and amoral reality."[54] To the extent that Pendennis accepts Laura's version of the world he blinkers himself, as Thackeray himself noted in his comment that he meant Pen's "uxoriousness and admiration for Laura . . . to show that he is a weak character & led by women."[55]

Thus, through provision of female monsters to contrast with truly virtuous heroines and emphasis on the hypocritical selfishness underlying virtuous femininity, Dickens and Thackeray respectively undermine the rhetoric about feminine gentleness in which their narrators indulge. While there has been considerable critical attention paid recently to putative Victorian fears of female sexuality and considerable debate about the extent to which Victorians acknowledged its existence, an even more important component in Victorian constructions of womanliness perhaps is the ideal of caretaking. In other words, while the Victorian cultural climate may have effaced aspects of female physicality, it imposed extravagantly high demands on female spirituality—demands so high as to ensure women's inability to meet them. That inability, however, then becomes evidence not of quotidian humanity but of monstrosity. As stylized and poetically extreme tributes to female delicacy helped create the famous Victorian dichotomy between "whore" and "angel," so the insistence on female tenderheartedness may account for the plethora of female monsters in Dickens's and Thackeray's fiction. The high proportion of nonnurturing and shame-inducing women in their novels, the rarity of Dickens's Esthers and Amys[56] and the ambiguity of Thackeray's Helens and Lauras,[57] expose the fragility of the dream of all-giving female love. Mary Burgan has cogently argued that "Dickens could not detach himself sufficiently" from an impossible feminine ideal of "perfect nurture" to "permit [the] compromis[e]" of what modern psychologists have defined as "'good enough' mothering" (86–87). In a similar vein an oft-quoted passage from one of Thackeray's letters reveals the pain he felt in growing out of his childhood perception of his mother as "an angel" to the realization that, like anyone else, she could be "cruel."[58] In the traditional sexual double standard, female modesty must be extreme to compensate for the supposed deficiencies of male modesty. In the same way, the double standard of tenderness apparently requires unvarying kindness from women precisely because men are allowed—expected to take—a far greater latitude in aggression and hostility.[59] Perhaps the inevitable falseness of exalting the virtue of nurturance while insisting that its practice belongs primarily to only half of humankind helps explain the ambivalence with which Dickens and Thackeray treat the idea of the nurturing female. Clearly both men were deeply attracted by the idea of a boundlessly giving and loving femininity, and just as clearly both had a keen eye for the selfishness and malice that could be found in actual females. In acknowledging this division between the ideal and the actual, however, these authors push female evil—or even moral mediocrity—into a realm of rhetorical horror as exaggerated as the rhetorical excesses surrounding female virtue. Male villainy, of course, is prominent in their works as well, but it is not as pronounced a deviation from the norm—not apparently as *unnatural*—as the female variety, which perhaps explains the fear of women at work in much of Dickens's and Thackeray's fiction. An impossible ideal creates its own shadow image: the dream of heavenly love creates the fear of hellish cruelty.

4 | Spinsters and Food in *Cranford* and *Villette*

WHILE CHARLES DICKENS and William Makepeace Thackeray are two male authors concerned with women who provide or withhold food, Elizabeth Gaskell and Charlotte Brontë in *Cranford* and *Villette* (both published in 1853) less conventionally focus on women who must find a role other than the traditional family nurturer and nourisher. Nor is this the only difference between the male and female authors' imagining of their female characters. Whereas Dickens and Thackeray imagine women powerful enough to satisfy or deny male appetites while apparently functioning themselves without the vulnerability of desire, Gaskell and Brontë envision needy, hungering women who cannot satisfy even themselves, let alone others. To describe the spinster heroines of *Cranford* and *Villette* in these terms is by no means to concur in earlier assessments of them as impoverished by a specifically female incapacity to thrive without men.[1] On the contrary it is to recognize these characters' participation in the general human misery that arises partly from economic and social pressures and partly from the insufficiency of *any* humans even to assure their own happiness, much less to ensure happiness for others. Thus, this chapter stands as an alternative to readings that see women without men as necessarily incomplete as well as those that celebrate a female strength so miraculous as to eliminate human need.[2]

Both *Cranford* and *Villette* amply set forth the multitude of needs that women, as well as men, experience, including the needs not only for human relationships but for meaningful occupation.[3] Such work as is available for

Miss Matty or Lucy Snowe is complicated, even distorted, by its always mim-
icking women's traditional domestic role.[4] Thus in addition to all the other
possible problems associated with employment, women must face the awk-
wardness of earning their living through functions by which women traditionally have expressed their love. Yet Gaskell's and Brontë's handlings of
women's relationship to the ideology of domestic love obliquely reveals the
craving for self-satisfaction inherent in romantic expectations. Whereas
Dickens and Thackeray pay uneasy lip service to the ideal of female selflessness, Gaskell and Brontë are comparatively open about women's desire for fulfilling, rather than effacing, themselves even through domestic devotion.

Not surprising, food becomes an important metaphor through which various emotional and ideological conflicts are expressed. But Gaskell and Brontë
differ crucially from Thackeray and Dickens in their greater emphasis on men
as providers of food for women; for them it is a way to dramatize the benefits
that men empowered by their society can confer upon disenfranchised women.
Equally important, Gaskell and Brontë focus on women's provision of food to
others and their own feelings about eating as a way to explore the tension
between social expectations of female nurture and women who have no one to
nurture but themselves. The heroines of *Cranford* and *Villette* urgently need to
carve out roles for themselves that do not depend upon caring for others
because in a society that defines women as caretakers they have no one to take
care of but themselves. How, then, can they define themselves? Sarah Stickney
Ellis's famous—or infamous—claim that women are "relative creatures"[5]
whose duties arise naturally from their relationships with others finds an echo
in Lucy Snowe's complaint about having to take up the burden of egotism.
Plaintively Lucy asks,

> is there nothing more for me in life—no true home—nothing to be dearer to
> me than myself, and by its paramount preciousness, to draw from me better
> things than I care to cultivate for myself only? Nothing, at whose feet I can will-
> ingly lay down the whole burden of human egotism, and gloriously take up the
> nobler charge of labouring and living for others? [6]

Lucy's desolation at this prospect seems ironic considering the attractions that
egotism holds for most, if not all, human beings. Yet, whatever the tempta-
tions to make oneself the center of the world, what does one do when there is
no socially approved way to live for oneself? Victorian discussion of women's
issues includes not only the sentimentality of homemaking as women's near
holy vocation (as in John Ruskin's "Of Queen's Gardens") but also the practical assumption that marriage constituted the sole female "business." Why
open up more jobs for women, one 1859 *Saturday Review* essayist argues,
when marriage *is* a woman's job? The failure of individual women to marry—

to succeed in their inevitable career, that is—no more validates other options for female employment than the failure of individual businessmen invalidates a market economy (what would this essayist have made of Marxist theory?):

> Married life is woman's profession; and to this life her training (that of dependence) is modelled. Of course by not getting a husband, or losing him, she may find that she is without resources. All that can be said of her is, she has failed in business; and no social reform can prevent such failures. The mischance of the distressed governess and the unprovided widow, is that of every insolvent tradesman. He is to be pitied, but all the Social Congresses in the world will not prevent the possibility of a mischance in the shape of broken-down tradesmen, old maids, or widows.[7]

In the same age that saw duty as central to the conception of human character a *Blackwood's* essayist could write of the spinster's "absolutely disengaged state" and "narrow sphere." [8] The old maid will remain youthful compared to the matron, this writer claims, because her shallower life renders her relatively impervious to pain. What suffering she experiences will be largely vicarious, and "sympathy in other's trials, however deep and long sustained, does not inflict on the countenance the permanent lines that the like cares do in our own case." Such an assertion, however, nullifies the essayist's earlier bland claim that "Trial comes to all." Clearly the assumption here is that the old maid does not experience life as deeply or as fully as the married woman and consequently "will carry about an atmosphere, as it were, of her calling, a virginal over-trimness . . . [and the signs of] unchecked particularities" (100). In other words, as Victorian society defined the spinster's life as incomplete, it defined the spinster herself as an only partially developed person. The central issue in *Cranford* and *Villette* then is the single woman's struggle to define herself when female singleness violates society's prescriptions.

Whereas Dickens's and Thackeray's novels demonstrate an overriding fear of cruel women, in *Cranford* and *Villette* the women themselves—single women—are afraid. They fear the loss of self in a society that threatens to erase them. In this context even the eagerness to win romantic attention, to be seen as attractive in conventionally feminine terms, emerges as not mere coquetry or pathetic middle-aged vanity but a desire to claim validation in one of the few ways open. Although the Cranfordians fear male aggression, the worst aggression they face is that which ignores rather than openly attacks them. Thus even Miss Matty's bluffly loving brother, Peter, betrays a typical insensitivity by reminiscing about her former suitor and informing his sister that she "must have played [her] cards badly" to lose him.[9] Too inattentive to notice his sister's distress until it has reached an uncontrollable state, Peter fails to understand even then that his own crudity is the cause of her pain (213). He is too immersed in his own condescension toward old maids (as witnessed in his telling of tall tales to his sister's friends) to credit them with the full range of feeling. Likewise, although Lucy has one unpleasant experience of being followed at night by lecherous males, male indifference is a far more pervasive threat. Men from Mr. Home to Dr. John see her only as a shadow, a background figure to the more graceful Paulina or the flashy Ginevra. As Jill Matus points out, Lucy's near invisibility complicates our contemporary focus on male spectatorship of women as oppressive. Matus observes, "The fact that Lucy is often unseen, overlooked and unrecognised provokes both resentment and hurt." Lucy *wants* to be seen "as an admired and desirable self." [10] Meanwhile female friendship in *Villette* and *Cranford* has some practical constrictions: it "is inevitably defined and limited by woman's economic position." [11] Men's greater social authority and opportunities mean, as Miss Matty wistfully puts it in *Cranford,* that "a man has a sort of knowledge of what should be done in difficulties, [so] that it is very pleasant to have one at hand ready to lean upon" (180). Because a man's romantic interest can determine the course of a woman's life, her dwelling place, and her social and economic status, this relationship has practical implications absent in most relationships between women. One result of the power men's marital choices have over women's lives is that an "unchosen" woman may lose some value even in the eyes of family and friends, as witness Miss Matty's brother, Peter, or Lucy's friend, Polly.

Both Gaskell and Brontë emphasize their heroines' existential quandaries by strictly limiting any subsidiary attachments that might replace the marital bond. This in itself is a departure from "most of the women writing in the eighteen-forties and fifties [who] do manage to provide their unmarried protagonists with people to whose needs they can 'minister'—dependent mothers, sisters, nieces and nephews, or, at least, pupils who require the moral influence of the heroine." [12] Although Lucy teaches, her pupils are hardly susceptible to her moral influence. She is an orphan and an inhabitant of a foreign country, albeit one wherein some long-lost English friends also reside. Miss Matty has outlived her parents long before the opening of *Cranford,* loses her sister early in the book, and does not encounter her brother again until the novel's conclusion. She has closer friends than Lucy ever cherishes, but neither woman has the family that Victorians found so sacred. [13]

This separation from family, the symbolic source of comfort, peace, and a stable identity, is indicative of wider social alienation. Lucy is not merely without relatives, she has no form of social and financial backing. Even her standing as a "lady" is threatened by financial necessity, as Polly's amazement at her employment indicates. Throughout *Villette,* moreover, Lucy faces even grimmer threats than loss of caste. She is frequently reminded that she has no support other than herself and no assurance that her attempts to earn her own living will end in anything other than destitution.[14] Miss Matty, meanwhile, faces a genteel poverty that constricts her psychologically as well as materially. Yet no form of employment is acceptable to Cranfordian propriety until Miss Matty's financial ruin forces her into refined retailing in tea.

Gaskell is more willing than Brontë to detail the financial concerns of her spinsters, perhaps because she is working in comedy, where the mundane and material are typically used to deflate pretension. Thus the opening pages of *Cranford* juxtapose the euphemistic circumlocutions of the Cranfordians in their attempts at exalting "elegant economy" with the prosaic clatter of pattens on the pavements: one form of elegant economy being the refusal—or rather the inability—to pay for a chair. This typically farcical touch, however, should not disguise the very real restrictions upon the women's lives, restrictions arising from limited means, which are themselves a reflection of the women's lack of "success" in the only female career, marriage. The Cranfordians struggle to maintain their status despite their straitened means, just as they struggle to maintain their claims to "femininity" despite their single state (itself a violation of Victorian feminine norms). The situation is exacerbated by certain female roles being inseparably linked to class and money. W. R. Greg, after all, perceived female servants as one class of women who could acceptably remain unmarried because even as spinsters, "they fulfil both essentials of woman's being; *they are supported by, and they minister to, men.*"[15] The real difficulty, for Greg and other Victorians as well, lay with "ladies," who by their gender should be "attached to others and . . . connected with other existences, which they embellish, facilitate, and serve," but who by their class must not "become drudges—either mere nursemaids or mere housewives" (Greg 451, 447). One result, as Greg acknowledges, is that gender identity often conflicts with class identity, and since both are indispensable to a satisfactorily constructed self, unavoidable tension arises.

Faced with the problem of how to remain "ladies" despite their poverty, and women despite their single status, the Cranfordians resort to strategies that camouflage their social reality while acquiescing in social expectations. Thus they display the dainty appetites that meet standard expectations of femininity and class refinement. Yet this action is essentially a way to avoid shaming themselves by acknowledging that they are too poor to feed themselves (41–42). These women try to hide their preparation and need of food; Mrs. Forrester doesn't admit that she makes her pastries herself (41), and her guests don't acknowledge that they might want something heartier for their repast. Mrs. Forrester's evasion in particular is an instance of two clashing ideals that run throughout *Cranford:* traditionally nourishing femininity and dainty gentility. The domestic duties that she tries to hide from her guests are part of the household routine for Matty's mother, who is making cowslip wine when her son comes to bid her farewell (96–97). Ironically, however, the tasks that appear necessary and even dignified for a family matron apparently are inappropriate for a single woman acting as hostess for her peers. She clearly is not playing the mother's role of nurture but rather is acting out of economic necessity. Family responsibility brings dignity with it, but financial constraints corrode social position. Likewise, the Cranfordians' eagerness to deny their own appetites is an instance of their more general denial of their poverty. Gaskell indulges in some painful play with the old joke that spinsters insist they chose to remain single: the assumption, of course, is that such an insistence must be false. The Cranfordians, much more poignantly, attempt to claim as voluntary the financial limitations of their lives (41–42). As Eileen Gillooly puts it:

> Where silent disavowal fails to ward off the stark character of reality, euphemism generally succeeds. "Elegant economy" is the Cranfordians' description of the penury they suffer in having to eke out an existence from diminutive incomes, which they are prevented by gender and class from increasing through professional employment. Even while this description of their finances cheats the socioeconomic truth of the situation—that these women are hounded by worries of insolvency—it also disarms the pain of poverty, by making money seem ungenteel.[16]

The truth is obvious, however, whenever a brush with affluence enables the women to experience real satisfaction. When the parvenue Miss Barker serves an abundance of food, the genteel Cranfordians eat as in a trance, even then refusing to acknowledge the hungers that they nonetheless are sating (111).

Such a refusal arises from a sense of shame about not simply the body's needs but the monetary inability to meet those needs. The women in this book always feel ashamed of their relations with money. Miss Matty feels personally responsible for the failure of the bank in which she has invested her money (177), and the friends who contribute to her support feel compelled to apologize for their proffered amounts, regardless of whether they consider the sums too small or too large (193–94). The only satisfactory way for them to possess money apparently is through domestic connection: as a daughter, wife, mother, or sister, a woman can draw upon masculine resources without guilt. No wonder then that men are necessary for last-minute rescues from catastrophic poverty.

The nervousness that afflicts all of Cranford's women, their susceptibility to "panics" about prowlers, their superstitious anxiety about the apparently supernatural tricks of a conjurer, especially their horrific stories of bloodshed and unnatural death (141–42), are legitimate expressions of a far profounder anxiety. They can express only through such indirect means the lack of social stability inherent in their position as women without men or children—women who cannot be relative creatures because they have no one to be related to and who have no social backing for lives as autonomous beings. The most obvious means by which these women are continually reminded of their own contingency is their poverty, and it is poverty—not spinsterhood per se—that haunts this book like a specter. Miss Jessy Brown, for instance, is an object of intense concern after the deaths of her father and sister because she is left bereaved and virtually penniless. The "romantic" happy ending to her story, in which she is conveniently reunited with a long-lost suitor, is happy not so much because it satisfies expectations about heterosexual mating patterns, but because it saves her from a precarious existence as a governess (59).[17] Money is what matters here, as we are reminded by Miss Matty's parallel rescue at the end of the novel. Miss Matty's long-lost brother, not her long-lost suitor, restores her fortunes at the story's climax, with the absence of heterosexual romance in this rescue underscoring the irrelevance of romance in the previous one.

In addition to their making dramatic rescues, however, men in *Cranford*—at least, good men—make their infrequent appearances mostly as figures of bounty. They, not women, are the providers and servers of food, roles that their greater strengths enable them to fill.[18] Captain Brown, for instance, is admirable primarily for his willingness to serve food, from his desire to pass around the trays at an evening party (46) to his solicitude in carrying home an impoverished old woman's supper for her (49). In both cases his superior strength makes him a "natural" server of relatively fragile women. The irony is that as a man Brown is socially as well as physically more powerful than the women around him: his greater access to the professions, to travel, and to knowledge derives from his sex as much as his muscular development does. Gaskell, however, emphasizes his physical capabilities—his handiness around the house, even his athletic death—as the source of his difference from the women and the compelling reason why he should minister to them as women traditionally have ministered to men: by attending to their wants and appetites. This idea of a man as an inexhaustible provider of support, of course, is as much a fantasy as the same idea of a woman, and Brown's prompt demise at the end of the first chapter emphasizes that he has no real existence.

His appearance, however, lasts long enough to demonstrate that the standards for judging men should include their abilities as providers. Unfortunately, although men may be responsible for most of the best food in the book—reasonably enough, since the women are too impoverished to provide it themselves—they too often lack the nurturing qualities allowing them to serve that food effectively. For instance, Mr. Holbrook serves his female guests a feast of fresh peas as part of their dinner with him, but he is too inattentive to notice that most are unable to eat with the implements he has provided (74–75). Holbrook's lavishness provides a poignant contrast to the stinted fare of attenuated bread and wispy pastries that the women serve among themselves, but his abundant food does not ultimately nourish because he does not create the conditions in which it can be eaten.

Gaskell in the Holbrook dinner scene uses the same Arabian Nights allusion as Thackeray: the ghoul Amina's dinner of rice grains. Yet while Thackeray uses Amina as a parallel to threatening, falsely fastidious females, Gaskell emphasizes Amina's deprivation. This Amina is not a ghoul but a hungry, underfed woman, partly pathetic, partly comic, and entirely unthreatening. The Arabian Amina starved herself at civilized meals so that she could gorge herself in bloody feasts afterward, thus showing a savagery that Thackeray suggests is endemic to other "respectable" women. To him, in short, the woman who deprives herself can be as threatening as the woman who is openly selfish. After all, the original Amina fed on corpses late at night, and Thackeray's Blanche Amory gobbles sweets in her bedroom. Gaskell, on the other hand, suggests that women have nothing to gorge upon; the women in *Cranford* have no possibility of a nocturnal feast once Holbrook's fresh peas have been carried away from the table. This paucity of food is one way to symbolize the more general paucity of the women's lives, which in turn accounts for the prevalence of fantasy in these lives. Thus after Holbrook's death Miss Matty clings to the notion of herself as his semiwidow, even the fantasy of a bereavement being preferable to the limitations of reality.

This fantasy is worthy of more detailed consideration. Miss Matty's abortive love affair with Holbrook perhaps is the most blatant example of class pressures in the book. Yet the episode shows more than the sundering of two people by social conventions. Holbrook, when we meet him, is forgetful of the past, unselfconsciously friendly toward Miss Matty, yet incapable of being moved to renewed ardor by an old woman. Time, which has only decreased Miss Matty's value, has added to Holbrook's. He has had the opportunity to enlarge his talents and improve both his fortune and social standing. As a successful gentleman farmer, he would be a worthy match for Miss Matty, but gender conventions prove less malleable than class ones: as an old woman, Miss Matty is definitively outside the marriage market. While men have at least some limited opportunities to improve their class standing over time, women must always lose ground through the years since they lose the youthful looks that give them value as sexual objects. Only by using their period of youth to establish connections with a man, thus gaining the stable position of a wife and mother, can women ensure their own continued value during middle and old age. As a result, the identity they gain through romantic love dominates their imaginations as much as it determines their actual lives. In one of the novel's most poignant moments Miss Matty claims at least the pretense of an established social role by requesting a widow's caplike headgear after Holbrook's death. Whereas ironically Holbrook's death stems from his passion for France, an aspect of the unquenchable appetite for more experience that defines him—and exactly the type of experience unavailable to Miss Matty—she meanwhile perforce defines herself through an imagined relationship. The fictitious marriage to Holbrook is the only experience on which she can unleash her imagination.

It is no wonder that Miss Matty regrets that lost opportunity, for Gaskell shows how marriage and—even more—motherhood are the formative experiences that her society provides for women. Miss Matty's own mother unwittingly illustrates this process through her letters, in which courtship evokes only her pettish vanity and small concerns while motherhood draws from her a rush of nurturance. Maternity allows the mother to "grow up" in the conventional sense, by turning her from self-absorption to nurturance (86–87). This role also allows her power, however, for as a mother she can legitimately be superior to her children. Even her ignorance is no obstacle to her dignity (88). Miss Matty's mother cannot write English without "fault in grammar, and often in spelling," but she maintains her authority nonetheless. When the eldest daughter, Deborah, precocious even as a child, "*would* ask questions her mother could not answer, . . . she did not let herself down by saying she did not know, but took to stirring the fire, or sending the 'forrard' child on an errand" (88). Motherhood had (and still has) abundant opportunities for self-sacrifice, thus enabling women to wish for it without fearing accusations of selfishness; it also offers opportunities for power and for self-assertion (157–59). The childlessness of the Cranfordians is as significant a feature of their lives as their singleness, for by not being parents they lose one guaranteed form of stature. Rather than possessing parental authority over children who owe them deference and attention, they lose with age most of whatever status they had, so that Miss Matty, for example, apologizes for seeking the young Mary Smith's company.

Miss Matty herself acknowledges that she has missed her vocation when she regrets her failure not so much to find a husband as to fulfill her potential as a housekeeper and mother. This is explicitly given to us as the one occupation in which Miss Matty might have really succeeded. "I never was ambitious," she says wistfully, "but I thought I could manage a house (my mother used to call me her right hand), and I was always so fond of little children—the shyest babies would stretch out their little arms to come to me; when I was a girl, I was half my leisure time nursing in the neighbouring cottages" (158). Miss Matty does show the one form of ambition Victorian society emphatically approved of in women: that of being everything to a child. She dreams of "a little child—always the same—a little girl of about two years old; she never grows older, though I have dreamt about her for many years" (158). Perpetually unformed and dependent, this dream child is also permanently silent: Miss Matty never "dream[s] of any words or sound she makes; she is very noiseless and still, but she comes to [Miss Matty] when she is very sorry or very glad" (158–59), and Miss Matty's maternal kiss is her utmost desire. This dream girl is thus the very quintessence of the child as a passive reflector of adult power and bounty: without personality of its own, its existence is a mere unchanging affirmation of parental importance. Miss Matty's fantasy is touching—indeed, deeply moving—but its pathos is not limited to that of a woman yearning to give nurture: at least as much it is a woman's longing to receive the tribute of dependent love. Yet Miss Matty's "natural" affinity for tending children is limited to the domestic sphere: after her financial debacle, her ignorance rules out the prospect of earning a living as a teacher (185–86). If Matty were her pupils' mother, instead of a potential teacher, her own lack of education would be no problem: she could still command respect and exact obedience—as her own mother did. But ignorance is unforgivable in a professional educator: another sign of her—and the other women's—estrangement from a world that has constructed them so that *only* domesticity offers a viable role. Indeed Miss Matty's wish for motherhood is her strongest aspiration toward authority. Although the life of a Victorian matron was certainly limited in many ways, she represents it as providing scope for action and decision: rather than being "in the power of her clever servant" (67), she dreams of running an entire household.

In the novel's slyest allusion to motherhood, the comic subterfuge by which Deborah Jenkyns decrees that she and Miss Matty will enjoy their oranges without risking the appearance of suckling infants is an attempt—no matter how farcically exaggerated—to maintain a dignity perceived as under attack (66). The breast-feeding woman, after all, is the most visible emblem of the woman whose very existence is nourishing to others, while the suckling infant represents the most extreme helplessness. Both aspects of this figure have the potential to disturb Deborah and Matty. Obviously their own lives have not run along the traditionally feminine lines of the nurturing mother. In a culture that exalts the mother their own lives appear unsuccessful. In addition to this harsh reminder of cultural norms, however, the Jenkyns sisters provide the even more ominous reminder of human helplessness. They, like all the Cranfordians, want to avoid the dependence of the infant. Even such a minor character as Miss Brown suffers her worst affliction not in the agony of prolonged illness but in the knowledge that her invalidism is a burden to her family (50). Miss Matty herself, the "perpetual child" (Gillooly 893), regards visible dependence with such horror that her friends feel compelled to disguise their aid to her, even at some cost to their honesty. The Cranfordians attempt to live independently in a society that neither recognizes nor honors female independence. It is no wonder then that the Jenkyns sisters shun reproducing the image of a nurtured child: an image that threatens their dignity.

The whole issue of dignity is further complicated, of course, by the significance of class. Overtly *Cranford* privileges gender status over class: Miss Matty's separation from Holbrook (and therefore from marriage and motherhood) is poignantly sad; Lady Glenmire's inversely parallel willingness to marry a doctor and thereby live according to feminine norms at the expense of social status is one of the few bright spots of the story. Yet the book's opening declaration that there are no men in *Cranford* when it means only that there are no gentlemen (39) suggests the extent to which class influences gender categories. The treatment of Martha's husband (188–89) as half-clownish, half-pathetic, and always subordinate to the interests of his wife's employer sufficiently suggests that *he* does not benefit from gender norms. Martha fulfills her role as a nurturing woman not through devotion to husband and child but to Miss Matty (204). No less than a spinster, she does not live her life to serve a man but does devote it to serving her mistress: an instance, sadly, not of female bonding but of class hierarchy.

Thus the working-class family inevitably must fail to follow the pattern of patriarch, wife, and angelic children that is sentimentalized in Victorian rhetoric and implicitly is the goal of Miss Matty herself. Martha fails the norms of femininity even when she becomes a wife and mother because her duties of nurturance are directed toward following class not gender norms. Jem is emphatically not in the privileged position of a man because even his house is not his own to inhabit freely (190). As for maternal pieties Martha considers her own children mainly in the light of whether they will be acceptable to Miss Matty. She dreads the idea that "the new claimant [her expected infant] would require attentions from its mother that it would be faithless treason to Miss Matty to render" (204). Martha's fears on this score might seem ironic, in view of Miss Matty's sentimentality about children in general, but these are working-class children and hence not subject to the same idealization as the offspring of the wellborn.

On a somewhat higher level Miss Matty's abortive entry into trade involves her in a subtle clash between gender and professional norms. As we have seen, Miss Matty, although apparently born to be a mother, cannot be a teacher: she is equipped to fill the domestic not the professional role. Likewise when she becomes a retailer of tea and candy, she cannot fulfill her duties as a merchant because she is absorbed in attempting to fulfill the traditional duties of a mother. As a shopkeeper she should sell what customers want while maximizing her own profits. But as a would-be nurturer she frets over the possibly deleterious effects of green tea on her adult patrons (202) and converts profit to loss by indulging her child customers with extra candy (204–5). Apparently she cannot bear to be in a business relationship with children rather than a traditionally feminine nurturing one. She cannot let her own need for self-support in the masculine world of business outweigh the caretaking and pleasure-giving aspects of the feminine role. Her anxious query to the town's other grocer about how her mercantile enterprise will affect him underscores her belief that she cannot abandon domesticity without doing injury to others (200). Her insecurity about selling food at all and her further anxiety about the effects of what she sells are emblematic of her insecurity about her own status as a nurturing woman: can anything she provides really satisfy others' needs? Since she does not occupy the matronly position that supposedly facilitates a woman's ability to do good, what good can she do?

Miss Matty's continuing insecurities fuel the book's sadness, so that appropriately the food that appears is mostly "comfort food," not the celebratory fare of the pages of Dickens or Trollope. The Cranfordians show their sympathy for the invalid Miss Brown and her long-suffering family by gifts of food (54–55); later Martha prepares a lion couchant as consolation for Miss Matty in her penury (184); and later still, the country folk bring offerings of eggs and other farm produce to Miss Matty in lieu of cash (205). The kindness of these people toward one another is luminous, but such gifts of food are more effectual as symbols of sympathy than as alleviations of difficulties. For the provision of bounty sufficient to last a lifetime, men are necessary.

Cranford at least ostensibly is a comic novel; *Villette* is so bleak a book that at least one contemporary critic believes that only childhood sexual abuse could account for the heroine's consistently despairing outlook.[19] As with Gaskell's characters, however, other threats appear far more terrifying to Brontë's heroine than the specter of aggressive sexuality. Lucy Snowe is trapped by poverty in an essentially unsatisfying career, deprived of familial support, and faced with a financially precarious future. In the light of her very real practical worries it becomes all the more interesting that she herself lays the blame for her depression primarily upon emotional causes: specifically upon the absence of romantic love in her life.[20] Even more particular, Lucy despairs that she will never have the opportunity to sacrifice herself for another. She is forced (according to her argument) into egotism and selfishness, yet (she protests) she would prefer self-abnegation. Brontë herself expressed sentiments that imply values similar to Lucy's. Gaskell's *Life of Charlotte Brontë* has Brontë writing in 1851 that a *Westminster* article "on the Emancipation of Women" (Harriet Taylor and John Stuart Mill's "Enfranchisement of Women") is "clear, logical—but vast is the hiatus of omission" because

> the writer forgets there is such a thing as self-sacrificing love and disinterested devotion. When I first read the paper, I thought it was the work of a powerful-minded, clear-headed woman, who had a hard, jealous heart, muscles of iron, and nerves of bend leather; of a woman who longed for power, and had never felt affection. To many women affection is sweet and power conquered indifferent—though we all like influence won.[21]

Brontë's novel, for all the piercing longing it expresses for an ideal communion, nonetheless depicts with equal forcefulness the nullity of unsatisfactory relationships. Her heroine consistently is torn between craving for companionship and disdain for inferior associates. Although food plays an important role in all of Brontë's novels in both scenes of communion and metaphors of hunger and satisfaction, Lucy Snowe has a particularly tortured relationship with it because it represents her ambivalence toward human interrelatedness, something she both desires and disdains.

This ambivalence expresses itself in other ambiguous attitudes as well. Above all, Lucy cannot find any acceptable ways for female flesh to represent and express inner emotions and personality. She seems to wish for what is humanly impossible: disembodied feeling. Other people routinely regard Lucy as without deep feeling, yet for her, deep feeling is the touchstone of personality and the foundation of merit. In fact she ends up emphasizing feeling in opposition to flesh, not as part of a traditional angel/whore dichotomy but as a way to claim a space for emotion apparently untrammeled by the reality that she finds drearily sordid. Lucy detests materialism, but she pits it not against etherealism, supposedly the crowning attribute of Victorian femininity but against passion, an attribute that she simultaneously prizes and fears. As if in compensation for other people's assumption that she neither feels nor expresses much, Lucy chooses for her heroine the figure most associated with undiluted emotion and its expression. Her ideal of the nonmaterial is Vashti, a scandal-ridden actress named after Esther's biblical predecessor, a woman who defied her husband. The actress Vashti is no more traditionally feminine than the biblical character had been, but she is lifted by sensibility above the confines of body and convention. Vashti is "not good," but she *is* undeniably spiritual: "scarcely a substance herself" (340). Yet her spirituality contains a potential for good denied to the mere mass of "full-fed flesh"; "if so much of unholy force can arise from below, may not an equal efflux of sacred essence descend one day from above?" (340). Meanwhile, Vashti's intensity, whether good or evil, is the touchstone whereby Dr. John reveals his superficiality; unable to appreciate her "Pythian inspiration" (341), his "branding judgment" of her actually damns himself (342). It is no wonder that Lucy, also passion-ridden and also unappreciated by Dr. John, feels a kinship with Vashti, but she can acknowledge a bond between them only by imagining Vashti as "an inordinate will" at odds with "a perishing mortal frame" (342), not as a woman who has both will and body.

Vashti at least is heroic. On the other hand, the painted Cleopatra whom Lucy observes at an art gallery is entirely earth-bound and ignoble because of her slavish sensuality; her beefy body symbolizes a coarse soul. Caustically shredding the conventional glamour of the figure, Lucy describes her with rich detail:

> I calculated that this lady, put into a scale of magnitude suitable for the reception of a commodity of bulk, would infallibly turn from fourteen to sixteen stone. She was, indeed, extremely well fed: very much butcher's meat—to say

nothing of bread, vegetables, and liquids—must she have consumed to attain that breadth and height, that wealth of muscle, that affluence of flesh. She lay half-reclined on a couch: why, it would be difficult to say; broad daylight blazed round her; she appeared in hearty health, strong enough to do the work of two plain cooks; she could not plead a weak spine; she ought to have been standing, or at least sitting bolt upright. (275)

Fleshiness here suggests not simply the voluptuousness that men might find desirable but also the woman's sloth, her vulgarity (she is fit to be only a plain cook), her less-than-human mental and physical inertia. She is thus equivalent to the "swinish multitude" of Lucy's pupils, whose "robust and solid" "contours" and greed in eating (291–92) signal that they are devoid of "self-respect," and composed entirely of "incapacity, ignorance, and sloth" (146–47). Brontë thereby draws a damning parallel between grossness of the Labassecourian schoolgirls, reared in an artificial and hypocritical "innocence," and that of the Egyptian femme fatale whose allure Brontë strips ruthlessly away. This Cleopatra is a "slug," a "pulpy mass" compared to the "scimitar"-like Vashti (340). Only "materialists" would "worshi[p]" (340) the Cleopatra and by implication would revere the Labassecourian maidens. Thus the traditional opposites of exotic eroticism and domestic purity are equated here as variations on sordidness.

For Brontë passion is an important component of spirituality; she uses the Cleopatra to symbolize stolidity rather than feeling. Male observers who find the Cleopatra titillating reveal only their own shallowness. Passion opposes mere meatiness, however, and also what is "as bad in [its] way" (278): the bloodless insipidity of the female celebrated in "La vie d'une femme." This woman resembles M. Paul's first love, Justine-Marie, in being nothing, a mere compound of "a weak frame, inactive passions, acquiescent habits" (484). Not "le type du voluptueux" like the Cleopatra (282), she yet lacks the substance of mind and spirit. Such women are not "anges" but "cold and vapid . . . insincere, ill-humoured, bloodless, brainless nonentities" (278). This creates a double bind for women: erotic fleshiness is ignoble but so is wholesome milk-and-water insipidity, for both imply a mental torpor. The only appropriate food imagery for women uses food as a metaphor for intense passions rather than a suggestion of either female voluptuousness or feminine wholesomeness.

Along with the painted Cleopatra and the eponymous "Femme," Paulina and Ginevra also prove unsatisfactory models of female physicality for Lucy. Instead, Paulina and Ginevra could represent the positive and negative models for traditional, marriage-focused femininity. Ginevra, despite her surface fragility and her unending desire to be taken care of, is one of the most robust characters in the book. Yet her strength is that of the baby whose utter self-absorption and persistence in wailing ensures its being fed. Ginevra constantly filches food: she gets "the lion's share, whether of the white beer, the sweet wine, or the new milk" of Lucy's portion (313).[22] Her buxom beauty reflects her ardent appetites: Lucy emphasizes Ginevra's weightiness, which is a part of her seductiveness for men imperceptive enough to prize flesh for its own sake (470). In her fleshy style of beauty Ginevra is akin to Mme. Beck, another buxom belle and materialist.

Paulina, meanwhile, is virtually weightless: light as a child when Dr. John carries her out of the theater (344). Although Helena Michie uses Paulina as one of her key examples for the abstemious woman as a "model of feminin- ity,"[23] Lucy herself despiritualizes even this ethereal creature by comparing her to a dog. Describing M. Paul's spaniel, Lucy remarks, "She was very tiny, and had the prettiest little innocent face, the silkiest long ears, the finest dark eyes in the world. I never saw her, but I thought of Paulina de Bassompierre: for- give the association, reader, it *would* occur" (510). Even if one ignores the implication of bitchiness, further hinted at in mentions of Paulina as a "vexed, . . . naughty being" capable of "transient perverseness and petulance" (389), the comparison suggests her limitations of mind and feeling. She does repre- sent a type of perfection, but the perfection of conventionality that distrusts passion. Even the way in which she squeezes the "flavor" out of her reply to Dr. John's proposal, rewriting three times in order to "confec[t] . . . a morsel of ice flavoured with ever so slight a zest of fruit or sugar" (466) before she sends it, shows caution as well as purity. Paulina does love Dr. John and admits as much to Lucy, but both women know that strong feelings—even of love— could disgust Dr. John, whose "tastes are so fastidious" (466). Even the delec- table Paulina knows that her love must be mild to tempt his appetite. Thus, in *Villette* as in *Cranford* women need not fear aggression so much as rejection. Women must be wary of not showing too little emotion but too much because men neither credit nor want to credit women with having the same strength of feeling as males. One reason for this masculine reluctance obviously is that female feelings—even of deep attraction—can be as invasive and unwelcome to men as male encroachments to women.

While Paulina's modest fears about her letter only hint at the threatening potential of other people's feelings, Lucy's ambivalence about human relation- ships much more fully illustrates that threat. This ambivalence deserves par- ticular examination because it is one way Brontë, whether wittingly or not, undercuts the sentiments about "self-sacrificing love and disinterested devo- tion" she expresses above. A striking element of this novel, a novel that Harriet Martineau criticized for its excessive emphasis on love and outraged some readers because its heroine was attracted to two men at one time, is the gener- ally unloving nature of its heroine. In her infamous review of *Jane Eyre* Elizabeth Rigby complained that Jane looks down upon her Lowood com- panions and chooses the isolation of which she is simultaneously the victim.[24]

Whether or not one agrees with Rigby's overall assessment of Jane, she is correct in asserting that Jane judges most of her fellows and finds them wanting. Lucy is even more judgmental, declaring frankly, "I might have had companions, and I chose solitude. Each of the teachers in turn made me overtures of special intimacy; I tried them all" (194). None of her colleagues survives that trial, and Lucy despises her students and Mme. Beck as well. Her condemnations are so frequent and so severe that it begins to appear that Lucy finds something demeaning, even degrading in human contact. More than four hundred pages into *Villette,* Lucy says of Paulina, "I liked her," only to add immediately, "it is not a declaration I have often made concerning my acquaintance in the course of this book" (461): a statement with which the reader can only concur. Lucy clearly is proud of her fastidiousness, however, which she exhibits in both her emotional and nutritive needs. To her, as self-indulgence in food betrays a coarse materialism, so pleasure in unworthy companions suggests a corresponding lowness. Unlike the gross Labassecouriennes, she herself needs coffee (a nerve stimulant) more than the roll that accompanies it (312), and more than either does she need the manna of ideal love. "[A]nimals kept in cages, and so scantily fed as to be always upon the verge of famine, await their food as I awaited a letter," Lucy declares at one point (350). The simile is instructive. Animals hunger for food, but a person—or at least this person—hungers for affection, in this case affection conveyed through the disembodied and thus asexual form of a letter. This emotional hunger is implicitly more crucial even than bodily hunger, if one judges by the amount and detail of Lucy's attention to it. When affection comes, it is "the wild savoury mess of the hunter, nourishing and salubrious meat, forest-fed or desert-reared, fresh, healthful, and life-sustaining" (318). Thus material food is rejected in favor of inherently spiritual love, only for that love to be metamorphosed back into food, a physically as well as psychologically sustaining force. This image, however, makes a mockery of Mme. Beck's advice to Lucy to "eat your supper, drink your wine, oubliez les anges, les bossues, et surtout, les Professeurs" (489). Mme. Beck assumes that self-nourishment exists independently of interest in others; Lucy assumes—perhaps more correctly—that people can never fully nourish themselves and that consequently everyone needs, in a sense, to "eat" and "drink" others. Yet this metaphoric pattern undercuts the idea that the longing to love represents an escape from egotism, just as Lucy's contemptuous dismissal of would-be companions undercuts the pathos of her solitude. No one eats altruistically: if love is food, then Lucy's desire for it is by no means a simple wish to "lay down the whole burden of human egotism" (450). When Paulina artlessly wonders why Schiller declares that *to* love is "the summit of earthly happiness, the end of life" and decides that "[i]f Schiller had said to *be* loved, he might have come nearer the truth," Lucy sees Paulina as merely ignorant about the subject (389). Yet the nature of love makes both claims potentially false, since—as the book makes abundantly clear—to love or to be loved can sometimes "be the extreme of mortal misery, . . . sheer waste of time, and fruitless torture of feeling" (389). To love, however, is no more inherently unselfish than to be loved. As Paulina's caution in revising her letters suggests, proffered love may even repel its intended recipient because love is not simply benevolence.

Villette consistently points out the irony that love itself can be an act of aggression, because human love is inseparable from the desire for response. In this twist Brontë offers a different model of human relations than, say, the Dickensian ideal of female love as so selfless, pure, and all-giving that it would be hard for anyone to demur at being its object. Brontë knows that an unwanted offering of love can be as offensive as reciprocated love is attractive. Like food, love has the potential either to be appetizing or to turn the stomach. Unlike food, which exists only to be eaten in a one-sided act, however, the female lover in Brontë seeks to satisfy her beloved's appetites as well as gratify her own. Women in love hunger for not only sexual pleasure but attention, tenderness, affirmation of their worth. As a result men do not simply receive; they must give, and the offering of love is itself a demand to receive love in return. The child Polly (the young Paulina) finds this out to her grief when she attempts to join the party Graham (the young Dr. John) holds for his schoolmates. Happy to accept her lavishly proffered attentions when they fit his mood, Graham imperiously repulses his adorer when he is engaged with other companions. Neither the child nor the woman repeats that one mistake, but this abstinence is as much self-protective as altruistic. Paulina will not risk another rebuff because Graham/John's approval is crucial to her own happiness. In a similar fashion Lucy's insistence upon the modesty of her requirements underscores the intensity of her desire, and that intensity amplifies her apparently minor claims to extraordinary proportions. Thus in a striking manifestation of Victorian gender ideology Lucy can express her longing for love—a longing that inevitably is egotistical and self-serving—as a longing to have someone *to love* and thereby a way to fulfill the caretaking responsibilities Victorian society assigned to women. Brontë herself, as her remarks on Taylor/Mill's "Enfranchisement of Women" indicate, endorsed that ideology, even though its prescriptions for female love clearly do not describe actual human emotion. Far more sharply, Lucy's emphasis on her own emotional hunger conveys the reality of the desire for reciprocation and nourishment. Through this means *Villette* undercuts her apparent desire for selflessness and also by abundantly revealing her dissatisfaction with the caregiving role of her job.

As many commentators have pointed out, the first employment opportunities for middle-class Englishwomen came through paid forms of typical domestic roles. Even when "[w]ider educational and employment opportunities for women were demanded because the 'facts' of increasing spinsterhood demanded them[,] the kinds of female employment recommended were those such as nursing, teaching children, and helping the poor, all of which embodied quasi-maternal virtues of service and self-abnegation" (Foster 12). Certainly Lucy's options revolve around domestic nurturance of others. As companion to an invalid, governess to Mme. Beck's children, even as a teacher in Mme. Beck's school, and as a possible companion to Polly (a role that both Polly and Mr. Home propose for her [382]), Lucy essentially does what a daughter, mother, or sister might do for family members, especially in a time when family members did far more nursing and teaching of one another than is common nowadays. All these jobs regularize and professionalize women's traditional roles of caring for the feeble and the young. The practical and emotional stresses and strains of such roles are enormous, of course, no matter how much sentimental rhetoric about motherhood has presented such labor as natural and pleasurable to women in the domestic sphere. Yet most of that rhetoric disappears when the work is paid; during the nineteenth century women who pursued such work for pay were the targets of hostile attacks rather than objects of sentimental rhetoric. Wet nurses, medical nurses in pre–Florence Nightingale days, and nursery maids were generally shown as tawdry figures, as likely to mistreat and corrupt as attend to their charges.[25] Attitudes in general toward servants' caretaking seemed to deny it the moral uplift that distinguishes the nurturance given by ladies. Ironically the closer such caretaking came to the purely domestic model, the more suspect it seemed: the more helpless the recipients of care, the greater the distrust of those who dispensed it—*unless* they dispensed it out of "natural" affection.

At the same time as women in caretaking jobs were implicitly rebuked for wanting their wages, they were discouraged from attaining a family intimacy that might inspire them to serve from pure affection. Winifred Gerin's biography of Charlotte Brontë presents the famous anecdote wherein one of Brontë's charges declared, "'I love 'ou, Miss Brontë,' which," Gerin records, "called down on him his mother's equally famous rebuke: 'Love the *governess* my dear!'"[26] Jeanne Peterson has amply established that status incongruence was one primary source of tensions in a governess's life.[27] The lack of an established status for governesses in highly class-conscious Victorian society meant that no one knew quite how to treat them. This concept of "incongruence" applies as well to the emotional status of paid caretaking women. As Mary Poovey points out, "Because the governess was like the middle-class mother in the work she performed, but like both a working-class woman and man in the wages she received, the very figure who theoretically should have defended the naturalness of separate spheres threatened to collapse the difference between them."[28] Since such caretakers supplied services in return for money, they were subject to evaluation and dismissal as family members could not be. Remember that Miss Matty's inadequate knowledge made her unacceptable as a teacher despite her love for children, while her mother's even greater ignorance never imped-ed her revered maternity. Moreover, even while a mercenary motivation for their work deprived them of moral status, any attempt to develop close emo-tional bonds with their charges or employers could be viewed as inappropriate and intrusive.

Lucy does not desire a close relationship with those whom she educates and tends, of course, and since she is not familially connected with them, there is little external or internal pressure to pursue intimacy where none originally exists. But accordingly she also cannot derive emotional support or sustenance from them. She cannot live "through" her pupils as women were expected to live through family. Nor for that matter can she get the gratification of social approval for her duties to them because that is just her job; teaching, no mat-ter how conscientiously done, does not win her the accolades that might go to a wife and mother.

Yet the very fact that teaching (like nursing or governessing) is devoid of the familial satisfactions that supposedly accompany domestic versions of its duties could make its performance an even greater example of self-denial. To abnegate herself for her pupils' sakes is one of Lucy's options. A recurring theme in nineteenth-century writings on single women indeed was the spin-ster's option—sometimes regarded as a duty—of finding ways to devote her life to others outside a romantic context. Although tendance upon family and charitable objects was more often proffered as a model than was woman-to-woman devotion, even the latter possibility was not entirely ignored. In *A Tale of Two Cities,* for instance, Dickens sets up one of his spinsters, the middle-aged, ugly Miss Pross, as a paragon of selflessness for her loving chaperonage of young, beautiful Lucie Manette. Miss Pross is "one of those unselfish crea-tures—found only among women—who will, for pure love and admiration, bind themselves willing slaves, to youth when they have lost it, to beauty that they never had, to accomplishments that they were never fortunate enough to gain, to bright hopes that never shone upon their own sombre lives."[29] Yet Brontë's Lucy rejects the temptation to form semimaternal links with her pupils and—even more striking—with the two young women with whom her greater intimacy might naturally lead to a greater inclination toward devotion. Both Ginevra Fanshawe and Polly Home give Lucy the opportunity to per-form a "mothering" role—which in both cases Lucy decisively rejects.[30] That she is drawn to that role in some ways is clear, although her motivation—equally clearly—is not a traditional quasi-maternal tenderness. Yet the situa-tion is ripe to allow a mentoring/mothering relationship to develop. Although only a few years older than Ginevra and Polly, Lucy is perceived and perceives herself as significantly older and more mature. In the early chapters of *Villette* Brontë makes Lucy virtually Polly's superintendent and unofficial nursemaid. From her first meeting with Ginevra, Lucy is in a position of trust over her, whether chaperoning her during their shared voyage to Labassecour or teaching in the school where Ginevra is a pupil. She is a confidante for both women and even goes so far as to mend Ginevra's hose for her (149) and to assist in the undressing and bedding of the injured Polly (345–46). Yet, though she has that option, Lucy will not simply devote herself to either of them. Moreover, as if to drive home the nullity of the maternal ideal, Brontë has Ginevra (of all people) become absorbed in her child. Child replaces husband in her concern, probably because a child is even more likely than a lover to be viewed merely as an extension of self. Ginevra does not become less selfish in her possessive maternity: she simply finds a new way to express her inexhaustible egotism.

Yet the Victorian myth of motherhood was designed to obscure maternal egotism, and unassisted motherhood (as opposed to Ginevra's pampered playing at maternity) is replete with enough demands to threaten the selfhood of one who tries conscientiously to fulfill them. Lucy confronts the possibility of just such an effacement of her being when she is abandoned during the long vacation to tend a cretin, her only companion in what is otherwise complete isolation. This experience in having to practice total nurture leads Lucy to revulsion and near breakdown. Left in charge of the cretin's feeding and domestic routine, she recoils in horror from the sordid details involved. "[T]here were personal attentions to be rendered which required the nerve of a hospital nurse," Lucy declares, "my resolution was so tried, it sometimes fell dead-sick." These "menial and distasteful" duties, she adds, "deprived me often of the power and inclination to swallow a meal" (229). The result is like a nightmare vision of maternity with Lucy as the mother/victim of a monster-child that disgusts while it consumes the mother whose role is to give selflessly. Lucy's distress during the weary vacation period is almost unbearably poignant, yet her very awareness of her own desolation emphasizes that she understands her own needs. The dream that drives her almost to frenzy is that of having those needs rejected: of meeting "the well-loved dead" and finding them "alienated" from her (231). Lucy's desires to love and to be loved are inseparable. She cannot and will not simply nurture.

As Lucy herself is painfully aware, however, almost all those around her see her as lacking a full emotional life. Consequently they cannot offer her significant support; they are neither aware of her emotional needs nor interested in finding out about them. Drily she records that "Madame Beck esteemed me learned and blue; Miss Fanshawe, caustic, ironic, and cynical; Mr. Home, a model teacher, the essence of the sedate and discreet: somewhat conventional perhaps, too strict, limited and scrupulous, but still the pink and pattern of governess-correctness" (386). Perhaps most hurtful of all, Dr. John thinks her "the most peculiar, capricious little woman he knows; but yet . . . excellent'" (520), a dismissive assessment to which Lucy responds that Dr. John "'think[s] what [he] know[s] not'" (520). M. Paul may be overbearing, but he alone treats Lucy as a passionate, fully feeling creature: "a fiery and rash nature—adventurous, indocile, and audacious" (386). In a society that refuses to recognize the idea of androgynous personality, he treats her "like a woman" even if that means according to somewhat oppressive conventions, the point being that if she is not treated like a woman (and she certainly can't be treated like a man) then she can't be considered as anything deeply feeling and profoundly human. This need for recognition as an individual with strong emotions and with urgent psychological wants explains Lucy's "eagerness to marry" even after Brontë has ensured that she is "not compelled to fall back on marriage for financial independence."[31] In a novel that insists upon Lucy's passionate personality Paul provides the only external recognition and validation of that passion ("passion" here meaning the full range of human emotion, not merely sexual feeling).

Fittingly Paul's recognition of Lucy as a personality in her own right parallels his consistent feeding of her. While Lucy gives Ginevra her roll, thus playing with her the mother's role of feeding a child, Paul shares with Lucy the sweets on which he himself dotes. Both the act of feeding and the type of food involved are significant here. Paul nurtures Lucy in a way that nobody else in the book does, by consistently paying attention to her, but he feeds her on the same childish sweets that he consumes: emblems of both the tenderness and egotistical pettiness of his nature (434). Lucy, as a quasi-mother to Ginevra, gives her the same types of treats that Paul bestows Lucy, yet her passing this same kind of food to another suggests that it in and of itself is not attractive to her. Lucy is perfectly capable of using the very food that Paul sees as providing a communion between them as a way to evade and escape him (444).

Paul's reliance on sweets to show and gain affection is perhaps the sign that Lucy's relationship with him is not fully adult for either of them. It is easy to say that Paul "infantilizes" Lucy by censoring her reading materials (434–35), teaching her (439), and referring to arranging "Lucy's cot" during his time away from her (586). Yet it is also possible to see Paul himself as the child. He is, as Nina Auerbach remarks, "the Grand Turk [as] a man of straw" (109). His emotionalism, egotism, vanity, transparency, even demonstrativeness are all childish, and his control over Lucy is as much the control of a child who demands his mother's undivided attention as it is that of a patriarchal man over a submissive woman. Lucy sees through him even as she feels tender toward him, and despite her hand-kissing at the end there is a sense in which she always feels superior to him simply because she understands him so well.

Thus one result of Paul's death is that Lucy ends up with no maternal role at all. She is not biologically a mother, and those adults in her life toward whom she could have adopted a quasi-maternal role are all gone. Ginevra has fled to become a mother herself, Paulina is married to a protective man, and Paul is dead. Lucy is thrown entirely upon herself, to be as egotistical as she dares in a society that frowns on female self-centeredness. Lucy's response to this opportunity is left deliberately unclear: whether she experiences it as tragedy or triumph is up to the reader to decide. In that context, however, remember that the "three happiest years" of Lucy's life are during her separation from M. Paul. Through this period Lucy has both the assurance of total love and untouchable self-containment. After the storm Paul's death confirms her proud solitude: Lucy now exists alone in a world apparently otherwise populated by the sordidly greedy and mercenary only. If misfortune only deepens Miss Matty's credulous faith in universal kindliness and rectitude, deprivation seems to intensify Lucy's sweeping suspicions of those who surround her. The result is that her spinsterhood symbolizes a human estrangement far more radical than the simple lack of a marital relationship. We get no sense that Lucy has *any* relationships at the end of the book. Her isolation stands as the polar opposite of the family web that enmeshes a domestic woman, yet this freedom is not merely liberatory. Lucy alone is responsible for her own happiness: the terrifying possibility is that she may not be up to that task.

Yet in this deeply ironic book there is another layer of irony to discover. We have no assurance of Lucy's happiness at novel's end, but we are fully informed that we need not fear material distress for her. The ending of *Villette* would have been different indeed had M. Paul died before establishing her professionally. If Lucy didn't have her school, there would be not only psychological attitudes to consider but also unemployment, poverty, possibly even destitution. As things stand, the emphasis can be entirely on her emotional condition. Once set up, whatever her feelings about Mme. Beck as romantic rival, she need not fear her as a treacherous employer. Lucy's economic security thus allows the emphasis to remain on her supposedly thwarted femininity rather than on her plight as an under- or unemployed female worker. Brontë ends by highlighting the affective life that supposedly is everything to women. Yet inevitably there linger considerations of the social and financial aspects of existence that—while less glamorous than erotic fulfillment—are at least equally important.

Whereas Dickens's and Thackeray's novels highlight men's fear of the punitive woman, these two novels by female authors focus on women's fear—not, as in Burney's fictions, of sexual aggression—but of indifference, of being overlooked rather than looked at. This fear is not simply of sexual unattractiveness, either; one of Lucy's shrewdest—and most damning—insights into Dr. John is that his love for Polly partially depends on her socially acknowledged value: "he was not the man who, in appreciating the gem, could forget its setting" (459). To be socially marginal—"alone, unguarded, . . . a dependent worker" (459)—can also mean being emotionally marginal: subject to casual sexual exploitation, perhaps, but handicapped in the competition—and it *is* a competition in these novels—for serious regard. Miss Matty and Lucy lack the material advantages as well as the personal attributes that might attract the attention of others; above all, they lack a respected social role and an occupation they find meaningful. The heterosexual union that both crave would mean not only the presumed joys of love but significant material and psychological advantages, most notably a sphere for self-development. In craving a husband whose home she could manage and in fantasizing about a dream child whose only support she is, Miss Matty envisions greater power for herself than she has ever actually possessed. Lucy, who longs to labor for others instead of for herself and who regards Paul's mind as her library, believes that attachment to others would inspire her to make more of herself. Thus Gaskell and Brontë, like Dickens and Thackeray, undercut the idea of totally selfless female love, but whereas the male authors conjure up a female monstrosity as the diabolical mirror image of angelic femininity, Gaskell and Brontë eschew both angels and monsters. Their women seek satisfactions of their own not because of inhuman selfishness but because of human neediness. Operating out of constriction rather than plenitude, unable even to ensure their own happiness, much less anyone else's, Matty and Lucy aspire toward a connection that will enrich and empower them as well as others. That connection, indeed, appears a precondition for their having much to give at all, for neither Gaskell nor Brontë has any use for the rhetoric of inexhaustible feminine bounty. Interplay and exchange are built into the models of connection that these two female novelists offer, and the threat facing their heroines is that no exchange, no reciprocation, will be forthcoming. Without that reciprocity, both Matty and Lucy face diminished lives. It is no wonder, then, that masculine unresponsiveness is as painful to them as female punitiveness is to Dickens's and Thackeray's men. If men in Thackeray's and Dickens's novels fear women's power to make them suffer, Gaskell's and Brontë's spinster heroines fear suffering as a result of being powerless to affect men at all.

5 | Women's Work and Working Women

THE PREVIOUS TWO CHAPTERS have explored the ambivalent attitudes of male and female authors toward female provision of and associations with nourishment. But the provision of food is only one form of service, and this chapter contends that Victorian heroines were expected to "serve" in a variety of ways. So emphatic is this focus on service that it links the figure of the delicate Victorian lady with her apparent polar opposite: the members—both male and female—of the supposedly crude and coarse working class. Although ethereal, the lady nonetheless has to be strong enough to serve or else suffer condemnation. Yet while ladies are meant to devote their energies to their family circle, working-class families are not supposed to receive such devotion even from their own womenfolk. Rather, working-class women and men alike are shown ideally to direct their attention upward toward the comfort of the leisure classes.

This chapter therefore counters two current theories: first, that invalidism or at least extreme debility constituted part of the Victorian feminine ideal,[1] and second, that there was concerted pressure, both practical and rhetorical, from the Victorian bourgeois to force the working-class family into aping the bourgeois patriarchal structure. Instead, I argue for the Victorian insistence on female strength, albeit female strength represented differently for leisure-class and working-class women. This chapter draws from various texts, but the primary material comes from the novels of Charles Dickens[2] and Elizabeth Gaskell, two authors crucially concerned with facilitating friendly relations between the classes and with celebrating domesticity.

In these novels important aspects of Victorian thinking about bodies and gender emerge: first, that most Victorian literature, far from endorsing female invalidism (or even extreme fragility), instead treats it as a culpable failure of the proper feminine role. Second, the conception of "femininity" as a universal norm potentially linking all women means that feminine instruction could be transmitted either way across class lines. Consequently, a womanly working-class female could serve as an example and a rebuke to undomestic leisure-class women. Nonetheless, as the Victorians were disquieted by the ambiguous status of governesses, so they obviously were uneasy about placing working-class women—especially working-class surrogate mothers—at the level of ladies. One way to overcome this unease was to accentuate the supposed bodily differences between working-class and leisure-class women in order to retain a greater aura of idealism about the latter.

Moreover, the novels under examination here provide examples of attempts not so much to "reform" working-class families into a bourgeois model as to incorporate working-class individuals into leisure-class families. Such assimilation operates literally when such families take in working-class people as servants and psychologically when working-class individuals—like Miss Matty's Martha in the preceding chapter—become involved with leisure-class persons and concerns, sometimes to the detriment of their own families. Although it obviously reinforces class hierarchies, such assimilation removes the working classes from many traditional gender norms. In other words, working-class individuals absorbed into the lives of their social superiors cannot identify primarily with traditional gender roles, since for them loyalty to the class above them is potentially more important. This absorption can transform independent factory operatives into facsimiles of domestic servants identified with the families they serve. The virtual domestication of factory work through the establishment of personal relations between factory masters and operatives is crucial in many industrial novels.

Thus throughout the handling of women's work, class and gender expectations exist in an uneasy tension. Although working-class women pursued a wide variety of occupations, many of them brutally demanding physically,[3] reform movements throughout the nineteenth century attempted to restore them to their "rightful" domestic labor. One concern of humanitarian leaders such as Lord Ashley was that work outside the home in a factory might lead women to an unnatural and destructive independence.[4] Work inside another person's home apparently did not have these insidious effects, since it kept women firmly in a domestic role, albeit as facilitators of another woman's wifehood and motherhood rather than as wives and mothers themselves. (Most employers discouraged romance and marriage among their servants.) W. R. Greg explicitly distinguishes female servants from the mass of unmarried women on the grounds that through domestic service they live out their feminine nature as fully as any wife.[5] And the middle-class wife's labor, as Patricia Branca points out, could be extensive and fairly arduous, since the average Victorian household might easily demand more maintenance than many middle-class families could afford to pay for.[6] Yet when wives and housemaids performed similar labor—indeed, when one signifier of normal femininity was that a woman should labor exclusively in the home—how could one easily distinguish between the work of the servant and that of the mistress? How, in short, could one maintain a hierarchy of values that dignified the work of the latter as homemaking while treating the efforts of the former as merely manual drudgery? Certainly, the idealizing rhetoric about homemaking that surrounded the iconic Victorian lady did not apply to the scullery maid or cook, no matter how valuable she might have been in maintaining a clean house and healthy family.

This difficulty in defining and distinguishing between genteel and mundane domestic work is indicative of the difficulties in defining women's work generally. Conduct-book writers and novelists alike condemned idleness and uselessness among self-designated "fine ladies,"[7] and yet most mid-Victorians distrusted the idea of women working outside the home, let alone entering traditionally masculine professions. One typical strategy of novelists such as Dickens was to show vain socializing rather than a professional career as the alternative to domestic homemaking. Women in Dickens's novels and in many others need to shun the temptation to pursue not medical studies or business interests so much as a life of fashion and worldliness. This temptation, which temporarily ensnares Bella Wilfer, blights Edith Dombey's and Lady Dedlock's lives, and ruins Fanny Dorrit's existence, is the shallow and ultimately unsatisfying alternative to the quieter yet deeper pleasures and spiritual contentment of domestic usefulness.

In this context invalidism, real or imagined, would be problematic by preventing such usefulness. To that extent it is a flaw, even when involuntary, in the person suffering from it. More perniciously still, invalidism may reveal other flaws. Genuine bodily pain and weakness may induce or exacerbate the irritability and peevishness that should be anathema to a Victorian lady. When the invalidism itself is mere hypochondria, it becomes a particularly repellant form of self-indulgence. In any case the concentration upon one's own symptoms and physical state that is part of invalidism (genuine or hypochondriacal) constitutes a self-absorption that separates the invalid from the other-focused ideals of Victorian femininity.

The mildest treatment of the invalid woman is simply to make her the target of humor. Mrs. Wititterly in Dickens's *Nicholas Nickleby* [1839], for example, who has a "faded look about her" and "a face of engaging paleness,"[8] prides herself on being "of a very excitable nature; very delicate; very fragile; a hothouse plant—an exotic" (267). Her doting husband praises her in the terms she finds most congenial when he assures her, "'Your soul is too large for your body. . . . Your intellect wears you out" (267). According to Mr. Wititterly, the doctor has told him, "be proud of that woman—make much of her; she is an ornament to the fashionable world and to you. Her complaint is soul" (267). This absurd rhetoric, with its grandiose claims for Mrs. Wititterly's spirituality (reflected in her physical debility), actually assures the audience of her mendacious materialism. Mr. Wititterly's uxoriousness makes him a willing partner to this fraud, since female invalidism here—as throughout Dickens—often gives wives a way to dominate their husbands. The headaches, fainting spells, and hysterical fits of Mrs. Varden in Dickens's *Barnaby Rudge* [1841] and Mrs. Wilfer in *Our Mutual Friend* [1865] are not only demonstrations of the women's self-righteousness but also bullying ways for them to maintain an illegitimate domestic authority over their husbands. Mrs. Clennam in *Little Dorrit* [1857] is far less humorous, but she no less than the others inflicts supposed physical ills upon herself that she then uses to increase her power over others.[9]

Female invalidism generally is shown to arise from a failure to accept normative femininity. Mrs. Varden, Mrs. Wilfer, and Mrs. Clennam are all inappropriately power-hungry and punitively minded females, and their literary companions in ill health, even when generally more sympathetic, usually show a similar dissatisfaction with their female roles. The sisters Mrs. Shaw and Mrs. Hale in Gaskell's *North and South* [1855] consider themselves invalids, a belief that becomes self-fulfilling for Mrs. Hale when she develops a fatal disease halfway through the book. Mrs. Shaw's "invalidism" on the other hand is cause for some caustic satire on Gaskell's part. Even in widowhood Mrs. Shaw is unable to break her

> long habit of considering herself a victim to an uncongenial marriage. Now that, the General being gone, she had every good of life, with as few drawbacks as possible, she had been rather perplexed to find an anxiety, if not a sorrow. She had, however, of late settled upon her own health as a source of apprehension; she had a nervous little cough whenever she thought about it, and some complaisant doctor had ordered her just what she desired,—a winter in Italy.[10]

Mrs. Hale is more genuinely feeble than her sister, but she sinks into quasi-invalidism long before experiencing actual illness. Marital dissatisfaction has obviously been the trigger for the pervasive malaise that renders both women mildly querulous. Significantly, although neither has to endure a marriage of real misery, each vaguely craves the blessings (whether financial or emotional) that she does not have in addition to those she already enjoys. This inability to be satisfied, typified by Mrs. Hale's dismay at leaving the village she has found fault with during her entire tenure there, is the antithesis of the grateful acquiescence, especially of marital happenstance, held forth as an ideal response for Victorian women.

The most pointed satire of feminine invalidism as an inappropriate form of discontented "fine ladyism," however, emerges through the treatment of working-class women raised to gentility who respond to their new leisure by fancying themselves ill. Mrs. Carson in Gaskell's *Mary Barton* [1848], Fanny Thornton in her *North and South* [1855], and Mrs. Scratcherd in Anthony Trollope's *Doctor Thorne* [1858] are all former working-class women ill suited for their new positions. Mrs. Scratcherd maintains what equilibrium she has by not entirely foregoing her earlier habits: an unexpected visitor can still catch her "with her housekeeper in a small room in which she kept her linen and jam, and in which, in company with the same housekeeper, she spent the happiest moments of her life."[11] Mrs. Carson is less industrious and consequently less healthy. On a typical morning

> Mrs. Carson was (as was usual with her, when no particular excitement was going on) very poorly, and sitting up-stairs in her dressing-room, indulging in the luxury of a head-ache. She was not well, certainly. "Wind in the head," the servants called it. But it was but the natural consequence of the state of mental and bodily idleness in which she was placed. Without education enough to value the resources of wealth and leisure, she was so circumstanced as to command both. It would have done her more good than all the ether and sal-volatile she was daily in the habit of swallowing, if she might have taken the work of one of her own housemaids for a week; made beds, rubbed tables, shaken carpets, and gone out into the fresh morning air, without the paraphernalia of shawl, cloak, boa, fur boots, bonnet, and veil, in which she was equipped before setting out for an "airing," in the closely shut-up carriage.[12]

What is true of Mrs. Carson's situation holds true for Fanny Thornton as well. Unsuited for leisure by temperament and training, both are inadequate as domestic women because they aspire to be ladies. The irony is that they fail to recognize that true ladies are useful, not idle: the distinction between a working-class woman and the best type of lady is not that one works and the other doesn't, but that the lady's work is more refined and elevated.

Not only does much apparent invalidism emerge as self-indulgence in Victorian fiction, genuine physical debility is often linked with other forms of self-indulgence. A true invalid, of course, would have difficulty with the physical aspects of domestic labor, but sickly women often are shown as being deficient in providing even the emotional efforts that homemaking requires. Jane Wilson in *Mary Barton,* Mrs. Boucher in *North and South,* and Miss Brown in *Cranford* are all afflicted with acute physical suffering, but their prolonged and disabling debility makes them psychological as well as practical burdens to those around them. They react to their conditions with what Elaine Scarry describes as the typical response of the "body in pain": the entire world shrinks to the exigencies of their own physical state.[13] They are irritable, self-absorbed, and demanding: not only do they require care, they attempt to procure it in excess while neglecting the claims of others, thereby violating the other-centered duties of the Victorian feminine ideal.

Far from ennobling the invalid, debility even distorts basically loving personalities. Jane Wilson, for instance, who denounces women's factory work for driving husbands to public houses and mourns that her own factory girlhood deprived her of much housekeeping knowledge, wishes eagerly to serve her family (113–14). Yet the factory accident that left her permanently "poorly" (82) has also rendered her perpetually irritable:

> [I]t was her way to prepare some little pleasure, some little comfort for those she loved; and if they, unwittingly, did not appear at the proper time to enjoy her preparation, she worked herself up into a state of fretfulness which found vent in upbraidings as soon as ever the objects of her care appeared, thereby marring the peace which should ever be the atmosphere of a home, however humble; and causing a feeling almost amounting to loathing to arise at the sight of the "stalled ox," which, though an effect and proof of careful love, has been the cause of so much disturbance. (350)

In the same way Miss Brown in *Cranford* is "cross . . . at times when the nervous irritability occasioned by her disease became past endurance" (50). Requiring patience in her spasms of irritability and "the bitter self-upbraidings by which they were invariably succeeded," Miss Brown "would so fain have . . . lightened [her family's] cares, that the original generosity of her disposition added acerbity to her temper" (50). Under the constrictions of illness this distorted generosity results only in "querulous and never-ending complaints" (57). In short, whether genuine or hypochondriacal, invalidism is often presented as a form of rebellion against or failure in the feminine role because invalid women frequently are shown as peevish, insufficiently loving, and uncomfortable domestic partners.[14] Ironically the invalid woman usually remains in the home, but her "homemaking" is confined to making home life a misery, rather than a pleasure, for those around her.

Despite the negative effects associated with prolonged invalidism, one common feature of Victorian plots nonetheless is a dramatic illness for the heroine or other significant female character. In a sense women must earn illness by long usefulness: thus there are vivid periods of delirium for Mary Barton and Alice Wilson in *Mary Barton* and for Esther Summerson in *Bleak House* [1853], and momentary fainting spells for *North and South*'s Margaret Hale (who lapses into weakness only after saving her beloved from an enraged crowd) and for *Little Dorrit's* Amy Dorrit (who faints only upon leaving the prison that has been the scene of her labors). Yet the collapse of these women only emphasizes that their heroism is consistent with their delicacy; their weakness allows a space for traditional male protectiveness, without diminishing their record as exemplary female caregivers.[15] The woman who *is* too weak to labor (even or perhaps especially in the sense of successful child bearing) is often suspect as a caregiver. Consider, for example, the way the gradual declines of Clara and Dora Copperfield (the one precipitated by childbirth, the other by a miscarriage) connect with their inability to nurture David Copperfield as mother and wife respectively.[16]

In short, the Victorian heroine's sickness does not make her permanently too weak or passive for traditionally feminine caregiving work; it simply reemphasizes and valorizes her typical energy while simultaneously insisting that this energy exists only for domestic functions.[17] When domestic functions are carried out as fully as such lifelong functions can be, female energy is temporarily gone. Hence one finds the brief lapses into illness (or weakness) of such heroines as Esther Summerson, Mary Barton, Amy Dorrit, and others. Thus women can at once be superlative workers and unfit for nondomestic work.

Women can even become invalids by work outside the home. For example, both Jane Wilson in *Mary Barton* and Bessy Higgins in *North and South* are permanently weakened, and in Bessy's case even killed, by factory work, while Margaret Legh in *Mary Barton* is rendered blind by seamstressing, a condition that is suddenly cured almost immediately prior to her marriage. Although Gaskell based the strike in *North and South* on events in the actual town of Preston, she failed to note that most of the Preston labor force was female. As one critic puts it, Gaskell "shrink[s] that female majority into a solitary disabled worker": Bessy Higgins, who "has been forced to leave work because of lung disease contracted in the carding room" and who eventually expires from that disease.[18] Nondomestic work apparently only exercises a strengthening function when it ultimately serves the cause of domestic devotion. Thus Lizzie Hexam's rowing exertions on her father's scavaging expeditions are little more than preparation for her love-inspired rowing to save Eugene Wrayburn's life. Even then, only a vulgar and coarse mind would ascribe her feat to mere physical prowess. The dinner guest who speculates about the amount of beef and porter that Lizzie would need to continue in proper rowing form thereby damns himself as irredeemably materialistic. To him

> [t]hese things are a question of beefsteaks and porter. You buy the young woman a boat. Very good. You buy her, at the same time, a small annuity. You speak of that annuity in pounds sterling, but it is in reality so many pounds of beefsteaks and so many pints of porter. On the one hand, the young woman has the boat. On the other hand, she consumes so many pounds of beefsteaks and so many

pints of porter. These beefsteaks and that porter are the fuel to that young woman's engine. She derives therefrom a certain amount of power to row the boat . . .[19]

The truth is that Lizzie's "power" is not provided by caloric intake; rather it is the power of her love. Feminine devotion, not beef, strengthens her.

This character-based strength is an essential element in differentiating the lady from the servant. Thus, although Florence Dombey is less obviously vigorous than her maid, Susan Nipper, she nonetheless is able to sit up and study while Susan, "asleep in some uncomfortable attitude, reposed unconscious by her side" (231). Love for her brother—a self-sacrificial, maternal love—sustains Florence and means that sleepless nights cause her no fatigue. Susceptibility to slumber, indeed, seems to be one of the ways in which servants show their mundane natures. In *North and South* Mrs. Hale's maid, Dixon, adores her mistress with an intensity that even Mrs. Hale's daughter, Margaret, cannot surpass, yet the latter nonetheless is able to stay wakeful by Mrs. Hale's sickbed when Dixon cannot. Despite her protestations "Dixon sat, and stared, and winked, and drooped, and picked herself up again with a jerk, and finally gave up the battle, and fairly snored" while Margaret's "senses were acutely vital, and all endued with double keenness, for the purposes of watching" (224). Sensibility substitutes for sleep.

As a lady Margaret is superior in being able to meet both the physical demands of a laborious life as well as other, subtler ones. After her family's financial decline Margaret prides herself in being able to perform a servant's tasks while remaining unalterably and unmistakably a lady. Circumstances may require her to act as "Peggy the laundry-maid" on occasion, but she is always "Margaret Hale the lady" (115). As Margaret herself asserts, "'I am myself a born and bred lady through it all, even though it comes to scouring a floor, or washing dishes'" (116). Even her physical attributes reveal her gentility. The wealthy manufacturer Thornton no sooner meets Margaret than he is vanquished by her queenly elegance, "her superb way of moving and looking" (100). He correctly perceives that "her round white flexile throat," "full, yet lithe figure," the "one lovely haughty curve" of "her lips," and "her eyes, with their soft gloom" indicate sensibilities too fine to tolerate the vulgar wallpaper that he previously had thought would be good enough for a relatively impoverished family (100). Even more striking, he is erotically stirred by the combination of her service and queenliness. When she serves tea (something delegated to servants in a household affluent enough to afford abundant domestics), Margaret is hampered by her bracelet (a piece of adornment that no servant could wear while working). Her ladylikeness again is shown by her elegance, which here translates into unobtrusiveness in the work she does: "her round ivory hands moved with pretty, noiseless daintiness." Yet the bracelet makes her the cynosure of Thornton's eyes. He watches, fascinated, while it falls repeatedly down her arm; each time she "push[es] it up impatiently, until it tightened her soft flesh" (120). To Thornton, Margaret seems to hand "him his cup of tea with the proud air of an unwilling slave," yet her pride does not prevent her from catching "the moment when he was ready for another cup" (120). Even more enticing than this subservience, however, is the prospect of its being offered in a spirit of domestic love: Thornton envies Margaret's father because she lovingly submits when "compelled" by "her father, who took her little finger and thumb in his masculine hand, and made them serve as sugar-tongs" (120). The grace of a lady makes servile work deeply stirring, in short, while the transfiguration of that work into a love offering is more exciting still. The active arm and the disruptive bracelet capture these permutations: Thornton is fascinated by the lady's arm at work in a household task while the bracelet demonstrates that her servitude is voluntary.

Margaret's ornamented and smoothly plump arm also indicates the extent to which a lady's "work" must not interfere with her ability to retain the conventional signs of feminine gentility and sexual appeal. Few Victorian men appear to have shared Arthur Munby's attraction to muscular and grimy women whose bodies bear the marks of hard manual labor. As the respectable professions required intellectual rather than physical effort by their gentlemanly practitioners, so the household duties for ladies had to demonstrate more managerial than manual skills. Elizabeth Langland, describing Dickens's "angels of competence," remarks that female "angelic nature [in Dickens's novels] is informed by a ready resourcefulness, energy, and efficiency," so much so that "virtue subtly becomes defined for us as managerial skill."[20] Such a definition, of course, makes the lady's virtue even easier to separate from the mere usefulness of the hardworking servant. Yet management remains a relatively more amorphous activity than servants' domestic work.[21] It is easy to define and describe a maid's tasks: scrubbing floors, washing and ironing clothes, preparing meals, and all the other household chores that were especially time-consuming and physically draining in a premechanized age. Such duties clearly require effort and some physical strength; it is easy to classify them as "real" work. At the same time, because the work is manual, it is subject to the contempt that often falls upon both physical labor and its practitioners. Yet the same work that is *merely* manual when relegated to servants can become unexpectedly heroic when undertaken by ladies. Dickens writes with heavy irony of the noble-spirited Harriet Carker in *Dombey and Son* that she is never "long idle" for she has "daily duty to discharge, and daily work to do—for such commonplace spirits that are not heroic, often work hard with their hands." The same irony underscores Harriet's virtue when the passage continues with a reference to "the lives of such low natures, who are not only not heroic to their valets and waiting women, but have neither valets nor waiting-women to be heroic to withal!" (557). The point of course is that Harriet's lack of servants in her self-imposed poverty with a disgraced brother is ample proof of her heroism. Moreover, her cheerful execution of household tasks raises her heroism to the sublime. In like fashion Bella Rokesmith in *Our Mutual Friend* demonstrates her improved character by joyfully maintaining her husband's home with only one young servant girl to help. Even more dramatically, Florence Dombey dismisses her servant, Susan Nipper, specifically to show that she is prepared for the hardships of her new married life. Although Susan implores to be allowed to serve Florence without wages, Florence must part with her to launch this new career. As she explains to the sobbing maid, "'I am going to be his wife, to give him up my whole heart, and to live with him and die with him. He might think, if you said to him what you have said to me, that I am afraid of what is before me, or that you have some cause to be afraid for me. Why, Susan, dear, I love him!" (882). Thus one sign of the virtuous woman is her ability to do without servants as a demonstration of her commitment to serve her husband. Ironically her willingness to provide such service ennobles the work itself, although the same tasks in a servant's hands would be only menial.

Sarah Stickney Ellis, the best-selling author of conduct books, argued that because a woman is typically the "least engaged of any member of [a family], [she is] consequently the most at liberty to devote [her]self to the general good of the whole." [22] As Ellis explains, women should actively look for ways to be useful. Since they exist in and through their relationships with others, the more perceptive and inventive they are in finding or devising modes of service, the better. In short they must in a sense invent their own careers as homemakers and as nurturing domestic women. Ellis's examples of a domestic woman's duties range widely. In many cases the domestic woman simply substitutes for a servant (34–35) with the crucial difference that she is motivated by "the disinterested kindness of a generous heart" (23), not money. Ellis claims that "the feminine qualification of being able to use the hand willingly and well, has a great deal to do with the moral influence of woman" (22). At the same time manual dexterity is the least of the virtuous woman's attributes: she is responsible for the emotional and moral well-being of all around her, even when her means of ensuring it consist only of "'cultivating cheerful conversation, adapting [herself] to the prevailing tone of feeling, and leading those who are least happy; to think and speak of what will make them more so'" (34–35).

However unlikely the success of such procedures, it was crucial to domestic ideology and to fiction's advocacy thereof to treat this behavior as serious work that could produce significant results. Sarah Winter's argument about *Little Dorrit* applies to domestic novels generally: the ideal woman is responsible for emotional labor, through which she wins respect. [23] The psychological dimensions of this work distinguish it from more mundane labor: the narrator of George Gissing's "Foolish Virgin" sums up the difference thus:

> A woman of the ignorant class may keep house, and bring up a family, with her own hands; she has to deal only with the simplest demands of life; her home is a shelter, her food is primitive, her children live or die, according to the law of natural selection. Infinitely more complex, more trying, is the task of the educated wife and mother; if to conscientiousness be added enduring poverty, it means not seldom an early death.[24]

This passage clearly does not exempt the "lady" from providing for her family's physical needs; she must provide as much material care as the "ignorant" wife and mother does. The better-born woman simply is responsible for subtleties of effort beyond the comprehension of her untutored sister. The "work" of human relationships can stretch out indefinitely, however. Thus Dickens apotheosizes Lucie Darnay in *A Tale of Two Cities* for "being true to her duties . . . truest to them in the season of trial, as all the quietly loyal and good will always be."[25] These duties include deeds that externally are almost entirely passive. Every day for two hours, for example, Lucie stands on the street outside the prison where her husband languishes. Dickens's description emphasizes the disparity between the time Lucie devotes to her vigil and the brief, infrequent glimpses her husband gets of her. Her husband's access to the window from which he might view her "'depends on many uncertainties and incidents,'" and he only "'thinks'" that "'he might see [Lucie] in the street, if [she] stood in a certain place'" (304–5). If he is able to get to the window at all, it will be only for a moment at three o'clock in the afternoon, and since Lucie is not able to see him, she will not know whether he has seen her that day or not. Nonetheless, "[f]rom that time, in all weathers, she waited there two hours. As the clock struck two, she was there, and at four she turned resignedly away. . . . [S]he never missed a single day" (305). Here a self-imposed duty relies for its nobility on the importance of symbolic action. Lucie's "work" here is largely to incarnate love for and faith in her husband; in the world of the book that work is vital.

Similarly the would-be pathetic descriptions of Florence Dombey's struggles to win her father's love (most fully detailed in chapter 24, "The Study of a Loving Heart") must be accepted as descriptions of real work if they are to have any effect. Even the account of Florence's love offerings (although sounding ludicrously like satire on Victorian ladies' pursuit of futile hobbies to fill time) is poignant if one accepts such handicrafts and their bestowal as a significant form of domestic nurture. Only during her father's absence, after all, can Florence

> render him such little tokens of her duty and service, as putting everything in order for him with her own hands, binding little nosegays for his table, changing them as one by one they withered and he did not come back, preparing

something for him every day, and leaving some timid mark of her presence near his usual seat. Today, it was a little painted stand for his watch; tomorrow she would be afraid to leave it, and would substitute some other trifle of her making not so likely to attract his eye. (395–96)

The type of domestic work in which Florence and those like her engage comes to seem all the more substantial because mid-Victorian novels typically offer female characters the alternative of social frivolity.[26] The contrast for women is therefore between domestic work and purposeless pleasure: fashionable society, not work typically identified with men, is the alternative to women's "real," if immaterial, work.[27] Lady Dedlock, Edith Dombey, Mrs. Skewton, Mrs. Merdle, and Mrs. Gowan are all examples of social women whose lives are empty because they are devoid of domesticity. To be a nondomestic woman is to be socially pernicious; at an extreme, for instance, Dickens identifies women who refuse to devote themselves to being mothers with the causes of French Revolution. In *A Tale of Two Cities* the throng of wealthy parasites who flock to Monseigneur's halls are "all totally unfit for their several callings, all lying horribly in pretending to belong to them" (136). The "leprosy of unreality" that infects these idle men also contaminates "the angels of that sphere," but whereas the men have a multitude of possible occupations to dishonor, the women have only one: motherhood (137). Not "one solitary wife," intones the narrator, "in her manners and appearance, owned to being a Mother. Indeed, except for the mere act of bringing a troublesome creature into this world—which does not go far towards the realisation of the name of mother—there was no such thing known to the fashion" (137). The dereliction of domestic duty, according to the logic of the novel, helps prepare the way for the bloodbath to come, even as the same logic confines women inexorably to the maternal role as their only proper one.

Dickens also emphasizes the same univocal femininity when he shows the sisterhood beneath the skin of social queen Edith Dombey and convict and vagabond Alice Marwood.[28] Neither Edith nor Alice, although living in disparate social spheres, adheres to domestic norms: both prostitute themselves (Edith through a mercenary marriage), and—even more damningly—both choose pride and vengefulness over feminine tenderness. Thackeray, likewise, denounces upper-class "Traviatas" in *The Adventures of Philip* when he declares that the "[u]nfortunates . . . whom I should like to see repentant and specially trounced first" are the very ones who "are put into reformatories in Grosvenor Square . . . [and] wear a prison dress of diamonds and Chantilly lace." "[C]all a midnight meeting of those who have been sold in marriage," *Philip*'s narrator remarks, "and what a respectable, what a genteel, what a fashionable, what a brilliant, what an imposing, what a multitudinous assembly we will have; and where's the room in all Babylon big enough to hold them?"[29]

The socialite woman therefore is implicitly a prostitute, whose "work" is sin. As such, she is a destructive rather than productive member of society, since prostitution itself is seen as one of the great social vices of the day and a general drain upon the country. By denouncing upper-class women who marry for money as prostitutes, these authors reinforce the sense that class differences between women don't matter: females are the same universally, and their roles and responsibilities remain the same across class lines. By making Alice and Edith cousins and emphasizing their physical similarities (just as he emphasizes those of Good Mrs. Brown and Mrs. Skewton), Dickens reinforces gender norms across class lines. At the same time it is striking that the worst divergence from female norms is the departure from feminine tenderness noted above. Despite the associations with and accusations of prostitution the socialite woman is rarely a sexually desirous figure, however attractive she might be. Fanny Dorrit, like Thackeray's femmes fatales, is too narcissistic to respond to any man except for his wealth and social status. Edith Dombey is frigid toward all men, especially Carker, and her supposed elopement with him merely reveals her detestation of him. Yet even prior to that elopement she has effectively destroyed her marriage by refusing to accept the domestic responsibilities of a wife. It is surely inappropriate to suggest, as has been done, that Edith's nonsexual "marital duties" are "merely ceremonial and decorative."[30] Dombey himself, though too emotionally frozen to seek household warmth, certainly wants a woman who will support his domestic and social position. As the Dombeys' disastrous dinner parties show, Edith fails to provide precisely that social management at which women were supposed to excel. Meanwhile, Lady Dedlock's "sin," as one critic points out, is that "she thought of herself instead of thinking of others, she was proud where she should have been humble, she was insensitive where she should have been loving."[31] Lady Dedlock's lack of domestic femininity, not her youthful love affair with Captain Hawdon, damns her. Although both Dickens and Thackeray often contrast their acquiescent heroines with rule-breaking, defiant antiheroines, it is not a "problematic, assertive, adult sexuality" on the part of the latter that creates the division but their total lack of the heroines' "self-sacrificing, loving, forgiving humility."[32] A sexually inflected warmth that inspires feminine tenderness and self-abnegation is an asset to the female character; the self-absorbed remoteness of a Lady Dedlock is a sin worse than sexual misbehavior.

Even though feminine norms are supposed to operate across class lines and Dickens strives to show the commonality of Edith Dombey and Alice Marwood, higher class status still serves one sexually linked function: it makes Edith more desirable than her impoverished cousin. In sharp contradiction to some modern claims that the working classes were always erotically charged for their social superiors,[33] we find (as perhaps we might expect) that wealth and status only add to Edith's icy appeal. Carker, who is able to abandon Alice without a second thought, finds himself drawn, manipulated, and destroyed by Edith. Both women are beautiful and strong willed, but Edith is also a trophy; consequently Carker desires her as he does not ultimately desire Alice. Edith meanwhile destroys her marriage's slim chances for success and lays herself open to Carker's encroachments by refusing to do a wife's work. Mingling in a social circle that she despises, she refuses to fill the role of homemaker, social facilitator, and domestic support that even the cold Mr. Dombey requires. Her redemption, such as it is, comes when she turns away from society to become a caregiver for her decrepit cousin Feenix. By assuming responsibility for his well-being Edith finally takes on female work.

Edith has the option of losing herself in a social whirl because her high class and, after her marriage to Mr. Dombey, her great funds enable her to move easily in the fashionable world. Ultimately, despite the genteel poverty that drives her into a mercenary marriage, Edith fits neatly into the pattern of the aristocratic woman who, according to Nancy Armstrong, is eclipsed and replaced by the domestic woman as the novel develops through the nineteenth century. According to Armstrong the bourgeois domestic woman becomes the model for femininity generally and the instructor of both aristocratic and working-class women in feminine norms. Yet it is by no means clear, as one examines the range of nineteenth-century novels, that the transmission of feminine norms invariably proceeds from the middle classes. Since femininity is presumably a universal given, linking women of all classes, there could be positive value in showing its appearance in females of all social strata. Thus in *Our Mutual Friend* the river scavenger's daughter Lizzie Hexam instructs middle-class Bella Wilfer in feminine devotion to an all-important man (527–29).[34] The working-class Polly Toodle, moreover, is an exemplar of femininity in the bleakly masculine world of *Dombey and Son.* Her ministrations to both Florence and Paul Dombey put to shame the posturing of that "common-place piece of folly" Mrs Chick (106) and of the faded spinster Miss Till.

Despite supposedly universal feminine norms, nonetheless the difference between leisure-class and working-class women is that class hierarchy can displace gender hierarchy for the latter, so that (in fiction at any rate) the centrality of husband and children is not always invariable. Ironically enough, rather than a liberating abolition of hierarchy, such a variation simply leads to stronger emphasis on class ranking. It is less important perhaps for working-class women to maintain proper deference for their husbands because their husbands are already socially "unmanned" by their subservience to upper-class men. Since these husbands are not "men" in the sense of possessing significant social power, the traditional hierarchical structure of marriage need not apply.

This claim goes against some current arguments that the Victorian leisured classes tried to shape the working class in their own image (patriarchal husband/father, stay-at-home wife, dependent children) in order to induce social stability, with lower-rank divergences from this bourgeois model seen as a threat.[35] Yet in fiction it appears that the working class family was not allowed to center around itself; the demand that their first allegiance go to the leisured classes (especially their own employers) preempts the psychological self-sufficiency typical of bourgeois domestic units. In a sense the working classes were supposed to be emotionally as well as economically dependent upon the leisure classes.[36]

One sees this psychological "colonization" of the lower ranks perhaps most strikingly in the phenomenon of working-class surrogate mothers and caregivers. The long list of such characters includes Peggotty in *David Copperfield,* the Little Sister in *The Adventures of Philip,* both Susan Nipper and Polly Toodle in *Dombey and Son,* Miss Pross in *A Tale of Two Cities,* Martha in *Cranford,* and Dixon in *North and South.* These caregivers are maternal, not erotic, nor disciplinarian, nor angelic: the mother as servant (one way a child might view her) rather than the mother as an intimidatingly powerful female icon. Even the association of these characters with the physically coarse has its advantages: the maternal servant can be a nurturing figure even while the child retains his or her sense of superiority. Thus Peggotty not only submits to instruction from David, but, although a maternal wonder woman in many ways, she cannot be the feminine ideal that Clara Copperfield and, later, Dora are. Her body, unlike that of David's biological mother, is comic, "with no shape at all," and "cheeks and arms so hard and red that [David] wonder[s] the birds didn't peck her in preference to apples."[37] Perhaps most telling of all, she snores when she sleeps, thus blurring gender markers even as her heartiness mocks the delicacy associated with a "defenseless woman" (22).[38] Peggotty's lack of erotic appeal matches the noneroticism of her marital life: she marries, with no discernible sexual feeling, a man who has barely seen her and apparently is attracted primarily by her cooking. The union is childless, except in being motivated by the child David: Peggotty decides on the match to establish a refuge for the now orphaned boy should he need one and to ensure their continued contact. In all this Peggotty is a contrast to Clara, who marries Murdstone to fulfill her own erotic needs, a deed that the novel—or at least David—presents as a betrayal of her motherly duties. The result of the twin characterizations (Peggotty and Clara even share the same first name) is like a split version of motherhood: the mother who has desires of her own (for a man) and sacrifices her child to them, and the mother whose relations with any man (in Peggotty's case, Barkis) are entirely for the child's sake.

In purely material terms Peggotty is by far the more satisfactory of David's two mothers, yet it is dainty, pretty, elegantly ladylike Clara whom David tries to replicate through Dora. Only after marriage does David discover (again) that the unsatisfactory (because insufficiently service-oriented) wife is also an unsatisfactory mother (Dora miscarries). Peggotty, as the alternative ideal of total service, could almost be the model for service-oriented Agnes, but David rigorously, thoroughly separates them as physical presences. Agnes is ethereal, Peggotty is coarse; Agnes is quiet, Peggotty is noisy. Yet Agnes gets more done without noise than Peggotty at her loudest. When Agnes works, David knows "who had done all this, by its seeming to have quietly done itself" (420), so that she is able to perform household tasks without bearing the marks of them, unlike Peggotty with her work-roughened fingers (10–11). Service remains the ideal, and Agnes provides service: even as a child, she is her father's house-keeper, and the term implies her usefulness. She fills the role of not only wife but chatelaine.[39] The crucial distinction, of course, is that Agnes is a subordi-nate who commands reverence as well as offers obedience: David imagines her as above him even while he happily accepts her life's devotion. The rhetoric surrounding her is reverential rather than comic; indeed, it would be almost sacrilegious to imagine a sense of humor operating too close to Agnes's hushed, stately presence.[40]

Agnes's solemn sanctity perhaps is part of what endears her to her real-life creator and her fictional husband. Peggotty, although wonderfully comic, would be a frightfully humiliating "connection" for anyone as priggishly self-conscious as David. She is simply too banal, too materially coarse to be accept-able as the source of the self who perceives her as lovable but laughable. This sense of the comic nature of the lower-class body may explain why blood ties hold sacred in the Victorian novel even when lower-class surrogates substitute for inattentive or cruel blood kin. In Freud's account of the family romance the developing child begins to imagine that his *real* parents must be far more socially elevated and glamorous than his mundane mother and father.[41] The developing child in much Victorian fiction has servants who perform the daily work of parenting, but distant biological parents capture the child's imagina-tion and admiration. David patronizes Peggotty but worships Clara. Mr. Dombey by any reckoning is an abysmal father, but he commands Florence's adoration in a way that Susan Nipper, infinitely more loving and protective, does not. The lower-class woman, then, may fill a mother's role, but she can-not expect a mother's recompense.

Lower-class men in the counterpart position of surrogate fathers are often ambiguous figures, however. Perhaps this is because a father's role is typically that of mentor and lawgiver as well as loving caregiver. Intelligence, discipli-nary abilities, and both social and familial authority are necessary to the father's traditional role. Yet since the working-class male typically lacks social authority and often has not been credited with either intelligence or the self-control necessary for disciplining himself or others, he fails in paternal quali-ties even in his own household more often than he can exhibit them in anoth-er's. Indeed, for a male servant to take a *father's* place can be sinister. Littimer's hold over Steerforth in *David Copperfield* is that of a tempter and a corrupter over a potentially noble youth. Steerforth dimly recognizes his need for a father, but Littimer becomes the obverse of all a father should be: corrupting and betraying rather than guiding and supporting.

In *Our Mutual Friend,* by contrast, the idealized working-class Boffins are admirable protectors of the terrorized Harmon children, though Mrs. Boffin is far more explicitly and recognizably a maternal figure than Mr. Boffin is a paternal one. While both Boffins regularly defend the children from the father's abuse, apparently only Mrs. Boffin engages in intimate interaction with them. Certainly it is she whom the adult, disguised John Harmon singles out by treating her with the tender attention due a mother (331). It is she who originates the idea of adopting an orphan to bear the supposedly deceased John Harmon's name. Most striking of all, Mrs. Boffin's "haunting" by the Harmon children (189–92) marks the dawning of her intuition that Mr. Boffin's secretary is the vanished John Harmon.

When working-class men do figure as crucial parental surrogates (Joe Gargary, Captain Cuttle, for example), they are regardless of their gender more like mothers than fathers. In other words they are simple sources of nurturing love rather than figures of instruction and power. Joe Gargary, already "unmanned" by his hapless submission to a shrewish wife, assumes a more positive femininity in his "womanly" tenderness toward Pip. Yet if the simple-minded and truehearted Joe eventually gains Pip's respect, it is a tribute to his earnest virtue, not his intellectual or other authority. *Dombey and Son* further destabilizes the surrogate father's gender by feminizing the male body. The novel's narrator muses about the Almighty's beneficence by paralleling "the delicate fingers that are formed for sensitiveness and sympathy of touch, and made to minister to pain and grief, . . . [with] the rough hard Captain Cuttle hand, that the heart teaches, guides, and softens in a moment!" (770). Here the hand that is implicitly masculine ("rough" and "hard") becomes feminine when it is engaged in the woman's work of nurturing. At a time when hands were sharply gendered (and class marked),[42] the practice of nurture diminishes the difference between men and women by making male bodies feminine.

Meanwhile, those working-class men who are not explicitly feminized are at least denied traditional masculine authority.[43] Polly Toodle provides an ideal figure of motherhood, but her husband by no means matches her stature. He is a passive figure: half-stolid, half-clownish. Endlessly procreative, he nonetheless is not a virile authority figure for he willingly concedes family authority to his wife, who dominates him not by "artificial accomplishments" (81) but because she is "a good plain sample of a nature that is ever, in the mass, better, truer, higher, nobler, quicker to feel, and much more constant to retain, all tenderness and pity, self-denial and devotion, than the nature of men" (81). Polly is thus part of a universal and never-changing femininity (a "mass") that links her with the eternity otherwise symbolized by the sea upon which Paul

Dombey loves to gaze. This placement of Polly within a framework of femininity naturalizes the class and gender hierarchy of which she is a part, so that her "womanly" authority is an inevitable part of her actual subordination. Toodle, on the other hand, as both the father of a multitude and a figure associated with the dark, driving railroad, might seem to represent masculine procreative power, but if so, his power is drastically undercut by his socially induced helplessness. Uneducated and illiterate, he is "all abroad" during the conference between his wife and Mr. Dombey (68) and confesses later that "'I heerd it, . . . but I don't know as I understood it rightly Sir, 'account of being no scholar, and the words being—ask your pardon—rayther high. But Polly heerd it. It's all right'" (69). Even the patriarchal Mr. Dombey cannot fail to recognize that in this case the husband is not "the stronger character" of the couple (69).[44]

In some ways the best thing that a working-class man can do is embrace the feminine (maternal) role. Nicholas Higgins in *North and South,* for instance, reaches his highest moral stature when he voluntarily cares for a group of orphaned children. Although an opinionated and sometimes violent man who had occasionally beaten his own daughters, Nicholas now lowers himself for the sake of his new "family," humbly asking for employment and patiently enduring rebuffs from an employer he had defied previously. Instead of acting as a disciplinarian for the children, he amuses them with toys that he enjoys as much as they do (402). He is gentler in his new incarnation as a father, and this new gentleness transforms his relations with his employer as well.

In contrast to the feminization of the working-class male, the "self-made" man assumes *more* gender authority as he becomes more socially significant. Thus it is important for Walter Gay to assume a "man's" role with Florence Dombey immediately prior to and after their marriage. Ironically, not only must Walter provide Florence with protection but the narrative must first strip her of protection: she must lose class privilege and wealth (including servants) before she can fully show that she deserves her future husband. In effect she must show her strength for domesticity, even on shipboard, and for childbearing. Meanwhile, that Walter does *not* marry "above" himself but is himself the marital prize amply illustrates that he is ascending in the world. Florence herself rejoices that her social fall enforces her marital humility by showing the world Walter's worldly superiority to her at the time of their marriage and his consequent condescension in marrying her, a "'cost'" to him and "'a poor disowned girl, who had taken shelter [with him]; who had no other home, no other friends; who had nothing—nothing!'" Florence herself is therefore "'nothing. . . . Nothing but [Walter's] wife'" (884–85). Florence's loss of social position therefore underscores Walter's masculine authority as a husband and anticipates his eventual elevation in class status: two situations that work together to increase his power.

If roles for adult men and women involve intricate adjustments of class and gender norms, what of the roles for children? More particularly, if the working-class person, male or female, is most necessary as a caregiver for leisure-class children, what about working-class children themselves? Who cares for them and for whom do they care? Generally speaking, even the youngest members of the working classes seem to need a more purposeful existence than do leisure-class children. As a rich man's son, for instance, Paul Dombey need do nothing except fade and die. Despite his pathetic eagerness during his final illness to be a comfort to those around him, his existence is good in and of itself: simply by living feebly and dying slowly he draws rapt attention and ready sympathy from all around him. Dickens makes ready use of the irony that the solitary Dombey son withers while the working-class Toodle horde thrives and expands. But there is more here than the implied answer to Paul's question, "'What can it [money] do?'" (152)—which in fact means "What can money not do?" (i.e. make Paul well). Paul is suitable as a cherished object of protection, nurture, and expensive care; among Mr. Dombey's characteristic sins are to desire that Paul be an active participant in his firm from the earliest possible age and to place him in Dr. Blimber's "forcing" school as a way of hastening that time. The narrative stresses that Dombey should allow Paul ample leisure and recreation. Paul needs a childhood in this novel that—for its upper-class characters, at any rate—emphasizes "constancy to a childlike state, as exemplified by Paul and Florence (among others), or a regression, a return to or rediscovery of the lost innocence of childhood, as exemplified by Dombey" (Pykett 17).

Yet the narrative places higher expectations of usefulness upon working-class children from the beginning. Also in *Dombey and Son* a working-class father is presented as anomalous for cherishing an incapable and sickly daughter. What is striking about his concern is that the invalid daughter is not the focus of sentimental attention—if anything, she is presented to the reader in distinctly unappetizing terms as "ugly, misshapen, peevish, ill-conditioned" and given only to "mutter[ing] . . . ungracious and sullenly" (425) in response to kind attentions. Rather, the father as caregiver is the natural target of sympathy and admiration, even to the neighbor who scolds him for "favor[ing] and humour[ing] her until she's got to be a burden to herself, and everybody else" (525). We can speculate that (regardless of real life behaviors and attitudes) in fiction the leisure-class child could be the most passive form of love object: an icon who need only exist to attract protective love. By contrast, both leisure-class women and working-class children (not to mention working-class adults) must prove their virtue not by passive suffering but by active work. Only when they do so can they receive a sentimental aura. Thus the working-class children who receive the most approval, such as Charley in *Bleak House*, are those who give care rather than require it. After losing both her parents

Charley assumes responsibility for her younger siblings by supporting them through labors as a washing-"woman" and later as a lady's maid. Even more significant, once she enters the Jarndyce household as Esther's maid, her brother and sister remain discreetly offstage, and Charley demonstrates her virtue mostly by her commitment to serving the social superiors around her.

The Toodles' son Rob the Grinder, on the other hand, is a troublesome working-class child because he is idle and spendthrift. The *Dombey* narrator explicitly blames Rob's immersion in a brutal charity school for the boy's later moral laxity, but the same narrator does not hesitate to show him as a grossly unappealing youth. The pairing of Polly Toodle and Paul Dombey usurps the weight of mother-child sanctity as Paul, the sweetly angelic boy, dies with Polly hovering nearby as a maternal figure of consolation. Paul, like Rob, has been the victim of a badly run school. The two boys are parallel in their unfortunate education and in their literal or symbolic orphanage: Paul losing his mother to death, Rob losing his to Paul. Yet Rob is comic and nasty, Paul poignant and perfect.

The combination of feminized men, class- rather than gender-subservient women, and caretaking children entails a shift in the way characters perceive their own and others' family roles. Martha in *Cranford*, for example, marries to provide her female employer with a home and worries about the impending delivery of her own child because she fears that caring for the child would be "treachery" to her mistress.[45] In the same way, even after *Dombey*'s Susan Nipper marries, her primary loyalty remains to her former mistress, Florence. Indeed Susan identifies herself as Florence's maid despite having become a leisure-class matron herself. When about to be reunited with Florence, who has been at sea with her sailor-husband, Susan insists on dressing in her old maid's uniform so as to be more familiar to Florence's eyes. Equally striking in another way, Dixon in *North and South* never marries at all but devotes herself to Mrs. Hale as the center of her life. More tellingly, Dixon positions Mrs. Hale as central in the way that men typically have been for women. When Dixon muses about her mistress's husband, she concludes that "Master was born, I suppose, for to marry missus" (179). For Dixon the entire world is relative to Mrs. Hale: she loves her mistress and her mistress's children, and the "rest be hanged, for I don't know what they're in the world for" (179). Dixon here offers a reversal of Sarah Stickney Ellis's claim that upper-class women exist only in relation to others: for Dixon the rest of the world exists only in relation to this one cherished woman.

The lack of normative femininity shown in these characters' preference for women over men helps account for their undesirability. Working-class bodies could be eroticized, but they also could be desexed: two class dynamics that emerge in Arthur Munby's fetishization of bodies ignored or despised by society as a whole. After all, however vulnerable working-class women were to sexual exploitation, their low prestige could strip them of some sexual appeal in a society that, like our own, invests eroticism in glamour and "trophy" status.[46] Dickens's *Barnaby Rudge,* for example, provides a three-step model of female appeal: the upper-class Emma Haredale is beautiful but ethereal, the solidly middle-class Dolly Varden is endlessly erotic and desirable, while the ignominiously lower-class Miggs (deprived alike of the title "Miss" and of a first name, as Matthew Arnold might point out) is a despicable pretense of a woman and a grotesquely unappealing figure.

Both Dolly and Miggs are associated with comedy in a way that Emma is not, but Miggs is exclusively, though savagely, comic, and as a result only she is totally unfeminine and unattractive. Even far more appealing working-class women retain an association with the comic. Dixon and Martha are both comic, as are Peggotty, Susan Nipper, and Polly Toodle. Mrs. Wickham of *Dombey and Son,* who gestures toward pathos, is nonetheless amusingly lachrymose rather than poignant. This then is another instance of an interesting Victorian phenomenon: despite the frequent willingness to sentimentalize over the poor, servants are not generally figures of pathos. They are somehow seen as privileged figures so that the rhetoric of oppression and injustice that often surrounds factory workers, for example, doesn't tend to occur as often with servants. Victorian writers therefore tend to make servants comic and only rarely to acknowledge the oppression of domestic servants (aside from "lady-governesses") with the same fervor they often display on behalf of factory workers and other working poor.

The degree of comfort with which middle-class observers could regard domestic servants accounts for the desire to mold factory workers into a domestic model of labor. Certainly one finds much championship of a domestic model of employment in industry—undoubtedly in part because of the widespread belief that fellow feeling between classes would largely avert social unrest. Both Charles Dickens and Elizabeth Gaskell, for instance, espoused the idea of uniting the classes through warm personal understanding.[47] Besides insisting on shared humanity as a link between classes, both consistently placed social problems within domestic narratives and constructed their novels so as to link the domestic and social resolutions.

This mixture of domestic ideology with social concern, however, sometimes leads both authors to using a gendered model of personal relations when they treat relations between the classes. Specifically, as these novelists' working-class men come closer to a social ideal, they also assimilate feminine modes of behavior more thoroughly, thereby placing themselves in a subordinate (because female) position to unambiguously masculine masters. Thus in Gaskell's *North and South* Nicholas Higgins's mother-surrogacy for the Boucher children mentioned earlier prepares for his gradual acceptance of willing subordination under virile Mr. Thornton's leadership. Originally Higgins is a fiercely independent factory operative and union man and therefore sees labor relations as impersonal, antagonistic, and contractually based. Gradually, however, he shifts toward a domestic model of interaction with his employer, in which personal feeling and loyalty supersede contractual requirements. Having "entered a little more on the way of humility," Higgins is "quieter, and less self-asserting" (427), more concerned with keeping peace than with claiming his rights. Thus he intuits Thornton's anxiety over a pressing deadline and works overtime and secretly to meet it, his motive being to restore Thornton to equanimity rather than to earn money or even acknowledgment for his services (513). His recognition that his master's peace of mind is crucial to his own suggests the internalized norms and delicate, often unstated negotiations of domestic life rather than the open and public contractual obligations of paid employment. Higgins gradually shifts toward seeing himself as someone bound personally to Thornton, as instanced by his writing of the round-robin in which he and others of Thornton's former employees "stat[e] their wish to work for [Thornton], if ever [he] was in a position to employ men again on [his] own behalf" (526). While not going as far as Dixon's willingness to work without wages, this act of allegiance is similar to her zeal to continue with the Hale family as though it were her own. Higgins now apparently sees himself in a quasi-familial relationship with his employer. The cash nexus is no longer paramount, but the diminution of its importance has also diminished Higgins's independence.

Meanwhile, for all their claims of impersonality, the factory owners in both *North and South* and *Mary Barton* also uphold a model of relationship between employer and employee that bears resemblances to the domestic model. True, while unreformed and unenlightened, both Thornton and Carson deny their responsibility to guide and educate their workers. They shun the caretaking aspects of the paternal role. Yet they would assume another aspect of the patriarch by demanding implicit personal trust and obedience from their workers. As the ultimate authority of the factory family they will make decisions that their workers, lacking the abstract knowledge and the worldly experience to judge for themselves, must accept as correct and act on accordingly. The workers therefore resemble children—despite Thornton's explicit denial of this similarity—and also women, whose limited sphere of knowledge and experience likewise render them dependent upon the insights and actions of their male protectors. Perhaps even more to the point, factory workers thus have a similar relationship with their employers as that supposedly experienced by domestic servants: servants, theoretically at least, identified their interests with those of their master's family, placed all their time at their employer's disposal, and executed whatever commands they were given without question. A family might run its home however it wishes; the factory owners implicitly wish to run their factories like so many homes, as entirely subject to their individual priorities and beliefs. Although Gaskell, through Margaret Hale in *North and South* and John Barton in *Mary Barton,* argues against this demand for blind trust, the endings of her novels show an only slightly modified version as praiseworthy.

Mr. Thornton concludes *North and South* by assuming just the kind of guardianship role over his workers that he has previously eschewed. By establishing a dining room for his men, he blurs the boundaries between their work and their domestic lives. One implicit aspect of this refectory is that it separates the men at mealtimes from their own families, since the atmosphere is as exclusively masculine as "mess at the barracks" (446). Thornton joins the men periodically, however, and his presence becomes a sought-after treat for them. Thornton thus maintains his psychological authority, although now it is the authority of popularity as well as of power. His goodwill is obvious, yet it remains the goodwill of condescension. In relating to Mr. Bell the origin of the dining hall Thornton claims credit for the idea, which he initially gave up, persuaded by Higgins's disapproval—until Higgins returned to him with virtually the same idea. By agreeing to the plan and giving Higgins "the honour and consequence due to the originator" (445), Thornton "coolly" humors the other man's egotism *and* supplies the stewardship that keeps the operation going (445). Here Thornton, like Higgins in the previous example, is accommodating another person and concealing his own initiative for the sake of overall peace. Yet whereas Thornton retains his dignity despite or even because of the deep concerns that motivate Higgins to secret work, Higgins is obviously "childish" in seeking credit for "a scheme so nearly the same as [Thornton's], that [Thornton] might fairly have claimed it" (445). In short, Thornton may be growing closer to his men as he "get[s] really to know some of them" (446), but he remains an authority figure similar to a husband.[48] He provides backing and worldly experience; the workers provide endearing personalities and a heightened level of emotion: as Thornton remarks, they have "humour, and such a racy mode of expression!" (446). While these are attributes more associated with working-class comicality than with ethereal femininity, they operate like femininity in rendering the employees harmless—disarmingly "cute."

Mr. Carson in *Mary Barton* provides an even more striking example of the ambiguity in Gaskell's "reform" of insufficiently caring masters. After John Barton's long tirade pleading for masters to talk with their men and show that they care about them, even if they deny them material assistance, Gaskell goes on to show that the reformed Mr. Carson still seems aloof and cold. He does good, but secretly, so that the idea of improving working class morale by showing them that the masters care for them as fellow human beings goes for nothing. The workers still need to take the concern and the compassion of the factory owners on faith.

If Thornton and Carson, then, maintain something of a master's condescension toward their respective employees, their workers—here represented by Nicholas Higgins and John Barton—assume a properly subordinate (and therefore implicitly feminine) relationship toward them. Nicholas Higgins's comic conversion to domesticity finds its tragic counterpart in John Barton's deathbed conversion. A broken and humbled man, John dies at the end of *Mary Barton* in an explicit parallel with the death of his sister-in-law, the prostitute Esther. In both cases the physical causes of death are secondary to the psychological ones: both John and Esther essentially die of guilt over their sins. These sins are basically the same moreover: both Esther and John have violated the proper domestic relationships they should have maintained by placing illicit relationships above them. Esther mistakenly believed that she could live as a wife and mother without the sanctification of legal and religious marriage; John placed his loyalty to his union "family" above the bond that he should have felt with Mr. Carson. For both Esther and John rejection of socially and legally endorsed submission, which implies a proper and hierarchical domestic model of life, leads to emotional decline and physical decay. Rejection of one's proper role deprives one of physical nutriment and substitutes corrupting substances (Esther drinks, John takes opium), doing so because the alienated mind preys upon the body. Both Esther and John know that they are in the wrong relationship with others, and this knowledge helps them to their deaths.

Not Gaskell but Dickens, however, is responsible for the novel that most neatly ties together the disparate strands of promoting service among the working classes and among ladies. *Our Mutual Friend,* Dickens's last completed novel, supplies ample examples. I have already touched upon the crucial role of Lizzie Hexam's strength: she assumes heroic status partly because she is physically able to row the wounded Eugene Wrayburn to safety. Lizzie's strength, of course, is the strength of submission and utter devotion, the qualities that make her a fit instructor in femininity for the willful Bella Wilfer. The Boffins likewise demonstrate the emblematic nature of the virtuous working-class by combining physical grotesquerie (Mr. Boffin's clumsy obesity is particularly relevant in this regard) with near apotheosis as the Harmon children's self-denying surrogate parents. But in this novel, which elevates the idea of work by examining the value of money and contemplating what people do (or don't do) to *earn* their money,[49] Bella's role is especially important. She initially assumes "fine-lady" airs without the finances or social position to support them. Useless both practically and emotionally from a domestic point of view, she aspires to a life of even greater and more luxurious idleness than that which she enjoys at the book's opening. She must learn how to be a wife, and her education involves embracing strength and service instead of daintiness and uselessness. Her mother and sister, with their fainting spells and fits, amply illustrate Dickens's satire of the female physical "weakness" that enables female domestic tyranny. Bella meanwhile must live with the former servants and now parvenus, the Boffins, and be in constant contact with the supposed servant John Rokesmith to learn the meaning and value of true domestic service. She attains illumination when she recognizes that Mr. Boffin, despite his power and wealth, deserves a subordinate position and that the supposed servant Rokesmith is meant to be a master. Ironically, of course, Mr. Boffin later willingly gives up his wealth and position to Rokesmith/Harmon. His sacrifice demonstrates his good-heartedness but also a recognition and acceptance of his ineffably lower-class position. Bella's true reformation comes with not so much her renunciation of Mr. Boffin's wealth as her subsequent dedication to a life of domestic work on behalf of her husband and child. While John Harmon/Rokesmith goes into the city daily, the novel never follows him there—understandably enough since we later realize that he has nothing to do there. He actually is living on his inherited wealth.

Bella's working days, on the other hand, are the subject of lovingly detailed description and full narration. At that late point she is the most active worker in the novel. Her chosen service is that of a wife, but it parallels that of the Boffins, who willingly return to the status of domestic servants to yield their wealth to the man who is at once their master and their surrogate son. Harmon himself, by contrast, pretends to take a servant's role only to protect the Boffins from the danger of their own inexperience and to observe, supervise, and instruct his future wife in her behavior and attitudes. The Boffins' submission, even though unrecognized by Bella at the time, foreshadows her own and, once she is acquainted with their true motivations, convinces her even more fully of the necessity for such submission and of her own need for subordination to her acknowledged superiors. Bella, moreover, demonstrates her fidelity in the same way demanded by Gaskell's factory owners of their recalcitrant workers: she accepts with blind obedience and trust commands and actions the reasons for which she cannot fathom. This form of loyalty both Thornton and Carson require from their operatives; it is the same form Harmon much more successfully exacts from his wife.

Our Mutual Friend, then, in particularly artful form combines the different strands traced throughout this chapter. This late Dickens novel shows the necessity for women to be strong to serve others and renders suspect that female sickliness (exemplified by Mrs. Wilfer and Lavinia) that prevents service. It promotes a domestic model of loyalty among members of the working-classes toward the leisure classes, with all the deserving poor in this book sooner or later entering into a quasi-familial relationship with an employer or other social superior. Here we see the same double standard of values at work between classes as we have already seen between sexes. Just as men and women are supposed to live by different values and different moral codes, so we see that the working classes were not meant to incorporate middle-class models and values in their own lives entirely. Specifically, members of the working class should not adopt middle-class gender constructions if those would interfere with class deference. Rather, the working classes are encouraged to adopt different models of behavior and affect that stress the hierarchical links between classes rather than the ones between sexes. Even the supposedly sacrosanct Victorian family is not meant to be a self-contained patriarchal unit among the working classes: rather, the relatively looser bonds among family members and the subversion of strict gender hierarchy allow for an emphasis on loyalty and service to the middle and upper classes. As between men and women, so the differentiation of values here suggests the variability of Victorian values depending upon the categories of persons to whom those values were meant to apply. Rather than a monolithic set of values imposed equally on all, we find a set of differences tending to support the existing power structure. The aura of comicality, meanwhile, naturalizes the low social status of even the most virtuous members of the working class.

Since femininity entails subordination, as does working-class status, working-class virtue will almost always be feminine in nature, whether its practitioners are male or female. Above all, this virtue will be focused on others, for both the lower classes and "ladies" will always be working *for* others. The physical labor performed by Victorian workers in fact and fiction is easy to verify and quantify. The type of work performed by Victorian heroines may often seem less significant to modern readers. But we should remember that the ideal of work—and of the strength necessary to perform to that work—was an essential component of the Victorian heroine's role. Far from idealizing female weakness, the Victorian novel valorized its own form of the superwoman who could—effortlessly—"do it all."

6 | The Servant's Body in *Pamela* and *Lady Chatterley's Lover*

WHILE THE PRECEDING CHAPTER examined, among other concerns, the differentiation of the lady's from the servant's body even as both lady and servant were consecrated to the ideal of service, this chapter explores the way in which shifting emphases upon class and gender in representations of the body indicate shifting fears about which figure—the lady or the servant—was more likely to withhold service. Although Samuel Richardson's *Pamela* (1740) and D. H. Lawrence's *Lady Chatterley's Lover* (1928) are separated by almost two centuries of radical transformations in English society, the two books share a common motif of the sexual attraction between and eventual union of servant and employer and a common concern with issues of power and self-definition beyond the personal affairs of two lovers.[1] Because they are organized around romantic relationships between people of unequal social ranks, both novels hinge upon gender and class identity. They differ dramatically, however, in the intensity with which they represent threats to those two aspects of selfhood.

Richardson, on the one hand, constructs a version of cross-class romance that highlights the potential instability of class hierarchy and the urgent need to safeguard established class relations—a strategy that Henry Fielding, perhaps Richardson's most famous critic, repeats in his parodic *Shamela*. While sexuality is open to negotiation for Richardson, status-based authority is not, apparently because any one of the available sexual options will maintain male power in one way or another and hence pose little danger to the established order. Since challenges to class apparently can provoke instability, however, Richardson's text expends considerable energy to contain and deflect them. For Lawrence, on the other hand, and for such immediate predecessors of his as George Gissing, sexual rather than social instability arouses the fiercest anxiety and the most vigorous response. Nor can Lawrence's own working-class origins account totally for this shifting emphasis.[2] While his political views ranged enormously during his life, he was never a straightforward democrat and spent his last years haunted by fears that working-class militancy would precipitate class warfare.[3] Richardson shares humble beginnings with Lawrence as well as an ambivalent attraction to hierarchy (even if in the form of meritocracy). Yet despite such biographical similarities differences in the cultural climate of their times lead them to place radically different emphases on which element in self-identity—class status or sexuality—is more vulnerable to attack. Richardson labors to maintain the authority of master and mistress over servant (whether male or female), while Lawrence struggles to show that male identity must include some mastery over subordinate females. The authors therefore employ cross-class couples for different purposes: Richardson traces Mr. B's progress from rake to paragon to illustrate the way domestic virtue can enable employers to justify their rule, while Lawrence establishes Oliver Mellors's unrivaled masculinity to demonstrate both the rarity of his virility and its necessity for personal and social regeneration.

The shift from Richardson's class vulnerability to Lawrence's gender risk takes place against a background of continuing anxieties evoked by the existence of a servant class. For centuries servants have been perceived as potentially threatening to their employers simply by their physical presence in the employers' home. After all, the servant's body, which employers would prefer to perceive as merely a domestic implement, nonetheless shares a common physiology with the upper classes that—as explored in chapter 5—challenges the hierarchy ordaining its subordination. As a result there must always be attempts, like those of Dickens and others examined in the preceding chapter, to imagine and represent the servant's body as essentially different from those of his or her "betters." Class identity, like sexual identity, is construed as inherent in the body and inseparable from it—but still frighteningly precarious. Like their peers Fielding and Gissing, Richardson and Lawrence use their characters' bodies to illustrate threats to selfhood: while the eighteenth-century authors see class as primary in defining identity, the modern ones focus on gender.

Servants, as Pamela Horn points out, have constituted a distinct class in Western society ever since its inception.[4] Yet during those centuries, Bruce Robbins observes, literary representations of servants have varied only slightly, if at all.[5] Without necessarily accepting such representations as archetypal "truths," we should carefully consider these longstanding traditions. Even from the mid-eighteenth through the early twentieth century there is astonishing continuity in the tone and rhetoric of servant conduct books, whether written as such or eventually as domestic management manuals. During this period, when the conditions under which English servants worked and the tasks they performed changed radically, there remain consistent concerns and priorities in the prescriptions for employer/servant relations and especially for servants' affective lives.[6]

One way to explain this continuity is by postulating that domestic servants, no matter how desirable the results of their labors, nonetheless constitute a threat as well as a benefit to their "masters." The idea that groups customarily define themselves by distinguishing themselves from a feared, often hated, and yet necessary "Other" has dominated recent theories of social, national, and psychological organization. What could be more "Other" than servants? Living among those from whom they must nonetheless remain always separate and to whom they must always be subordinate, servants combine physical proximity and psychological distance. Ironically enough, their presence, with the ample opportunities it affords for comparison between the classes, potentially threatens the very hierarchy it sustains. Only by creating definitions of selfhood that internalize hierarchical distinctions can a society maintain the fiction that such distinctions are natural—as natural as the body itself.

Servants threaten hierarchical boundaries in two especially important ways. First, living among the leisured classes, they could show themselves to be physically indistinguishable from their social superiors. Second, their proximity enabled them to observe and to judge their "betters." William Hazlitt reveals the first fear in noting the symbiosis whereby servants absorb the upper-class appearance of their masters. In his 1830 essay "On Footmen" Hazlitt describes "an old butler who had lived with a nobleman so long, and had learned to imitate his walk, look, and way of speaking, so exactly that it was next to impossible to tell them apart."[7] This imitation is virtually an act of aggression, however. It appropriates the physique and the manners that should distinguish the master and thereby reveals the unreliability of such social signifiers. This blurring of boundaries prompts Hazlitt's later speculation that there might be "no other difference between the retainers of the court and the kitchen than the rank of the master" (359). When the butler might be mistaken for the nobleman and "the maid has not seldom a chance of being taken for the mistress" (357), the institution of servitude potentially could undermine the very hierarchy it was supposed to maintain.

Besides the threat of servants looking *like* their masters, there is the danger that they look *at* their "betters" with a condemning eye. Certainly the terror of scrutiny by underlings runs throughout servant conduct books. Defoe's *Religious Courtship* (1722), for example, offers an extraordinary account of how demoralizing servant observation could be: one of the book's speakers describes a husband who refuses to continue family prayers once he discovers that his wife's maid has been mocking his piety.[8] Deeply embarrassed at the thought of such close-range contempt, the man feels too abashed to pursue his duty. Although Defoe's speakers agree that the man should be more steadfast, his extreme discomfort is a natural enough response to the ambiguity of the situation. As master he possesses practical authority, but in the inevitable intimacy of the household, he is subject to his servant's gaze when his dignity is most fragile—or when a servant could judge it so.

The enforced intimacy of a shared household could be especially detrimental to dignity. Focusing like Defoe on servants' potential to shame their employers, Swift is typically merciless in exploring people's unease about servants who could literally expose their dirty laundry or even, as Swift caustically points out, their dirty chamber pots. His *Directions to Servants* (1745), written in the persona of a footman advising his fellows, shows considerable sympathy for servants, according to critic Janice Thaddeus.[9] For Thaddeus, Swift's characteristic reiteration of the scatological nature of some eighteenth-century household chores reflects empathetic acknowledgment that "disposing of other people's excrement is demeaning" (119). Yet surely Swift's satire at least equally reflects the fear of being humiliated by those whose job includes assisting one's bodily functions. When Swift's narrator advises maids to carry their mistresses' brimming chamber pots "openly, down the great Stairs, and in the Presence of the Footmen" and to answer callers at "the Street-door, while you have the Vessel filled in your Hands,"[10] he envisions an apt retribution for the discomforts of servitude. Swift's "Lady" must fear the maid who can "expose her Filthiness to all the Men Servants in the House" (61), even though that "filthiness" is nothing more than the result of normal human physiology, shared by servant and employer alike. To maintain status, apparently, it is necessary to conceal or at least disguise such common elements.

Faced with the simultaneous desirability and threat of household help, the employing classes reacted by trying to neutralize these disturbing inmates of their houses. To do so required the construction of tangible and theoretical differences between employer and domestic. Servants obviously had to be separate, both physically and psychologically, from their "betters." Thus servant conduct books ceaselessly reiterated that servants should be nonpresences in the household, never reminding their employers of their personalities or their persons.[11] While servants should dress with respectable middle-class taste, eschewing the vulgarity of their origins,[12] their attire should preclude their being taken for their own employers or members of their employer's family.[13] While they should uphold standards of even fastidious cleanliness and daintiness in catering to their employers, they must do the actual dirty work that allows others to be clean. They must practice on behalf of their employers the delicacy that they must relinquish in their own lives. Thus *The Female Servant's Adviser* (c. 1829) admonishes servants to shop scrupulously for their employers' tables while it simultaneously adjures them to accept uncomplainingly the scraps from those tables.

> Nor should servants be too nice or dainty in their appetites. It is their duty to use at their table all the wholesome remnants of food which are brought from their employers' table; and not throw them, as is too often done, into the dust-hole, or the hog-tub. How often has it happened to a servant in after-life, with a hungry and famished offspring around her, to bear testimony to the homely and monitory adage, "That wilful waste makes woeful want." How gladly in those afflicting moments would she prize that food which, while in service, she often turned up her nose at, and spurned as the vilest offal, as the daintiest cheer, and primest blessing of life! But how just are the retributions of providence, and how guarded ought to be our conduct![14]

This insistence that a servant's palate should be undiscriminating and a servant's body inured to the dirt that it must remove from the employer's view implies a difference in both physical and emotional sensitivity. Speaking specifically of women in the nineteenth century, Helena Michie observes that "physicians had constructed two entirely different bodies for working-class and leisure-class women."[15] Her words, however, apply as well to perceptions of corporeal differences between the classes across a range of centuries. According to this perception, because servants are physically hardened as their employers are not, their labor comes naturally to them as it would not to members of the middle or upper classes.

Lower-class physical toughness, moreover, corresponds to an emotional dullness that shields workers from psychological stress. As Barbara Ehrenrich and Dierdre English put it, the lady's "physical frailty went hand-in-white-gloved-hand with her modesty, refinement, and sensitivity. Working class women were robust, just as they were supposedly 'coarse' and immodest."[16] Hence there is no cruelty in the lot assigned to servants, although there may be some danger for the more delicate people with whom their work brings them in contact. This conception of servants as incorrigibly insensitive appears prominently in the frequent discussion of servants' relations with employers' children. Commentators from John Locke to Charles Dickens condemn servants who traumatize their susceptible charges with horrific tales, the goriness of which has failed to disturb their own coarser sensibilities.[17]

As late as 1892 an article, "Ladies in Service," advocating the creation of a class of "lady"-charwomen, foresees that ladies entering domestic service would object most strongly to contact with "persons who do not obey a refined standard of manners."[18] The correlation between servants and vulgarity is absolute, and entails not only bad table manners but a "lack of self-control"

(92) that contaminates the entire personality. The article's "solution" is that the "lady-helps" enter service exclusively on a nonresidential basis. The point here is not to protect the genteel servant from exploitation: that potential problem is never raised, even though Victorian employers might demand sixteen-hour days from their domestics. It is the other, nongenteel servants who constitute a threat to the new lady-char: their presence alone is guaranteed to disturb her peace of mind. Differences in sensitivity, both of body and mind, here form a barrier between the classes that continues even when the apparent reality of class difference—the lady *is* now a servant, after all—no longer exists.

Samuel Richardson's *Pamela* at first glance might seem an odd choice for a book upholding class hierarchies: its plot of a servant girl marrying her master outraged contemporary readers who found such interclass marriage deeply distasteful. Fielding's parodic *Shamela* was only one among the many protests that greeted Richardson's first novel.[19] As the philandering of Fielding's own Tom Jones with the lowborn Molly suggests, however, it was the apparently antihierarchical implications of Richardson's *marriage* plot, rather than Mr. B's willingness to pursue sexual pleasure across class lines, that aroused unease.[20] The rather distasteful satire of *Shamela* is based on the assumption that Shamela/Pamela, as a typical servant girl, is a calculating slut whom a gentleman might bed but whom only a "booby" would marry.[21] For *Pamela* to succeed, the reader must accept the heroine's sincere desire to preserve her chastity; it is precisely this sincerity that Fielding is unwilling to credit.[22] In *Shamela*'s schema sexual manipulativeness is a servant's stock in trade, and sexual predatoriness is a master's natural response, however piously Fielding's Parson Oliver may hope that "our sons" will neither marry *nor* "debauch" their servant-maids (538).

Richardson, however, rejects this crudely physical model of cross-class relationships to substitute a far subtler yet still hierarchical one. Pamela's body, no matter how sexually desirable, is even more important as the vehicle for her sensibility. She most movingly asserts her willingness to reject Mr. B when she envisions transforming the ladylike "fair soft hand[s]" that Mr. B admires (1:55) into unmistakably working-class ones: "as red as a blood pudding, and as hard as a beechen trencher to accommodate them to my condition" (1:63). She will live upon "pig-nuts, potatoes, or turnips" (1:66), a working-class diet. In short she will live by the convention of servants' insensibility in a manner that exposes the falsity of that convention. It was this convention that servant conduct books upheld when they postulated a link between the physical hardiness servants require for their work and the psychological coarseness they supposedly show in their relations with children and each other. Sir Simon Darnford, to whom Pamela applies for assistance, uses this model of servant insensibility when he refuses to interfere on her behalf. "'Why, what is all this, my dear,'" he remarks to his wife, "'but that our neighbor has a mind to his mother's waiting-maid! And if he takes care that she wants for nothing, I don't see any great injury will be done her'" (1:118). Not only Pamela's "honesty" but her fear and humiliation "go for nothing" (1:118–19), for Sir Simon cannot credit that a servant girl would suffer psychologically from rape. In this attitude he resembles the parish minister Mr. Peters, who deems that Mr. B will provide Pamela with "'good terms enough'" to justify his violence toward her (1:119). According to this view of the matter, luxury—or at least physical comfort—will always adequately compensate a servant for a master's abuse because the working classes lack the emotional delicacy required to suffer inwardly. Pamela's willingness to live crudely, however, is the result of her allegiance to a higher standard of sensitivity than a merely physical one.

Yet if Pamela's sincerity paradoxically transforms the signs of working-class vulgarity into emblems of nobility, Mr. B's sexual predatoriness is not an aspect of his class status; instead, it is a diminution of it. As long as Pamela feels that he is lowering himself by pursuing her, she can and does defy him. The psychological distance that a master's authority and a servant's social inferiority are supposed to maintain dissolves here as Mr. B's passion reveals a humanity not similar to Pamela's but actually beneath it. She thus assumes the position of the servant who, having observed, can judge her employer. Having "lost all fear and all respect" Pamela informs Mr. B, "'Well may I forget that I am your servant, when you forget what belongs to a master'" (1:12). Mr. B may include sexual submission among a servant's duties, but Pamela fails to see the mastery in his assaults. To her Mr. B has "'lessened the distance that fortune has made between us, by demeaning yourself, to be so free to a poor servant'" (1:12). Even if she speaks disrespectfully of her employer, she observes, "it is his own fault if I do. For why did he lose all his dignity with me?" (1:11). Mr. B therefore violates his own class status as much as he attempts to violate Pamela's virginity. Although his aggression is based on the arrogance of rank, his actions destroy the hierarchy on which he relies. By trying to push his authority beyond its proper scope, Mr. B has "put it into the power of [his] inferiors to be greater than [he]!" (1:13).[23]

Mr. B's lust aligns him with the worst of his own servants: Mrs. Jewkes, who contrasts with Pamela's gentility by embodying the vulgarity and temper that the servant conduct books attribute to bad servants. At the same time Mrs. Jewkes avoids a servant's worst fault of all (according to the conduct books): insubordination. In Richardson's handling, however, Mrs. Jewkes's slavish obedience potentially endangers Mr. B's status. During most of Pamela's captivity Mr. B is not actually present. Instead he swoops down intermittently to terrorize the already frantic girl; his housekeeper meanwhile conducts the steady campaign to force Pamela into accepting sexual submission as one of a servant's duties. Mrs. Jewkes thus becomes a stand-in for Mr. B even in his sexual conduct.[24] She can do so only because, despite her massive bulk, procuress's role, and unceasing bawdiness, she represents a servitude so abject as to be essentially without qualities of its own. Mr. B, she declares, "'is my master; and if he bids me do any thing I *can* do, I think I *ought* to do it: and let him, who has power to command me, look to the *lawfulness* of it'" (1:93). Just as Mrs. Jewkes erases her own conscience by entrusting it to her master, so her body cancels itself out through a combination of contradictory attributes. Her obesity makes her at once grossly female in the exaggerated contours of her breasts and buttocks and yet masculine in the forcefulness of her hamlike arms. She *"waddle[s]"* (Richardson's emphasis) rather than walks, the verb suggesting, even as it satirizes, the sway and jiggle of heavy female flesh. Pamela describes her as "a broad, squat, pursy, *fat thing*" (Richardson's emphasis), the words "pursy" and "thing" balancing each other with their respective connotations of female and male genitalia. She has a "man-like voice" and "looks . . . deadly strong," with "a huge hand, and arm thick as [Pamela's] waist" (1:97). The mixture of male and female features makes Mrs. Jewkes sexless, and thus a conduit for Mr. B's sexuality rather than an agent for her own.

Consequently, although Mrs. Jewkes's advances to Pamela suggest sexual interest (1:91), Richardson does not raise lesbianism as a serious possibility. That would make her, in one sense at least, an alternative to Mr. B, whereas she actually is his assistant in his plans for seduction and/or rape. Indeed, only two pages after praising Pamela's charms and offering to kiss Pamela herself, she issues a heterosexual creed to counter Pamela's claims that Mr. B's aggression is an act of violence against her. "'Are not the two sexes made for one another?'" Mrs. Jewkes asks. "'And is it not natural for a gentleman to love a pretty woman? And suppose he can obtain his desires, is that so bad as cutting her throat?'" (1:93). Mrs. Jewkes's refusal to see violence, much less criminality, in Mr. B's assaults is a reflection of her identification with the lust possessing her master. Yet although she claims to "glory in my fidelity to my master" (1:144), she absorbs his autocratic wishes as her own only to intensify them, to the exclusion of any second thoughts of his own. Her delight in Mr. B's predatoriness and her zeal on behalf of his worst impulses suggest that she finds a vicarious pleasure in his aggression. During the bedroom encounter between Mr. B and Pamela, at which Mrs. Jewkes is a third party, she is less deferential than goading. While Pamela screams and writhes, and Mr. B straddles her naked body, Mrs. Jewkes urges Mr. B on to the rape that he does not ultimately commit (1:179). As an externalization of Mr. B's lust, Mrs. Jewkes does not damage Mr. B's masculinity (despite her own putative femaleness), but she does contaminate his status. Although Mr. B wishes to see his pursuit of Pamela as a gentleman's prerogative, his need for Mrs. Jewkes as an intermediary renders the matter not only immoral but déclassé.

Only when Mr. B disciplines himself sexually by offering to marry Pamela (a proposal that theoretically should erase the class difference between them) does she totally accept his class superiority. Then he becomes truly her "Master," and, Pamela adds, "I shall think myself more and more his servant" (1:271; see also 255 and 323).[25] Mr. B's self-restraint reestablishes the legitimacy of the class authority that Pamela earlier had defied on the basis on their spiritual equality. From fighting to preserve her sense of self-worth, Pamela comes to deplore her "own unworthiness" (1:246); from asserting her will to defend her honor Pamela melts into meekly assuring Mr. B, "I have no will but yours" (1:246). The irony is that Pamela's submission, while now no less slavish than Mrs. Jewkes's had been previously, does not debase Mr. B's authority but rather reinforces it. Now that Mr. B has accepted the duty of self-government that legitimizes his position as a member of the governing class, he deserves deference from his lawful dependents. Pamela's sudden humility springs from her recognition that Mr. B has now justified his mastery over her.

Richardson repeats this pattern of resistance to class authority that subsides into acquiescence with the parson, Mr. Williams. Like Pamela Mr. Williams contrasts with Mrs. Jewkes by his initial willingness to defy his master. Also like Pamela, once convinced of Mr. B's rectitude, Mr. Williams abandons all pretensions toward an independent conscience. His behavior is particularly interesting because his position contains so many tensions. Both man of God and a member of the domestic staff, a chaplain presumably has an authority that can supersede even his master's on occasion, but he simultaneously is a social inferior and financial dependent of that master. His ambiguous status is reflected in his physical location: unlike Pamela and other domestics he has a residence of his own, apart from his master's. Yet that residence is actually his master's "holding," and the church in which Mr. Williams preaches is likewise implicitly under Mr. B's jurisdiction. Although Pamela refers to Mr. Williams as a "gentleman," she knows full well that "all his dependence is upon my master"—who therefore is Williams's master as well (2:96). It is thus plausible for Mrs. Jewkes to terrify Pamela with the news that Mr. B plans to force her into marriage with one of his servants at a ceremony to be conducted by another (1:156), that is, by Parson Williams himself, who by this time has made his own marriage proposal to Pamela (1:124). Williams's ability to unite a couple in matrimony is indicative of his religious authority. The force of Mrs. Jewkes's disclosure, however, rests on the all-too-obvious fact of Williams's worldly subjection: presumably he *could* be made to do his master's will, even when it is as evil as Mr. B's. Richardson challenges that subjection's inevitability when he makes Williams the only servant at Mr. B's Lincolnshire estate who will assist Pamela in preserving herself from Mr. B's aggression. Williams renounces one ideal of a servant's unconditional loyalty to his master to assert another ideal of principled resistance to a master's unreasonable and immoral desires.

Williams, however, can assert himself only when Mr. B abdicates his own authority through his self-lowering pursuit of Pamela's sexual favors. Once Mr. B decides to marry Pamela, Parson Williams sinks back into humility and servitude. He must implicitly renounce the very ideal of independent virtue on which he previously had acted. "'Sir,'" Parson Williams declares, "'I shall be taught by your generosity, to think myself inexcusably wrong, in all that could give you offence; and my future life shall shew my respectful gratitude'" (1:274). Ultimately then, Mr. B's renunciation of his desire to establish himself through his sexual siege leads him to a greater mastery over his servants, including Williams.

Despite his ambiguous status Parson Williams possesses enough authority to make his initial resistance the most plausible subversion of class hierarchy that *Pamela* offers, which seems to be the reason why Fielding—himself a supporter of clerical dignity—responds to Williams in *Shamela* as vitriolically as he does. Shamela's promiscuity and scheming are predictable, typical, and therefore unlikely to undo anyone except an egregious fool like Mr. Booby. Who else would believe in the "virtue" and high-flown sentiments of a slatternly serving maid? Williams, however, demands more attention. Prior to his collapse in the final chapters of the book, Richardson's Williams has convincingly argued for, and acted on, the idea that a clergyman should attack and thwart the evil propensities of the upper classes as much as those of the lower. In Fielding's venomous version of these events, however, Williams loses clerical integrity altogether to become the mere embodiment of a domestic subordinate's treachery. Shamela's lover both before and after her marriage, he provides the justification for her various immoralities (549), cheats and flouts Mr. Booby (551, 562–63), and cross-examines Shamela upon the most intimate details of her wedding night (564). His probing into Mr. Booby's conjugal intimacies suggests a Swiftian fear of the body's exposure. Here is an almost paranoically concentrated vision of the upper classes, in the person of Mr. Booby, being betrayed through their own weak good nature and the vicious opportunism of their inferiors. Williams's most flagrant wrongdoing is his consistent aggressiveness, an overbearing energy that, ironically, meets many of the cruder standards for masculinity even while failing to satisfy the expectations for a servant's deference. In this context his willingness to lecture Mr. Booby on his religious duty is as insolent as the censoriousness that the falsely pious maid Jane shows toward her mistress in Defoe's *Religious Courtship*. Williams, like Jane, is among the "worst [servants] that ever were heard of" (327), not only because he is ethically lax but also because his egotism violates the religion that "never . . . privileges Servants from observing the due space which Nature has put between the Person to be served, and Person serving" (330). Yet fear as well as indignation seems to fuel Fielding's satire: although despicable, Williams is also scarily forceful, particularly in comparison with Mr. B's weakness. His cuckolding of his patron reveals Mr. B's deficiencies to both Shamela and the reader. This presumptuous servant-parson, "whose family hath been raised from the dunghill by [Mr. Booby's]" (562), nonetheless has a crude physical superiority to support him in his determination to "hate, detest, and despise" "fashionable . . . wretches" (548). As Shamela's constant comparisons establish, Williams's phallic prowess puts her husband's puny lovemaking to shame.

Whereas Richardson worries about the antihierarchical effects of upper-class sexual predatoriness, Fielding sees an upper class imperiled by its own lack of virility. As his tolerance of Tom Jones's philandering shows, Fielding is ready to smile on some upper-class "poaching" of available, and usually lower-class, women. But not all gentlemen are up to the sport and their spiritlessness is worrisome. Thus Fielding's Mr. Booby, unlike Richardson's Mr. B, is despicable because he is too *bashful* as a lover rather than too violent (544). All too easily rebuffed, all too easily moved by Shamela's fake hysterics, Mr. Booby is prey for his robust servants. Clearly Fielding does not endorse libertinism as a strengthening mechanism for the upper classes, but just as clearly he finds lower-class sexuality disturbing as an indication of lower-class vitality. Williams's and Shamela's ruthless energy, like their casual promiscuity, springs directly from their emotional coarseness. They are as much examples of lower-class insensitivity as are the master-ridiculing, ghost-storytelling servants deplored by Defoe, Locke, and other writers, but this insensitivity is their strength. Richardson, on the other hand, discerns no such vitality in crudeness, rather locating strength in the chastity that Mr. B eventually assumes.

Actually, his sexual self-discipline consolidates Mr. B's leadership qualities with the males of his own class. Just as the chaste Sir Charles Grandison is able to dominate the rakes he encounters, so Mr. B's newly discovered ability to control the urges of his own body elevates him above his dissipated former companions. Able to set rules by which his fellow rakes must abide (1:331–32) and to reduce the amoral Sir Simon Darnford to a ludicrous figure who "*wants* the example he ought to *give*'" (2:78), Mr. B gains stature in comparison to "simper[ing]" "libertines" (2:77). The same Mr. B who in the first half of *Pamela* is defined purely in terms of his private intrigues emerges after marriage as a public-spirited figure, the worthiest representative of English gentry. Early in the second volume of *Pamela* he even receives the offer of a baronetcy, only to reject the title as unnecessary to one who already has the honor of being a "*country gentleman*'" (2:96; Richardson's emphasis). To Mr. B at this point, "'Titles at best . . . are but shadows; and he that has the substance should be above valuing them'" (2:95).

As Mr. B's public authority emerges along with his newly discovered personal qualities of chastity and moderation, his servants also display new facets. In the first volume of *Pamela* Mr B's Bedfordshire servants respect and love Pamela without ever becoming highly visible themselves. At the Lincolnshire estate she is the single fount of sensibility among social peers who, from Mrs. Jewkes to the "hideous monster" Monsieur Colbrand (1:145), are grotesque instruments for their master's dirty work. While Pamela's body displays the fineness of her inner self through its tears, tremblings, convulsions, and faintings, the bodies of other servants are distinguished only by their grossness: the obese Mrs. Jewkes, the gigantic Colbrand with his "blubber lips" (1:145), the drunken Nan (1:174). In the second volume of *Pamela,* however, Pamela's example as mistress infuses with sensibility all those servants capable of being influenced for good.

While all the other servants who earlier conspired in Mr. B's plots simply reform once Pamela becomes their mistress, Mrs. Jewkes shrinks into nothing. Since Mr. B now manages his desires and channels them into domestic procreation rather than amorous adventures, Mrs. Jewkes, with her embarrassing bulk and her bawdy stories, represents an outmoded style of service. No longer necessary as the instrument of Mr. B's lust, she sinks into "an inward decay, all at once as it were, from a constitution that seemed like one of iron; and she is a mere skeleton" (2:355). In her new defleshed state she assumes Pamela's religious attributes in preparation for death. As Pamela's correspondent assures her, Mrs. Jewkes "made a very exemplary [end]—Full of blessings—And more easy and resigned, than I apprehended she would be" (2:358). Her death removes one of the last reminders of the libertine code by which Mr. B has previously lived.

By the end of the novel, therefore, servants' physical proximity to their masters no longer affords them a gratifying awareness of their employers' fleshly frailties, for those have disappeared from view. Instead, the family prayers that Pamela institutes establish "a family of love" (2:255) in which even physical appearance is transfigured into emotional and spiritual elevation. The butler Jonathan's "silver hairs" become a way for "Mrs. B always [to] distinguis[h] him" as "venerable" in a moral as well as physical sense. Another servant's "friendly salutatio[n]" to "'Good Madam Jervis'" that she "look[s] purely this blessed day, thank God!" signifies Mrs. Jervis's spiritual purity as well as her continued health. The experience of witnessing and participating in this love feast sends them back to "their several vocations, so light, so easy, so pleased, so even-tempered in their minds, as their cheerful countenances, as well as expressions, testify, that it is a heaven of a house" (2:255). In short, the family prayers not only unite the servants in worship of God, but allow them to witness in one another and thus implicitly in themselves the virtues of a good servant, which include cheerfulness as well as diligence and cleanliness. A smiling face in this household is not only the badge of a well-trained maid or footman but also the sign of someone touched by God. The deity, however, approaches the household staff only through the mediation of the household mistress, who organizes and monitors the twice-daily prayers.

That mistress, Pamela, also gives the most extended meditation on the meaning of a servant's transfigured looks. When the "silver hairs" by which she distinguished the butler Jonathan "are . . . laid low," she recalls them as hairs "which I have beheld with so much delight, and thought I had a father in presence, when I saw them adorning so honest and comely a face" (2:438). After quoting the biblical David on the fallen Jonathan, Pamela adds the following extraordinary commendation:

> I might have continued on in the words of the royal lamenter; for, surely never, did one fellow-servant love another in my maiden state, nor servant love a mistress in my exalted condition, better than Jonathan loved me! I could see in his eyes a glistening pleasure, whenever I passed by him: if at such times I spoke to him, as I seldom failed to do, with a "God bless you too!" in answer to his repeated blessings, he had a kind of rejuvenescence (may I say?) visibly running through his whole frame, and now and then, if I laid my hands upon his folded ones, as I passed him on a Sunday morning or evening, praying for me, with a "How do you, my worthy old acquaintance?" his heart would spring to his lips in a kind of rapture, and his eyes would run over. (2:439)

At this point it is clear that the real purpose of Jonathan's venerable hairs, streaming eyes, and miraculously rejuvenating frame is not to reflect credit on him so much as on his employers. That is why Pamela's two pages of praise for Jonathan and Mrs. Jervis on the occasion of both servants' deaths are ultimately self-reflexive. "['T]is almost a misery," Pamela sighs, "to have so soft, so susceptible an heart as I have, or to have such good servants and friends as one cannot lose without such emotions as I feel for the loss of them!" (2:438). Pamela's sensibility becomes self-referential: it shows *her* softness of heart more than the worth of the pair she mourns. In the same way even Mr. B's mention of their names shows his "generous concern" (2:439). Pamela's sensibility and Mr. B's generosity are not merely admirable qualities: they help to justify the pair's position as master and mistress. The butler "excelled all that excelled in his class" (2:438), but his greatest virtue of all seems to have been his rapturous love for his employers. By having the servant love them as he does, Richardson demonstrates the naturalness and beneficence of the system in question. Jonathan's characterization also provides the most comforting possible alternative to the conduct book's anxieties about servants who secretly mock their masters: his attentive gaze is a continual affirmation of the supreme worth of Pamela and Mr. B, whom he observes only to admire.

In short, servants in the second volume of *Pamela* are more concrete physical presences and more sentimentalized figures than in the first volume or than in *Clarissa* (where the Harlowe servants are among the heroine's persecutors). *Sir Charles Grandison,* which—like the second volume of *Pamela*—is essentially a celebration of reconciliation, also makes Sir Charles's servants, like those of the Bs, devout admirers as well as domestics.[26] These domestics, however, reflect rather than originate virtue; indeed, they show their virtue most when they recognize the worth of the paragons they serve. Whereas Mrs. Jewkes disclaims any need for "inferiors" to have a conscience, these morally refurbished servants can satisfy conscience and master at once, by finding religious exaltation in their service. The blessing of their expanded consciousness thus narrows down again to focus only on their employers.

It is fitting, therefore, that *Pamela*'s second and final volume close with a rewriting of the parable of the talents. Mr. Longman, the B. family steward, bequeaths the bulk of his money to his "honoured principal," "out of his great love and gratitude to the family, in whose service he had acquired most of his fortune" (2:482). Like the good servant of the parable, Mr. Longman not only increases the goods he has been given by his master but ultimately returns the benefit to the master himself. He has chosen emphatically to align himself with his master's family in preference to his own biological one. Yet while both his financial ingenuity and final generosity might redound to Mr. Longman's credit, they serve most as a tribute to Mr. and Mrs. B. They are the monetary equivalent of Jonathan's tremulousness in Pamela's presence: they direct our attention toward the attributes of the employers who inspire such devotion. Mr. B even countermands his steward's intentions by having Pamela redistribute the money to Longman's disinherited relations after first instilling a "due sense of their demerit" by "a just and effectual reproof" (2:482). Richardson thus dissolves the antihierarchical implications of granting servants the right to moral consciousness by imagining employers who make themselves responsible for that consciousness. Mrs. Jewkes's amoral zeal to do whatever Mr. B requires makes her a useful instrument, but Mr. Longman surpasses her: he puts his virtues at Mr. B's service, and in the process Mr. B's virtues efface his own.

Through the two volumes of *Pamela* then, Richardson raises the prospect of a radical class critique only to lay that threat to rest. He is refreshingly willing to endorse Pamela's initial fierce self-respect, but he does not acknowledge that sentimentality, like sexuality, can operate coercively. After all, in the first volume of *Pamela* sensibility is crucial to the heroine's self-defense. Once Mr. B adopts Pamela's fine feelings, however, sensibility turns from a means of self-preservation to an instrument of aggression. Due to this shift in perspective on the tactics of sensitivity, Richardson's conservatism takes longer to surface than Fielding's. Yet when it does emerge, it is as encompassing as the latter's. Mr. B's renunciation of his theoretical right to his female servants' bodies ultimately enhances his own authority as much as it protects underlings from sexual exploitation. By adopting an ideal of self-control rather than self-indulgence, Mr. B establishes a moral rationale for his worldly power. His newly self-disciplined body befits him for continued, even expanded, mastery. His servants, meanwhile, are now able to display the physical attributes of sensibility, but only in order to pay tribute to him. For all Richardson's playing with class-linked ideas about sexual authority and sensibility, he keeps traditional class structures firmly in place. Mr. B adopts a different ideal of manliness, it is true, when he accepts chastity as a masculine virtue. (In so doing, he prepares for Sir Charles Grandison, who goes further by incorporating premarital virginity into his ideal manhood—a step that even some of Richardson's admirers felt excessive.) [27] Yet Mr. B's willingness to redefine himself sexually only reinforces the comparative rigidity of his class-based authority. That Richardson wrote when class boundaries were—or were perceived as—shifting dramatically only increases his need to emphasize the status quo. Pamela induces Mr. B to abandon his plans for sexual mastery but in doing so confirms his class-based position of "master." Apparently in the negotiations surrounding sexuality and class, the latter, as a more significant element in identity, must remain relatively unchallenged.

Two hundred years later, physicality is increasingly a marker of sexual rather than class identity. Class identity does not disappear (far from it), but sexual identity becomes increasingly contested and controversial. There is evidence throughout English literature for some sense that sexual identity is primarily internal, frighteningly vulnerable, and potentially mutable; nonetheless, that sense grows sharper throughout the fin de siècle and early twentieth century.[28]

Although Lawrence may well be the supreme exponent of this sharpened sense, he is by no means the only one. The late-Victorian writer George Gissing, like Lawrence, started outside the upper-class world of privilege. Like Lawrence also, he transcended his low social origins through literary ability and ambition and went on to combine a fervent belief in hierarchy with a stinging contempt for the particular hierarchy the English had so far devised. He resembles Lawrence most of all, however, in the centrality of the sexual power struggles in his fiction. In both the novel *The Emancipated* (1890) and the short story "The Foolish Virgin" (1896) Gissing anticipates some of the configurations of sexuality and servitude that dominate *Lady Chatterley's Lover* [1928].

The Emancipated, like Lawrence's novel, relates the transformation of a merely biological female into a true woman: a process in which psychology and physiology are interlinked. Miriam Baske begins the novel as a convalescing widow whose emotional coldness and aesthetic philistinism are signs of her need for the rich masculinity of Ross Mallard, the man who later becomes her husband. His half-reluctant wooing of Miriam reaches its culmination when he summons her to his studio to do some mending for him while he works.[29] When he subsequently offers to make Miriam some tea before she leaves, she responds by suggesting, "Perhaps I could save your time by making it myself," an adaptation that he approves as a "capital idea" (3:327). This apparently minor moment is actually fraught with significance since Miriam's acquiescence signals her acceptance of the woman's role of handmaid. As Mallard declares during his veiled proposal to Miriam, "'I shouldn't dream of allowing [my wife] to come in the way of my life's work; if she cannot be my helper in it, then she shall be nothing to me at all'" (3:273). During this scene Miriam's willingness to accept tasks traditionally assigned to servants shows that she will be such a helper. Gissing eroticizes this subordination in traditionally sexual terms. Miriam is a tremulously receptive female, who obeys the masterful Mallard when he summons her to his studio, when he dismisses her with the words, "'Now don't hinder me any longer'" (3:274), and when he later directs her to "'take off [her] hat and [her] mantle . . . [to] see if [she] can feel at home here'" (3:276). This pattern of his strength and her submission culminates in their embrace: while Miriam's back is turned, Mallard "step[ped] up to her, till he was very close. Then she turned, and his strong arms were about her, and his strong heart beating against hers" (3:276). Miriam here is the passive recipient of Mallard's overtures, while the artist is a traditionally dominant lover.

Despite Gissing's acceptance of sexuality he remains a gender conservative. Miriam's "emancipation" is in many respects an assimilation of "feminine" qualities: softness, submissiveness, subordination. Yet Gissing's emphasis on the liberation of her senses obscures the extent to which he turns her into a latter-day "angel in the house"—albeit one as comfortable in the bedroom as in the parlor. The author subverts Victorian prudery even as he retains important elements of Victorian gender ideology. Although Miriam must give up her earlier unnatural independence, Gissing can include her among the "emancipated" because she is thereby freed from the small-minded Evangelicalism that considers the body shameful. She can now enjoy Italian art undaunted by its indulgence in nudes. Inspired by her new husband, Miriam even wishes to endow her hometown with a public bathhouse rather than a new church. The appreciation of the body now becomes as much a way to represent spiritual health as religious worship had been previously.

Even more significant, her new womanhood transforms Miriam physically as well as inwardly. Or, more precisely, Mallard's creation of her womanhood transforms her. She begins the novel as a convalescent, her "imperfect health of body" as much a reflection of her "troubled earnestness" and "weariness, even . . . ennui" as of physical disease (1:4). She finishes in marital happiness, not only "healthier and more beautiful" than ever before" (3:290) but an actual approximation of her husband's prescient vision of her. Before marrying Miriam, Mallard showed her his two portraits of her, "subtly distinguished from each other" (3:271). The first is Miriam as she had "looked altogether" when under the influence of Evangelicalism (3:273), with "a face fixed in excessive austerity, . . . with resentful eyes and lips on the point of becoming cruel" (3:271). In the second, "though undeniably the features were the same, all these harsh characteristics had yielded to a change of spirit." "Austerity" has become "grave thoughtfulness"; there is "a noble light" in the eyes; "on the lips was sweet womanly strength" (3:271). Under Ross's influence Miriam gradually resembles more and more the ideal portrait that her artist husband has painted of her. After a few years of marriage she has "not quite the second of those two faces that Mallard drew, but with scarcely a record of the other" (3:290). By transforming Miriam into his domestic handmaid, Mallard has simultaneously remade and improved her physically. From a frigid, sickly, independent female, she becomes a sensual, healthy—and dependent—woman.

Gissing further explores the idea that the domestic role is necessary for feminine fulfillment in "The Foolish Virgin." The "virgin" of the title, Rosamund Jewell, is a gentlewoman who decides to enter domestic service after hearing such a choice praised by the man she desires to marry. Although she does not thereby win a marriage proposal, she does gain increased health and vitality once she moves from idle gentility into a servant's life. Whereas being a "lady" involves "unwholesome habit of mind and body," domestic work gives Rosamund a "brisk step, . . . upright bearing, . . . clear eye, and pure-toned skin."[30] Rosamund's misfortune is that she will never have the opportunity to practice her "'vocation'" for a man of her own, but she at least is better off than those "'[t]housands'" of her sisters "all meant by nature to scrub and cook— [who] live and die miserably because they think themselves too good for it'" (237). Ironically the snobbish Rosamund stumbles into this rather bleak salvation by chance: she chooses domestic service as a stepping-stone toward marriage, only to discover that it is the end point.

Gissing is far from original, of course, in proposing household duties as the natural ones for the majority of women, but his willingness to accept class degradation is the crucial distinction from previous representations of female subordination, which had prioritized class over gender politics. Recollect social critic W. R. Greg's 1862 declaration that female servants fulfilled "both essentials of woman's being: *they are supported by, and they minister to, men.*"[31] Greg, however, had excluded the possibility of "ladies" laboring in homes other than their own. Gissing's portrayal of Rosamund attributes invigorating and beautifying qualities to a woman's domestic work even when her subordination lowers her original class status. To make this subordination seem both natural and attractive, the author must realign representations of the body to emphasize gender above class.

Like Gissing, Lawrence in *Lady Chatterley's Lover* unites a self-consciously daring emphasis on the importance of sexuality with a conventionally oppressive idealization of strict gender divisions. As David Ellis, Christopher Heywood, and James Cowan demonstrate in different works, Lawrence is eager to ground his ideas about human psychology in concrete facts about human biology and physiology.[32] His concern for bodies is far more for what they reveal about gender identity than what they signify about class position. While Richardson demonstrates that Mr. B's lust makes him resemble his lowest servant, Lawrence shows that lacking the right kind of lust makes men and women resemble each other, thereby sinking them all into sexual disarray. His primary interest is therefore in providing precise specifications for healthy sexuality, complete with models for true man- and womanhood. The three versions of the novel reveal a gradual shift from social criticism and realistic techniques to romance content and form. "In the final version of the novel," as one critic has observed, "'class' is abolished" in favor of exclusive focus on "the relationship between Connie and Mellors."[33] Since gender confusion spans the classes, corrupting miners as well as aristocrats and intelligentsia, Lawrence cannot align sexual health with any particular social stratum. Instead, he selects his two lovers from opposing classes, then mates each with a social equal who is also a gender failure. Throughout *Lady Chatterley's Lover,* then, Lawrence exploits the traditional connotations of different class positions to preach about sexual rather than social identity.[34]

It is especially in his descriptions of bodies that Lawrence uses and sometimes reverses conventional class associations to assert the priority of gender over social status.[35] To begin with, Clifford Chatterley and Bertha Mellors are the only two who actually look their roles. A country gentleman, he is blond and "almost . . . chirpy, with his ruddy, healthy-looking face and his pale-blue, challenging bright eyes. His shoulders were broad and strong, his hands were very strong."[36] His paralyzed lower body, of course, constitutes Lawrence's sardonic comment on the nature of that gentleman. "Gentleman" is always used to describe him, but Connie eventually realizes that to be a gentleman now means to be a "'dead fish'" with "'about as much feeling as celluloid has'" (194). Clifford clings to the ideal of upper-class sensitivity, intimidating Mrs. Bolton with the "higher fastidiousness" that makes him object to the scent of hyacinths (98). But in reality both his senses and consciousness are so dull that "the very stale air of the colliery was better than oxygen to him" (108). Lawrence thus attributes to Clifford the coarseness of sensibility that servant conduct books had previously identified with servants and with the lower-classes generally.

Although Lawrence insists on Clifford's vulgarity (100, 109), he does not deploy this as a social criticism. Rather he uses this insensitivity to stigmatize all gender-blurred individuals. Thus throughout *Lady Chatterley's Lover* aristocrats and miners are seen as alike in their insentience. Clifford is educated and "artistic" insofar as one considers his writing to constitute "art." Yet neither his upper-class refinement nor his miners' working-class hardiness is to blame for the emotional incapacities of the respective classes; instead, those capacities shrivel through the failure of gender identity. As we have seen in *Pamela,* the worst threat to the heroine is the upper-class assumption that servants' supposed lack of fine feelings justifies their sexual exploitation. Mr. B has to learn to respect Pamela's sensibility before he curbs his own rampant sexuality and, in the process, acquires sensibility of his own. Pamela's delicate emotions demonstrates that, although a servant, she is not mere sexual fodder for her master. For Lawrence, however, sexuality does not oppose sensitivity but operates in conjunction with it.

As if to drive home this point, Lawrence invents a parodic machismo for the impotent and unfeeling Clifford. A forceful industrialist, Clifford gets "his pecker up" in his "man's victory" with the mines that he operates, expands, and improves (107–8). He enacts with Mrs. Bolton a superficial show of masculine mastery, reducing her to being "flushed and tremulous like a young girl" (99), while he "feel[s] a lord and a master" (109). Yet this strength is false because it is based on his class position. He inherits the mines to which he devotes himself, and he continues their operation by insisting on his separation from the men who work in them. He intimidates Mrs. Bolton initially by being "a gentleman, a *real* gentleman . . . with a queer temper and a fine manner and money and power in [his] control, and all sorts of odd knowledge that she had never dreamed of, with which he could still bully her" (99). Yet Mrs. Bolton nonetheless can manipulate Clifford because her apparent subservience is based merely on class feeling. In gender terms, however, she sees him as a "baby" (99) and further diminishes his sexual identity by making him dependent on her, while "[s]he loved having his body in her charge, absolutely, to the last menial office" (98). Unlike the domestics in Swift's *Directions to Servants,* who are revolted at cleaning chamber pots, Mrs. Bolton is eager for apparently degrading offices. But the actual degradation is Clifford's. Although in every objective way she is a devoted servant, "she was getting him by the throat, and he was yielding to her" (98). Herself oblivious to the sanctity of virility, she encourages his false identification of authority with class status, rather than with the "'balls'" that keep a "'real man'" from being "'tame'" (217). Asserting himself through the privileges of rank and wealth, Clifford can be a magnate and a bully, but because he is cut off from physical life and the emotional riches inseparable from it, he lacks the genuine authority of the real man.

Consequently Mellors threatens him through masculine superiority. Clifford may attack Mellors as a "'disreputable character who walked about with [his] breeches' buttons undone,'" but Mellors can far more tellingly retort that Clifford has "'nothing to unbutton anyhow'" (270).[37] As G. R. Strickland points out, Lawrence specifically introduced this sort of cruel reminder of Clifford's physical disability into his third and final version of the novel, as though to intensify the wound's damning significance. "[P]resented with evident sympathy and admiration" while they jeer at Clifford's impotence, both

Mellors and Connie have authorial validation for their taunts. Lawrence, Strickland continues, can thus "invite us to amuse ourselves at [Clifford's] expense"³⁸ only because, in the novel's schema, Clifford's bodily condition degrades his spirit: it renders him not pathetic, but objectionable. In the same way Mellors's virility ennobles his entire character. Secure in the possession of a penis, the gamekeeper can defy the aristocrat's class power by not acknowledging it: he willingly leaves his job, refuses Clifford's offer of "a month's wages extra" (269), and plans a self-sufficient life of farming. Gender stability thus has social implications. By being man enough to grasp independence Mellors shows that Clifford's social powers are as incapable of controlling him as Clifford's disabled penis is of impregnating Connie. (As we see later, however, that individual freedom, not social influence of his own, is all Lawrence can grant this hero.)

While Clifford inadvertently undermines class privilege by looking the part of an aristocrat yet lacking substance, Constance does nothing to support the traditional associations of the "lady"'s physique with innate delicacy and sensitivity. Physically, Constance's ruddiness and heartiness make her appear a village girl rather than an aristocrat (6). Lawrence is at pains to emphasize the materiality of her femaleness: her round belly, her sloping buttocks, her full thighs (70–71) show that she is "'nice'" and "'real,'" (68), not one of the "'little jazz girls with small boy buttocks'" whose existence is a sign of modern degeneracy (39). Whereas Pamela's slightness helps separate her from Mrs. Jewkes's grossness, Connie's attenuation through frustration is a psychological as well as physical diminution. Pamela is more feminine as well as more ladylike because of her daintiness; when Connie loses weight, she lacks not only feminine contours but femininity itself. As with Miriam Baske in *The Emancipated,* ill health signals sexual maladjustment, while radiant wholeness accompanies sensual fulfillment. Like Miriam also, Connie experiences this physical change during a progress from perverse female pride to feminine subjugation, except that Lawrence is more precise and detailed in his contrasts than Gissing: he differentiates not merely between Connie's sexually unsatisfying marriage and her later love affair with Mellors but between Mellors's lovemaking and that of Connie's first lover, Michaelis. Whereas Michaelis's boyishness and passivity allow Connie to experience her own sexuality as active and to derive from "her own activity" a "subtle sort of self-assurance, something blind and a little arrogant" (29–30), Mellors's "penis rise[s] against her with silent amazing force and assertion" so that she can only go "all open to him and helpless!" (173). It is this acceptance of her own quiescent role in sex that allows Connie to be "born: a woman" (174), an event as spiritually significant as the conversion experience is for "born-again" Christians. By understanding the proper way for women to achieve orgasm, Connie breaks free from worldly corruption and redeems her soul and flesh. This understanding involves renouncing the class status of the "lady" for the ecstatic abjection of the archetypal female "slave" (135, 247) to whom Connie repeatedly compares herself in her relationship with Mellors.

Yet Lawrence does supply an iconic figure of delicacy, although through a masculine rather than feminine body. Initially, Lawrence's presentation of Mellors seems designed mostly to refute assumptions about working-class crudity, yet, ultimately that presentation has less to do with class than with gender.[39] Mellors's body, no less than his ability to speak "standard" English and his experience in the army, reveals that he is "no simple working man" (243).[40] "[H]is smallish, sensitive, loose hand" (243) is itself sufficient demonstration of that. Lawrence uses language laden with upper-class associations—purity, reticence, delicacy, fineness, refinement, sensitivity—to describe this working man's body. Within one page, for instance, Mellors is described as having a "slender white body" that is "white as milk, with fine slender muscular flesh," "white and thin," "white and fine, the small buttocks beautiful with an exquisite, delicate manliness, the back of the neck ruddy and delicate and yet strong. There was an inward, not an outward strength in the delicate fine body" (209). Strength is certainly important here, and Mellors's "'proud . . . lordly'" penis explains why he is "'so overbearing'" (210), but even more striking is Lawrence's emphasis on the delicacy and fineness of the male body. Consequently, the male body unites the most desirable attributes of male and female: strength *and* subtlety, power *and* delicacy. Most important, these physical qualities are the outward signs of inward states. Mellors is simultaneously stronger and more sensitive than anyone else in the book. As if to drive this superiority home in every detail, Lawrence even makes him "instinctively much more delicate and well-bred" in his table manners than Connie's defeminized sister, Hilda, who suffers from "a certain Scottish clumsiness" (244). One could hardly have a stronger reversal of the assumptions of the 1892 article "Ladies in Service" dreading the effects of servants' table manners upon the delicate sensibilities of "lady-help."

Lawrence also uses class-connotative language as a means of characterization in describing Bertha Mellors's body. Again terminology that originally implied class status is now more important for pinpointing gender identity. While aristocratic terms help to idealize Mellors's male power, associations with lower-class vulgarity condemn Bertha's sexual confusion. The reader already knows that Bertha is "common," but her commonness goes deeper than her "talking broad" or wearing cheaply "smart clothes" (201). Bertha's clitoral orgasms align her with "an old trull," with "the old rampers [with] beaks between their legs." Her urge for sexual satisfaction is a "raving necessity" like "how old whores used to be," and, most damning of all, "[i]t was a low kind of self-will in her, a raving sort of self-will: like in a woman who drinks" (202). Once Mellors leaves her, she takes up with her own kind: "[a] big baby sort of fellow, very low-mouthed. She bullies him, and they both drink" (202). The metaphoric picture that emerges is a composite of ragged, elderly streetwalker and worn-down, uncontrolled alcoholic: images of social degradation as much as of sexuality. Regardless of what Mellors's (and Lawrence's) misconceptions about women's responsiveness might be, the point here is not to prohibit female orgasms per se. Nor is it designed to dismiss Bertha altogether: Mellors would still prefer his "common" wife to the socially higher "never-never ones" who had frustrated him earlier (203). Rather, Lawrence uses negative class associations for the clitoris to lend additional emotional power to his con- demnation of whatever threatens phallic supremacy. As employers' sensibility in *Pamela* precedes and defines servants' consciousnesses, so the masculine body in *Lady Chatterley's Lover* should create as well as satisfy women's "feel- ing" and "sensation" (202). Lawrence insists on the moral element here as much as Richardson does, for he shows both the evil in Bertha's self-will and the redemption that Connie finds through renouncing the clitoral capacities she had exercised with Michaelis.

Ironically enough, however, Lawrence's interest in establishing masculinity as a supreme value on which all other values depend means that the book allows "clitoral" women one extenuation. Even when, like Connie, such women are essentially wholesome, the tendency of such "modern men" as Michaelis to be sexually "finished almost before he had begun . . . forced the woman to be active" (54). Mellors himself, never shy about expressing his aver- sion to unfeminine women, concedes that "[i]t's because th' men *aren't* men, that th' women have to be" (219). Men thus precede and establish female gen- der identity: their own sexual security or shakiness allows or prevents proper female development.[41] In a novel famous for celebrating the body, women have surprisingly little physical existence of their own. Just as employers in *Pamela* co-opt servants' affective lives, so "real" men in *Lady Chatterley's Lover* co-opt women's physical consciousnesses, which, in Lawrence, is also affective. Mrs. Bolton's husband Ted, for instance, feels his wife's labor pains more than she does herself. After witnessing her "bad time," Ted cannot have "any right plea- sure . . . at nights . . . —he'd never really let himself go"; men's superior sensi- tivity "spoilt his pleasure in his bit of married love" (163). Despite men's anatomical inability to experience labor, the birth of his child renders Ted more in need of "comfort" than his wife (163). Sexual intimacy even grants men a knowledge about women superior to that of the women themselves. Mellors, for instance, knows when a woman is a lesbian even when she does not (203). Despite Lawrence's insistence on knowing oneself through one's body, Mellors's intuitive prowess actually reveals women's alienation from their bodies and Lawrence's acceptance of that alienation: Lawrence here privileges men's expe- rience and knowledge of women's bodies over that of women themselves.[42]

To show how biblical "knowledge" of a sexual partner translates into knowledge of another's inner self, Lawrence all but personifies male and female body parts, using them as moral and spiritual signifiers in a psychomachia of sexual identity. Mellors's superiority to the other men in Connie's life is that "he was kind to the female in her, which no man had ever been. Men were very kind to the *person* she was, but rather cruel to the female. . . . Men were awfully kind to Constance Reid or to Lady Chatterley: but not to her womb they weren't kind" (121). Just as particular gender identity replaces general human identity here, so the womb becomes a synecdoche for the female gender. The womb, even more than "Lady Jane," represents womanhood at its finest— receptive, quiescent, and acquiescent—just as the clitoris represents the nega- tion of femininity. Mellors identifies female "will" with the clitoris, so that women who achieve orgasms through clitoral stimulation rather than through penile penetration of the vagina are asserting their wills *against* men, rather than simply experiencing sexual satisfaction.[43] Bertha is his prime example of this female "bullying," with both her "will" and her clitoris to blame.[44] He describes the latter with an intensely physical disgust as a "beak tearing at me" (202). The penile connotations of "beak," as much as Bertha's unsuitably aggressive behavior, suggest the woman's lack of gender stability. Bertha, like Mrs. Jewkes, is an unfeminine lower-class woman, but the ferocity with which *Lady Chatterley's Lover* condemns her has no parallel to the handling of Mrs. Jewkes in *Pamela*. Even the "problem" of insufficient femininity is different in the two books: Mrs. Jewkes is unwomanly because she assists a man in vic- timizing another female; Bertha's crime is that she is not sufficiently obedient to the man who should be her master.

Lawrence's suspicion of all female bonding, moreover, including Connie's early closeness to her sister, contrasts with Richardson's implicit assumption that women *should* help protect each other from masculine aggression, although not all do. For Lawrence the need for women's connection to men apparently outweighs any worth in female friendships, and lesbianism consti- tutes Mellors's most serious charge against sexually maladjusted women. Such lesbianism is not like Mrs. Jewkes's casually indicated tendencies, which actu- ally serve her master, and it is even further from the usual pornographic treat- ment, in which lesbian scenes serve to titillate the (presumably male) reader while reassuring him of the necessity for masculine presence.[45] In this novel a lesbian inclination, like a clitoral orgasm, is virtually an act of sex war. At the same time lesbianism's apparent exclusion of men only reemphasizes men's absolute centrality: the real importance of lesbianism is that it makes men suf- fer (203). As servants' virtues in the second volume of *Pamela* find their points of origin and completion in the sensibilities of employers, women's physicality in *Lady Chatterley's Lover* exists only in relation to men.

Yet even as *Lady Chatterley's Lover* postulates masculine men as the prereq- uisite for feminine women and a healthy society, it also makes masculinity the most threatened and the most precious of all qualities. The delicacy of Mellors's body, described above, not only translates the refinement of class into the fineness of true masculinity but suggests the vulnerability of the ideal male. The whole weight of society tries to crush Mellors because masculinity itself has become taboo. Yet his fragility is that of an individual outsider, not of an entire class. As Richard Wasson points out, Lawrence's "commitment to *eros* as the solution to class struggle" meant that his hero had to be "the beautiful male living in solitary beauty[, not] a member of the working class, suffering the indignities of industrial labor."[46] In an earlier version of the novel Lawrence's realistic depiction of a hero whose physique has been "notably damaged" from "a day's labor" makes it "difficult to imagine that [the man's] body can once more become that quick and love-giving flesh it was in the woods" (Wasson 302). It is part of Lawrence's move, Wasson explains, "from the realm of realism to the realm of romance" that he abandons this acknowledgement of "the dangers brought to the male body by industrial working conditions" (303, 290). In the third version of *Lady Chatterley's Lover* Mellors is more vulnerable to his wife's clitoral selfishness than to brutal working conditions. Society ignores, rather than maims, him. Yet even in those muted terms he is a victim and a social exile.

By contrast, various social rewards accrue to the unmanliest of his foils. We see this not only in the physically incapable Clifford, whose superior social standing and wealth are obvious, but also in the technically potent Michaelis, who in some ways parallels Mellors. Like Mellors, Michaelis is lower class but able to assume upper-class mannerisms when necessary (28). Like Mellors also he is fiercely antisocial (28). Unlike Mellors, however, he is a dismal lover. His habit of premature ejaculation, one the narrator ascribes to modern men generally (54), damningly reveals the emotional childishness that corresponds with his childish "unfinished, tender flesh" (29). Since his "male passivity" (30) does not allow him to establish satisfactory sexual relations with any woman, he is left to pursue the "bitch-goddess" success (53). It is only this socially constructed female icon that any of the half men in this book truly *can* desire. "Sexually, [Clifford and Michaelis] were passionless, even dead"; unable even to want real intimacy they long only "to make a real display—*their* display— a man's own very display, of himself" (51). The hint of exhibitionism here neatly captures the extent to which society in this book vampirically drains sexual energies by displacing them into the fight for "success" (51), a fight as sterile as masturbation and, according to Lawrence, likewise fueled by frustrated sexuality and psychological (if self-chosen) isolation.

In such a society Mellors *must* be vulnerable and even rather unsuccessful by society's standards. His pure flesh is the sign of his emotional distance from the decadence that engulfs the other male characters. But in a book where "success" is axiomatically a bitch, only "doggy" men, as Connie later dubs both Clifford and Michaelis (248), can succeed. Mellors alone is a real man, with a man's "[s]heer fiery sensuality," and not one of the men who really "are all dogs that trot and sniff and copulate." In a world of such dogs, Connie realizes "how rare a thing a man is!" (248). Yet a man's rarity does not enhance the value society places on him—wherein we see another contrast with Richardson. One common way for readers to attack the morality of *Pamela* has been to point out the material rewards that Pamela receives for her "virtue." Richardson has been characterized as naive or crass or both for making social elevation, wealth, and praise from all who meet her the vindication of his heroine's goodness. Lawrence takes an opposing approach: Mellors and Connie must end without any form of social affirmation because only thus can they demonstrate *their* virtue. In a book where Mellors holds out the vision of "alive an' beautiful" men wearing "close red trousers" with "buttocks nice and showing scarlet" (219) as a way to redeem society but where Lawrence vividly dramatizes the hurdles to realizing such a vision, the pure of flesh and spirit must remove themselves from society altogether. This perhaps is Lawrence's final step toward dissolving matters of class entirely into matters of gender. His wholesale rejection of modern society as artificial and false necessarily entails rejecting the existing class divisions as tainted by the superstructure that devised them. Such a rejection does not mean giving up all hierarchies, but it does require beginning from supposedly natural gender differences in order to construct an improved, because "natural," set of social arrangements.[47] Thus whatever hope exists in the novel's close comes from the potential of Connie and Mellors's projected life together, apart from the corrupt modern world. The sole representatives of true manhood and womanhood, these two must maintain the ideal and the example of proper relations between the sexes. From such beginnings only, Lawrence apparently believes, could a harmonious society grow.

Both Richardson and Lawrence, then, play with the signifiers of social and sexual identity, only to differ on which of the two is more subject to challenge and therefore more in need of stabilization. Richardson freely modifies concepts of masculinity but reinforces class entrenchment in the process. Lawrence uses the accumulated power of class connotations only to apply them to representations of gender. While the applicability to class may be gone, Lawrence retains the hierarchical assumptions. *Lady Chatterley's Lover* thus shows a new obsession with sexual classification, precisely because categories seem hard to maintain: it is crucial that people fully understand and accept their sexual "place." Mellors's laments over modern blurring of gender identity are reminiscent of the hand-wringing sentiments about modern servants in Defoe's *Religious Courtship*. Whereas Defoe's characters look back to a Golden Age of obedient, devoted subordinates and deplore underlings' current worthlessness, Mellors in *Lady Chatterley's Lover* and Lawrence in "Apropos of *Lady Chatterley's Lover*" deplore current sexual degeneracy and harken back wistfully to a preindustrial age of gender stability. As usual the past is being used to represent the "natural" that is also the ideal: what differs is only that natural/ideal sexual relations, rather than class interactions, now assume the status of threatened artifact.

Conclusion

Virtue's Reward or the Mother's Recompense

THIS BOOK BEGAN by pointing out that the conception of maternity as an inherently noble force expressing and gratifying a uniquely female need to nurture represents only one vision of motherhood, and by no means a universal one. Yet this vision has gained in recognizability and power over the years, even as—or maybe because—it has been challenged and disputed. A pattern of rhetorical idealization has fixed the concept of "motherhood" as a cultural icon quite distinct from the practices and treatment of actual mothers. Simultaneously recent centuries have witnessed an increasing interest in exploring childhood development and the processes by which human infants mature into a psychological and social equilibrium (or lack thereof) that is now seen as far more the product of human influences, initiative, and even biology than of divine will and unchangeable social caste. Perhaps not so coincidentally, the developing genre of the novel, which assumed recognizable shape during the same centuries, established a new literary interest in the childhood experiences of its protagonists and in the maturation of those protagonists along lines similar to those of a "narrative" of childhood development. Certainly, the longest-canonized of the novelists treated in this book are part of that history of the novel's generic concerns and master plots, from the tentative beginnings of Richardson through the solidifying forms of Dickens and Thackeray to the restless innovations of Lawrence.[1] Conversely, Burney's, Brontë's, and Gaskell's relatively late entry into the canon suggests not only a general suspicion of female authorship but perhaps also that the necessarily different forms of maturation for a female rather than male protagonist have stamped narratives of female development as comparatively trivial—at least until the recent advent of feminist scholarship. After all, the crucial lesson for women tends to be how to give love—a less enticing prospect than the alternative for men. Female novelists, of course, have often employed male protagonists as one way to broaden the scope and assumed seriousness of their books. And male novelists have sometimes employed female protagonists, although there is then a tendency to make those characters relatively static morally. Pamela is the intense focus of the book that bears her name, but she is a paragon from the novel's beginning to end. Amy Dorrit may be the central and title character of *Little Dorrit,* but she never needs to undergo the self-exploration and self-disciplining of the similarly eponymous David Copperfield.[2]

After all, the emerging vision of motherhood assumes nurturant femininity as a given for all "good" mothers and focuses attention upon the crucial matter of the child's successful or unsuccessful development, while many of the most famous eighteenth- and nineteenth-century novels trace the development of a male protagonist who is never believed—nor expected—to be as good as the idealized woman who loves him but whose struggles toward mature selfhood command the attention that her static virtue does not. This common pattern links even dissimilar novelists: it appears in the courtship between Tom and Sophia in Fielding's *Tom Jones* as much as in the romance between Mr. B and Pamela in Richardson's *Pamela,* and between Pen and Laura in Thackeray's *Pendennis* as much as between David and Agnes in Dickens's *David Copperfield.* Why then do so many authors of this period assign the excitement of aspiration to male and the monotony of achieved selfhood—whether virtuous or not—to female characters? The pattern that emerges is close to that of parenthood (which in our society mostly means "motherhood"), in which parents (mothers), simply through their physical adulthood and caretaking role, are expected to be beyond the deepest struggles of character formation and free to devote themselves to "forming" their children. That this pattern is much more a dream than a reality does not alter its powerful hold over the imagination. This modern dream-vision of childhood development—which always has the potential of turning into a nightmare through the figure of the "bad" mother who hampers rather than aids the child's growth—can provide the narrative model for a secular version of the "psychomachia." Whereas earlier religious writers could allegorize the soul's progress toward salvation through a world populated by the personifications of spiritual abstractions, so novelists could portray a protagonist's growth into maturity through an environment populated by other characters whose significance consists of their ability to aid or impede that process. The result is that those other characters exist mainly as instrumental figures, whose virtues matter mainly for their effect on that central character.

The correlation between child-focused theories of childhood development and protagonist-focused narratives in the novel might explain why material powerlessness for women—and for other groups as well—can coexist so easily with discursive idealization, and also why novels can idealize virtues their protagonists are never meant to acquire. The exalted heroines' crucial responsibilities fit neatly into the newly emerged paradigm of maternal nurturance. The heroines' "work" is overwhelmingly maternal in nature even—or especially—when performed for the good of the heroes they eventually marry. The hero then is rewarded for successful growth through union with a female figure of endless nurturance, while destruction often coincides with failure to attain or to keep such a figure as mate. In a sense, we might see this pattern as the child's fantasy of successful completion of a task: achievement will bring the eternal approval of an idealized maternal figure—a fantasy, one might add, that has its appeal for female as well as male readers. One might argue that the novel typically has relied upon human egotism to ensure its readers' identification with the protagonist and consequent willingness to invest emotion, time, and effort in tracing the protagonist's path to its end. Thus, any rewards the protagonist receives, no matter how stellar, and any special consideration the protagonist is shown, no matter how exceptional, can be accepted by the protagonist-identified reader as natural and deserved.[3] In that context any questions about the worthiness of a male to receive female attentions become irrelevant.

Even novels in which a woman is nominally the central character often show that woman as suitably mated with a male whose virtues might seem far less than her own. Thus Pamela marries Mr. B even though his despicable behavior could easily disqualify him from being the husband of such a paragon, and a century later the high-principled Jane Eyre is happy to marry Rochester, despite his history of deceiving, manipulating, and planning to betray her. *Clarissa,* on the other hand, continues to unsettle readers today precisely because its heroine refuses a man on moral grounds and even more emphatically refuses to accept that man's reformation as her responsibility. These refusals make Richardson's novel genuinely startling, even revolutionary in some respects, but Richardson cannot go further to conceive of an arena for female virtues outside masculine reformation and tendance: hence Clarissa's death. Likewise, in Dickens's and in Thackeray's oeuvre, one consistently encounters female characters whose moral resplendence illuminates the considerably less stellar males who surround them, but who nonetheless are destined for no other fate than life with those same men. The most dramatic shift allowed them is a transfer of attention from a less to a more appreciative male. Thus Amy Dorrit in Dickens's *Little Dorrit* first labors selflessly for her ungrateful and emotionally abusive father only to end up equally devoted to the gentler Arthur Clennam. Marriage to Arthur is presumably Amy's greatest fulfillment, the fitting reward for her spotless life, but Arthur, although certainly more attractive than the egregious Mr. Dorrit, nowhere matches Amy's consistent heroism. The difference in stature between hero and heroine, however, is nowhere a cause for concern: Arthur's acceptance of her love is justified by his passive gratitude for it, not by any need of his to equal her strenuous labors on behalf of those she loves. Likewise, Eustace Wrayburn in Dickens's *Our Mutual Friend* can bless Lizzie Hexam simply by bestowing on her his own disfigured person and shattered prospects in marriage. That Lizzie loves a man far below her own moral stature does not change the fact that the proper recompense for her is marriage to that man.

The idea of "reward" thereby plays a double-edged role in these marital narratives: the male partner gains the reward of endless female love as the prize bestowed on a maturation whose proof is willingness to accept love from the appropriate female—Agnes rather than Dora, marriage to Lizzie rather than seduction of her. Consistently a man proves his maturation in eighteenth- and nineteenth-century novels by learning what is best for himself: by recognizing that the woman who will most nurture and care for him is the one he should attach himself to for life. Attraction to women whose main appeal is sexual demonstrates male immaturity because such women ultimately are unsatisfying: their lack of nurturing qualities means that a sexually tantalizing woman might allure but typically does not offer consistent emotional sustenance. Rather she demands such sustenance, as Thackeray's Blanche Amory and Beatrix Esmond and as Dickens's Dora Spenlow illustrate. Men, then, demonstrate adulthood when they choose self-gratification or rather, the proper, most valuable form of self-gratification—the nutritive, rather than junk food, kind. The ideal women in many of these novels—Amy Dorrit is perhaps the best example here—never need to attain adulthood: they are born "little women" already mature in childhood. When a female character, like Dickens's Caddy Jellyby in *Bleak House* or Bella Wilfer in *Our Mutual Friend,* does need to improve, she usually must learn how to *be* nurturing rather than how to receive nurture. Once she is "mature," a woman theoretically will fulfill the same needs by giving nurture as men satisfy by receiving it. Even Jane Eyre, after all, who begins by hungering for experience, eventually finds her bliss in tending a blind and crippled husband, while Constance Chatterley, almost a century later, gladly gives up "emancipation" in exchange for Mellors's masterful lovemaking. Women's reward is to have their love accepted—and as love from a wife, not a mistress (a role with which Pamela and Lizzie Hexam are threatened), nor as a sister (Laura Bell and Agnes Wickfield), nor even as a mother (Rachel in *Henry Esmond*). But since female love is nurturant, this reward truly is the opportunity to practice female virtues indefinitely: to provide consistent nurture with the only return being the recipient's appreciation and gratitude.[4] This novelistic convention fits neatly into the paradigm that historian Joan Wallach Scott examines in her exploration of nineteenth-century discourses about female workers. According to Scott, theorists across the political spectrum removed female domestic labor from any consideration of economic factors—let alone economic recompense—by assuming that it was women's "natural" and always willingly undertaken work, work that really was its own reward.[5]

In the case of novelistic romances, then, the supposedly adult relationship between two lovers actually recapitulates the idealized form of parent-child—or, to be more specific, of mother-child. In the dealings between mother and child the child can offer virtually nothing in return for parental care except gratitude and affection, nor, as long as the child is a child, does the mother have the option—at least a socially and morally acceptable option—to withhold care. Furthermore, the focus of parental care is the child's development, the expansion of all his potential and capabilities (the male pronoun here is deliberate). The parent, as an adult, presumably already has developed, and therefore the total lack of provision for further development for her is a matter of course.

In a sense this model of male-female relations is a natural extension of the shift from political to domestic definitions of femaleness that Nancy Armstrong has noted. When previous centuries had employed the image of a king's relations with his subjects as a metaphor for a husband's relations with his wife, the result had been to emphasize the material power of the male and the practical obligations of the female. The emphasis was political rather than psychological. The eighteenth century's emphasis on the relations between mother and child as a way to conceptualize femininity itself had the perhaps unexpected result of introducing a factor of perpetual childhood into conceptions of masculinity. The increasing awareness of *male* sensitivity and sensibility at that time—noted by critics from Janet Todd to Claudia L. Johnson—can often figure into treatments of the ideal male-female relationship mirroring the child-parent one, with the woman called upon to nurse the emotionally needy man. This treatment certainly banishes overt political metaphors from the realm of domestic relations but does so at the price of figuring all domestic relations as some variation of the parental—or, more precisely, the newly valorized maternal. One might argue that the father's role in the emotional as opposed to material maintenance of a family has been so attenuated and often invisible in modern conceptions (as opposed to individual experiences perhaps) of domestic life that the parental role applies in its fullest force only to the mother. Although the father represents authority, it is most often the authority of forces originating outside the home. In the Victorian dichotomy of private and public realms, the father's role seems to be to introduce and enforce the tougher standards of public life, while the mother's is to soften those standards and to shield the home's inhabitants from their full rigor. Thus arises the oft-repeated cliché that only a mother's love is unconditional—a comment also sometimes applied, interestingly enough, to the love offered by dogs. In the "private" world of the home the father may be head, but the mother is heart.

This pattern of investing the mother with emotional resonance beyond that of the father might also explain the rhetorical insistence on female power, so baffling when one looks at the material conditions under which women lived. Some commentators have explained this belief in women's power as a sign of male fear of female sexuality. But while both men and women can experience sexual desire for another as a loss of control and as a manifestation of the other's power, the perception of sexual desire *in* another can just as easily serve as confirmation of one's own power over the aroused other. In short the woman who can be sexually aroused can thereby be "controlled" as much as men apparently always have feared being manipulated sexually by women. Perhaps, then, it is not so much the woman as lover as it is the woman as mother who arouses the deepest fears. The emphasis, originating in the eighteenth century, on women's formative role in child development seems to carry over into the realm of supposedly adult relationships, so that a woman is never free of the responsibility for another's psychological health and emotional security. The amorous male's perception of his female lover's power thus might have its roots in the child's sense of maternal power. This psychologically based "empowerment" theoretically replaces any need for women's practical authority even as it crushes women with the awesome responsibility for others' happiness.[6]

There are other figures of "instrumental" virtue aside from the redemptive woman, however. The effusive sensibility or sentimentality that marks so much late-eighteenth-century and nineteenth-century literature can also idealize members of the working classes. Earlier literature generally has no equivalent to the nobility that some Victorian literature in particular attributes to working classes—alongside of fearful depictions of them as monstrous. This alternation between idealization and denigration parallels the novel's treatment of women and perhaps for the same reason: both women and the working classes are perceived as important for their effect on "real" subjects—assumed to be upper class and male—rather than for what they are themselves. Virtuous members of the working class can tutor leisure-class protagonists in the art of cross-class interaction, but the emphasis remains on the protagonist's "enlightenment," not on the working classes themselves. One might wonder why the "enlightenment" of a leisure-class protagonist is worth so much effort and so much display of great working-class virtue and suffering: the effect, even if not intended, seems to be that the ultimate end is not so much political change as the further perfection of the leisure-class psyche. The attainment of proper cross-class sympathies becomes one more marker of the protagonist's successful development. Thus the entire working class, when in its supposedly ideal relations with its social superiors, is quasi-feminine and quasi-maternal:

like the ideal woman it displays its worth not by what it is in itself but by what it contributes to others. At the same time the emphasis on personal warmth theoretically makes those contributions reciprocal: there is no need for material equality when there is equality of goodwill. The irony is even sharper here than in male-female relations, yet novel after novel testifies to personal concern being the most valuable gift the leisure classes can bestow on the working class. Again, this emphasis on the personal disguises the practical power of the leisure class, just as men's practical power has been hidden in their relations with women. For all the emphasis on the leisure class's greater complexity, sophistication, and intelligence, that class almost plays the child's role here: requiring practical care and rewarding that care with fondness for the caregiver and with the opportunity for the caregiver to rejoice in the development it has helped to foster.

In the English novel women and the working classes in particular have received an undue proportion of sentimental idealization *and* of near hysterical vituperation. (In American novels African American characters have received strikingly similar treatment.) Whereas the working classes often have been blamed for the sorry state of the body politic, women additionally have been seen as causing the debility and decay of individual (male) bodies. When demonized, women and the working classes are distinctly and distinctively "Other"—objects of dread outside the realm of empathetic human relations. Unfortunately, when idealized—even, as often happens in treatments of the working classes, when idealized in the name of "fellow feeling"—they remain stubbornly "Other." If when unregenerate they are immune to moral appeals, then in their ideal form they respond to nothing else (we certainly cannot say that of the heroes they serve). Cheerfully giving of their spiritual abundance, they ask for nothing except to be allowed to keep on giving: this is virtue's reward.

Notes

Full reference is given at the first citation of a work in each chapter. Reference to subsequent citations will be given in the text in parentheses.

INTRODUCTION

1. See pt. 3, "The Bride from Heaven" (141–228) of Alexander Welsh, *The City of Dickens* (Oxford: Clarendon Press, 1971).

2. Alexander Welsh, *From Copyright to Copperfield: The Identity of Dickens* (Cambridge, Mass.: Harvard University Press, 1987), 100.

3. Nina Auerbach, *Woman and the Demon: The Life of a Victorian Myth* (Cambridge, Mass.: Harvard University Press, 1982).

4. See Nancy Armstrong, *Desire and Domestic Fiction: A Political History of the Novel* (Oxford: Oxford University Press, 1987).

5. Bram Dijkstra, *Idols of Perversity: Fantasies of Feminine Evil in Fin-de-Siècle Culture* (New York: Oxford University Press, 1986); Helena Michie, *The Flesh Made Word: Female Figures and Women's Bodies* (New York: Oxford University Press, 1987); Amanda Anderson, *Tainted Souls and Painted Faces: The Rhetoric of Fallenness in Victorian Culture* (Ithaca: Cornell University Press, 1993).

6. See Thomas Laqueur's *Making Sex: Body and Gender from the Greeks to Freud* (Cambridge, Mass.: Harvard University Press, 1990).

7. Jill L. Matus, *Unstable Bodies: Victorian Representations of Sexuality and Maternity* (Manchester: Manchester University Press, 1995), 34.

8. For a fascinating exploration of the traditional associations of women with peacemaking *and* the way in which women who oppose traditional gender associations nonetheless still struggle for peace, see *Rocking the Ship of State: Toward a Feminist Peace Politics,* ed. Adrienne Harris and Ynestra King (Boulder: Westview Press, 1989).

9. Adrienne Harris and Ynestra King, introduction to *Rocking the Ship of State,* 2.

10. In *Woman to Woman: Female Friendship in Victorian Fiction* (Atlantic Highlands, N.J.: Humanities Press International, 1988), critic Tess Cosslett, while conceding Nancy Chodorow's early influence on her own work, succinctly sums up her later uneasiness with the implications of Chodorow's "unacceptably ahistorical and essentialist . . . concept of 'female identity'" (10). Cosslett suggests that what "Chodorow presents as inevitable psychological characteristics of women" replicates the Victorian "programme of socialisation, based on ideological assumptions as to what women and men are and should be like" (10). While more convinced than Cosslett that Chodorow's theories potentially could be used to dismantle rather than to support gender roles, I share Cosslett's discomfort with Chodorow's apparent certainty that socialization works in the same entirely predictable and inescapable way for all women.

11. See Carol Gilligan's *In a Different Voice: Psychological Theory and Women's Development* (Cambridge, Mass.: Harvard University Press, 1982) and Nancy Chodorow's *The Reproduction of Mothering: Psychoanalysis and the Sociology of Gender* (Berkeley: University of California Press, 1978). Also relevant here is *Making Connections: The Relational Worlds of Adolescent Girls at Emma Willard School,* ed. Carol Gilligan, Nona P. Lyons, and Trudy J. Hanmer (New York: Emma Willard School, 1989).

12. See Dorothy Dinnerstein, *The Mermaid and the Minotaur: Sexual Arrangements and Human Malaise* (New York: Harper & Row, 1976).

13. Mary Daly, *Gyn/Ecology: The Metaethics of Radical Feminism* (Boston: Beacon Press, 1978), 17–18.

14. Susan Griffin, *Woman and Nature: The Roaring Inside Her* (New York: Harper and Row, 1978), xvi.

15. Hélène Cixous, "The Laugh of the Medusa," in *The Women and Language Debate: A Sourcebook,* ed. Camille Roman, Suzanne Juhasz, Christanne Miller (New Brunswick: Rutgers University Press, 1994), 82, 83.

16. Barbara Love and Elizabeth Shanklin, "The Answer Is Matriarchy," in *Mothering: Essays in Feminist Theory,* ed. Joyce Trebilcot (Totowa, N.J.: Rowman & Allenheld, 1983), 275.

17. George Eliot, a figure not treated here, deserves a study of her own for her complex and knotty struggles with the ideal of the nurturant female. Eliot's emphasis on sympathy commits her to accepting nurturance as a crucial moral quality, but she attempts to invest that ideal with a philosophical substructure and a range of applications that have the potential for revolutionizing it. Reality in the form of social constraints always intervenes, however, and the stories of all Eliot's heroines end up resembling that of Dorothea, her most famous: domesticity remains the arena in which good women practice their virtues, but such domesticity is at least a partial defeat.

18. The current anti-abortion movement, for example, also puts enormous influence upon the spiritual and psychological importance of women's gestative capacities. Thus in *Aborted Women: Silent No More* (Chicago: Loyola University Press, 1987), David C. Reardon argues that abortion access constitutes a form of sex discrimination since abortion prevents women from practicing a uniquely female ability.

19. Ornella Moscucci, *The Science of Woman: Gynaecology and Gender in England, 1800–1929* (Cambridge: Cambridge University Press, 1990).

20. Margaret Homans, *Bearing the Word: Language and Female Experience in*

Nineteenth-Century Women's Writing (Chicago: University of Chicago Press, 1986); Peter Gay, *The Bourgeois Experience: Victoria to Freud* (New York: Oxford University Press, 1984–).

21. Elaine Showalter, *Sexual Anarchy: Gender and Culture at the Fin-de-Siècle* (New York: Viking, 1990).

22. Bruce Robbins, *The Servant's Hand: English Fiction from Below* (New York: Columbia University Press, 1986); P. J. Keating, *The Working Classes in Victorian Fiction* (New York: Barnes & Noble, 1971).

CHAPTER 1: SENTIMENTAL AUTHORITY

1. Representative work here includes Lawrence Stone, *The Family, Sex, and Marriage in England 1500–1800* (New York: Harper, 1977), and Leonore Davidoff and Catherine Hall, *Family Fortunes: Men and Women of the English Middle Class, 1780–1850* (University of Chicago Press, 1987).

2. See Nancy Armstrong's *Desire and Domestic Fiction: A Political History of the Novel* (New York: Oxford University Press, 1987) and Thomas Laqueur's *Making Sex: Body and Gender From the Greeks to Freud* (Cambridge, Mass.: Harvard University Press, 1990).

3. As Felicity Nussbaum points out in the midst of her discussion in "'Savage' Mothers: Narratives of Maternity in the Mid-Eighteenth Century" (*Eighteenth-Century Life* 16, n.s. 1 [1992]: 163–84) of eighteenth-century "fascination with the maternal," medical innovations are making it increasingly possible to envision human gestation and childbirth as a nongendered activity (165–66). And even before medicine held out hopes for "male pregnancy," there was evidence of "womb envy" among men. The overwhelming tradition of writing and thinking about human procreation nonetheless assumes that the gestative process is essentially female. Nussbaum has since expanded and developed material from this article in her book, *Torrid Zones: Maternity, Sexuality, and Empire in Eighteenth-Century English Narratives* (Baltimore: Johns Hopkins University Press, 1995).

4. In *Realizations: Narrative, Pictorial, and Theatrical Arts in Nineteenth-Century England* (Princeton: Princeton University Press, 1983), Martin Meisel points out that the figure of the suckling woman could represent both "Christian Charity" and its "secular, humanistic cognate," both "a sacred, transcendental ideal" and an "admired 'natural' ethic and 'natural' feeling" (319).

5. Dolores Peters gives a useful overview of some eighteenth-century views on the relationship between body and mind in pregnant women in "The Pregnant Pamela: Characterization and Popular Medical Attitudes in the Eighteenth Century" *Eighteenth-Century Studies* 14 (1981): 432–51.

6. The attribution of specific psychological and moral qualities to women because of their particular parental role is not inevitable. Elisabeth Badinter's *Mother Love, Myth and Reality: Motherhood in Modern History* (New York: Macmillan, 1981) examines at length the historical development of the now widely held belief that "a 'maternal instinct' . . . [is] rooted in woman's very nature, regardless of the time or place in which she has lived" (xx). Marilyn Francus in "The Monstrous Mother: Reproductive Anxiety in Swift and Pope," *English Literary History* 4 (1994): 829–51,

points out that prior to the eighteenth century the "image of the fecund female has often been associated with monstrosity" (829). See also the work by Felicity Nussbaum cited earlier. Ruth Perry explores the eighteenth century's growing valorization of maternity in "Colonizing the Breast" *Eighteenth-Century Life* 16, n.s. 1 (1992): 185–213. Perry cogently argues that "[m]otherhood has not always carried with it associations of tenderness and unstinting nurture. Nor has it always been interpreted as a woman's ultimate fulfillment" (190).

7. Dorothy McLaren, "Marital Fertility and Lactation 1570–1720," in *Women in English Society 1500–1800,* ed. Mary Prior (London: Methuen, 1985), 28.

8. Stone, 271–72. For a complete survey of the subject, see Valerie Fildes's *Breasts, Bottles and Babies: A History of Infant Feeding* (Edinburgh: Edinburgh University Press, 1986).

9. Richardson's reliance on the doctrines of conduct-book authors has been noted frequently and documented carefully in Katherine Hornbeak, "Richardson's *Familiar Letters* and the Domestic Conduct Books," *Smith College Studies in Modern Languages* 19 (1934): 1–29; and Sylvia Kasey Marks, *Sir Charles Grandison: The Compleat Conduct Book* (Lewisburg: Bucknell University Press, 1986).

10. Jeremy Taylor, *The Life of Our Blessed Lord and Saviour Jesus Christ: The Whole Works,* ed. Reginald Heber and Rev. Charles Page Eden, 10 vols., 2 (Hildesheim and New York: G. Olms Verlag, 1969), 75.

11. John Tillotson, *The Golden Book of Tillotson: Selections from the Writings of the Rev. John Tillotson, D.D., Archbishop of Canterbury,* ed. James Moffatt (Westport, Conn.: Greenwood, 1926; reprint, 1971), 141.

12. Chaucer's version of the Griselda story appears in "The Clerk's Tale" in *The Canterbury Tales.*

13. Paula Marantz Cohen, *The Daughter's Dilemma: Family Process and the Nineteenth-Century Domestic Novel* (Ann Arbor: University of Michigan Press, 1991), 19.

14. Sally Shuttleworth in "Demonic Mothers: Ideologies of Bourgeois Motherhood in the Mid-Victorian Era," in *Rewriting the Victorians: Theory, History, and the Politics of Gender,* ed. Linda M. Shires (New York: Routledge, 1992), 31–51, argues that the fear of conflict between wifely and maternal roles remained in operation for the Victorians. As Shuttleworth acknowledges, however, this fear provides a half-buried subtext to "yet one more recitation of the maternal creed [in which w]e hear endlessly of the mother's sacred mission to rear children, and of her spiritual grace which, filling the domestic sphere, uplifts her weary husband on his return from the corrupting world of Mammon. Few ideological constructs seem to arouse such uniform responses in the era; men and women, conservatives and reformers alike, seem to endorse this identikit picture" (31). That there could be actual or perceived conflict between the husband's and the child's demands upon a woman's time and attention nonetheless should not divert us from the overwhelming assumption that a devoted wife yearns to bear and rear her husband's children and that a woman who seeks heterosexual union *without* an accompanying desire for offspring is both immoral and unnatural. Claudia Nelson's *Invisible Men: Fatherhood in Victorian Periodicals, 1850–1910* (Athens: University of Georgia Press, 1995) is an invaluable examination of the impact that this idealization of maternity had in the paternal role.

15. Toni Bowers, "'A Point of Conscience': Breastfeeding and Maternal

Authority in *Pamela 2*," *Eighteenth-Century Fiction* 7 (1995): 268.

16. The growing tendency to invest sentimental authority in the mother of course can create some tension about the father's role in the family's emotional structure. Florian Stuber, in "On Fathers and Authority in *Clarissa*," *Studies in English Literature, 1500–1900* 25 (1985): 557–74, illustrates this point when he argues that the novel's fathers collectively represent a failure to combine authority and nurture. Stuber suggests that ultimately the figure who best combines strength and nurture (and thus becomes a kind of father figure) is Clarissa herself.

17. Numerous critics have discussed this aspect of Richardson's work. Nancy Armstrong's *Desire and Domestic Fiction* has helped define the terms in which the "domestic woman" in literature has been discussed over the past decade. An earlier, less Foucauldian but still intriguing study of the place of Richardson's heroines in the history of ideas about women is Marlene LeGates's "The Cult of Womanhood in Eighteenth-Century Thought," *Eighteenth-Century Studies* 10 (1976): 21–39.

18. Despite the eighteenth-century interest in breast-feeding, critics of Richardson have only recently begun to devote much attention to this topic, although there has been earlier work on related issues. Dolores Peters's valuable study of Pamela's experience of pregnancy and Robert Erickson's examination of midwifery in *Mother Midnight: Birth, Sex, and Fate in Eighteenth-Century Fiction (Defoe, Richardson, and Sterne)* (New York: AMS Press, 1986), for example, do not include suckling in their treatments. Ruth Perry's "Colonizing the Breast," however, examines the subject in depth. More recently, Toni Bowers's rewarding article "'A Point of Conscience'" offers a sensitive and illuminating discussion of the cultural context for and power dynamics in the struggle between Pamela and Mr. B.

19. Ruth Perry's summary is apropos here: "Richardson's successive treatments of maternal breast-feeding can be read as stages in an advancing belief system whose tenets included the following: that women's essential nature was to be mothers; that men's rights in women's bodies extended to their reproductive functions and, indeed, that men's ascendancy over women was based on women's 'natural propensity' for motherhood; that maternal feeling was antithetic to sexual desire; and that men's heterosexual desire was an immature expression of the ultimate desire to procreate and to 'have' a family" (203).

20. The issue of mastery explains the apparent inconsistency of both Lovelace and Mr. B—otherwise quite different in their attitudes to the idea of breast-feeding—allowing one month of the practice. In Mr. B's case the insignificant concession emphasizes the firmness with which he vetoes sustained maternal nurture; for Lovelace the time limit suggests his own sexual hunger for Clarissa, a hunger stimulated by the idea of breast-feeding. The two men, far apart in their rhetorical treatments of the issue, are ironically close in their concentration on their own wills.

21. Samuel Richardson, *Pamela* [1742], intro. George Saintsbury, Everyman's Library, 2 vols. (London: Dent and New York: Dutton, 1914; reprint, 1926), 2:233.

22. See Susan Weisskopf Contratto, "Maternal Sexuality and Asexual Motherhood," in *Women: Sex and Sexuality,* ed. Catharine R. Stimpson and Ethel Spector Person (Chicago: University of Chicago Press, 1980): 224–40, at 233.

23. In *Clarissa* Belford implies a similar split between the physical and intellectual aspects of "mothering" in his declaration, "Were she [Clarissa] mine, I should hardly wish

to see her a mother, unless there were a kind of moral certainty that minds like hers could be propagated. For why, in short, should not the work of bodies be left to *mere* bodies?" Samuel Richardson, *Clarissa* [1747–48], intro. W. Lyon Phelps, Everyman's Library, 4 vols. (London: Dent and New York: Dutton, 1932; reprint, 1950), 2:244. Mr. B apparently hopes that Pamela's managerial duties in the nursery will ensure that the children under her care grow up with "minds like hers."

24. Lois A. Chaber argues that Pamela (and probably Richardson) misreads Locke in commenting on him in "From Moral Man to Godly Man: 'Mr. Locke' and Mr. B in Part 2 of *Pamela*," *Studies in Eighteenth-Century Culture* 18 (1988): 213–61.

25. No similar difficulties arise in *Sir Charles Grandison*, although Sir Charles is easily the paragon equivalent of Clarissa. His supreme moral stature only increases his desirability in women's eyes, even when that stature threatens to overshadow all around him.

26. Obviously this incident—in fact, *Clarissa* in its entirety—is ripe for psychoanalytic readings. Raymond Hilliard explores the novel's Freudian riches, while Katherine Cummings offers a Lacanian approach. Gerald Levin and Maurice Funke apply less rigorous models in their respective books. See Maurice R. Funke, *From Saint to Psychotic: The Crisis of Human Identity in the Late 18th Century. A Comparative Study of Clarissa, La Nouvelle Héloïse, Die Leiden des jungen Werthers* (New York: Peter Lang, 1983); Raymond Hilliard, "*Clarissa* and Ritual Cannibalism." *PMLA* 105 (1990): 1083–97; Katherine Cummings, "Clarissa's 'Life with Father,'" *Literature and Psychology* 32.4 (1986): 30–36, later expanded and developed in Cummings's book, *Telling Tales: The Hysteric's Seduction in Fiction and Theory* (Stanford: Stanford University Press, 1991); and Gerald Levin, *Richardson the Novelist: The Psychological Patterns* (Amsterdam: Rodopi, 1978).

27. As an example of Lovelace's consistent sexualizing of women's experiences, consider his belief that his cousin Charlotte complains of "a stomach disorder" because she's "a single woman" and therefore "dreary" and "desolate" (2:403). But no "vapours . . . would be known" if Lovelace's scheme of annual marriages assured all women perpetual sexual excitement and satisfaction (3:182).

Focusing more specifically on women's association with food, there is another aspect to this image of the female body as nutritive source: Hilliard has documented Lovelace's association with cannibalism. But while cannibalism assumes a human victim, Lovelace himself consistently discusses women as animal flesh: food that people traditionally feel free to eat without experiencing guilt. He imagines women not only as food (e.g., 2:147, 337) but as food that desires consumption (2:209). He even reverses accepted human/animal roles by wishing to exempt animals from the demands of human hunger, at the same time that he legitimizes women's sexual victimization as just punishment of them for their function as cooks. By distinguishing between the gourmet's cruel and ignoble appetites and his own valorized sexual desires (2:248), Lovelace suggests that an appetite that requires female suffering for its satisfaction is more innocent than one that necessitates animal pain.

Eira Patnaik's article "The Succulent Gender: Eat Her Softly," in *Literary Gastronomy*, ed. David Bevan (Amsterdam: Rodopi, 1988): 50–73, provides a capsule history of images of the female body as eager-to-be-eaten food.

28. Albert J. Rivero in "The Place of Sally Godfrey in Richardson's *Pamela*" (*Eighteenth-Century Fiction* 6 [1993]: 29–46) recognizes the importance for Richardson

of expelling Sally while arguing that this expulsion "establishes . . . nobility of character [as] best exemplified by submission to the patriarchal order, now redefined as providential" (35).

29. As Marlene LeGates puts it, "What is divine about the female, however, is her embodiment of the traditional pieties of religion, the family, and even the state" (29). She remarks further that "amiability . . . was seen as the positive contribution of the fair sex to civilization" (38). A perverse kind of amiability, of course, is exactly what Lovelace desires—and what he does not find in the women he has sexually initiated.

30. Veronica Bassil in "The Faces of Griselda: Chaucer, Prior, and Richardson," *Texas Studies in Literature and Language* 26 (1984): 157–82, documents Richardson's horror at Matthew Prior's heroine Emma, who disregards her lover's apparent lawlessness and even murderousness. Bassil argues that Richardson's condemnation of Emma springs from her choice of sexual over filial love, and it is certainly true that Richardson expresses his condemnation most forcefully through his attribution of sexual profligacy to Emma. Nonetheless, I am more inclined than Bassil to accept the sincerity and seriousness of Richardson's insistence that Clarissa manifests her own moral probity by her concern for the moral standards (not merely sexual, either!) of her suitors and that Emma, by contrast, disgraces herself by her indifference to her lover's possible crimes.

31. Robert D. Moynihan argues that Richardson accepted Puritanism's insistence that women's first duty was to God; see "Clarissa and the Enlightened Woman as Literary Heroine," *Journal of the History of Ideas* 36 (1975): 159–66.

32. Letter 93 of *Clarissa* (2:330–37) presents a sustained exposition of the folly of "keeping" over "marrying," an exposition to which Belton's case serves as illustration.

33. In *Samuel Richardson's Fictions of Gender* (Stanford: Stanford University Press, 1993), Tassie Gwilliam, in a perceptive discussion of Lovelace's relations with the whores, points out that he "becomes disturbed by the notion that the whores' desire to humiliate Clarissa supersedes and even replaces their desire for him." At the same time, however, he attributes their evil to his own sexual initiation of them and "tries to claim credit for having made them diabolical" (91).

34. In *Powers of Horror: An Essay on Abjection,* trans. Leon S. Roudiez (New York: Columbia University Press, 1982), Julia Kristeva writes on the split in images of maternity between the mother as guardian of the subject's "'own and clean body'" (53) and as a monster characterized by "the desirable and terrifying, nourishing and murderous, fascinating and abject inside of the maternal body" (54). The psychological implications of this concept of the female body emerge because "it is . . . not lack of cleanliness or health that causes abjection but what disturbs identity, system, order" (4). Kristeva's maternal figure is potentially disruptive and destructive to both society and her own children because her body is chaotic.

35. Judith Wilt forcefully argues that the whores are not only instigators but agents in a "rape" that takes place despite Lovelace's impotence. See her now classic article, "He Could Go No Further: A Modest Proposal about Lovelace and Clarissa," *PMLA* 92 (1977): 19–32. Gwilliam suggests potential rather than actual impotence because the whores "distur[b] Lovelace with the implication that they may be capable of usurping his power and of draining away his potency—and that *his* penis has become *their* instrument, not his own" (91). James H. Maddox Jr. in "Lovelace and the World of Ressentiment in *Clarissa,*" *Texas Studies in Literature and Language* 24 (1982):

271–92, sees Lovelace as physically potent but psychologically dominated by the need to impress bystanders, so that he rapes Clarissa simply to avoid losing face with the prostitutes who surround him.

36. Carol Houlihan Flynn examines Richardson's ambivalent handling of Charlotte in "The Pains of Compliance in *Sir Charles Grandison,*" *Samuel Richardson: Tercentenary Essays,* ed. Margaret Anne Doody and Peter Sabor (Cambridge: Cambridge University Press, 1989), 133–45.

37. Samuel Richardson, *Sir Charles Grandison* (Oxford: Oxford University Press, 1972), 7 vols., 4:340.

38. Elaine Moon in "'Sacrific'd to My Sex': The Marriages of Samuel Richardson's Pamela and Mr. B, and Mr. and Mrs. Harlowe," *AUMLA: Journal of the Australasian Universities Language and Literature Association* 63 (1985): 19–32, notes the importance of childbearing for the "diminution" of spirit in not only Charlotte but Pamela, Mrs. Harlowe, and (potentially) Anna Howe (32).

39. Stephanie Demetrakopoulos, "The Nursing Mother and Feminine Metaphysics: An Essay on Embodiment" *Soundings* 65 (1982): 430–43.

40. This attitude toward breast-feeding has its own history and provides one of the few instances when the female body has been granted a profound and positive moral significance, as Marina Warner, Marjorie Stone, and Stephanie Dematrakopoulos show in their different studies. Problems arise, of course, when the spiritual implications of this image are assigned exclusively to women, operating as an essentializing metaphor to define female selfhood rather than applying across gender categories. See Marjorie Stone, "Taste, Totems, and Taboos: The Female Breast in Victorian Poetry," *Dalhousie Review* 64 (1985): 748–70; and Marina Warner, *Alone of All Her Sex: The Myth and the Cult of the Virgin Mary* (New York: Knopf, 1976).

41. The relationships between eighteenth-century conceptions of physiology and psychology and of both to theories of sensibility were complex. In addition to the works on sensibility cited elsewhere in this chapter readers might consult G. S. Rousseau's "Nerves, Spirits, and Fibres: Towards Defining the Origins of Sensibility," *Studies in the Eighteenth Century,* vol. 3, ed. R. F. Brissenden and J. C. Eade (Toronto: University of Toronto Press, 1973), 137–58. R. F. Brissenden, meanwhile, reminds us of the blurring between the emotional and the intellectual in the ideas of "sentiment" and "sentimental." See his "'Sentiment': Some Uses of the Word in the Writings of David Hume," *Studies in the Eighteenth Century,* vol. 1, ed. R. F. Brissenden (Toronto: University of Toronto Press, 1968), 89–108.

42. In *Eighteenth-Century Sensibility and the Novel: The Senses in Social Context* (Cambridge: Cambridge University Press, 1993), Ann Jessie Van Sant points out that "sensibility defines a new male rather than female character type," partly at least because "*woman* and *woman of sensibility* might have been thought synonymous, while for a man to be so defined by delicacy was noticeable enough to require a label" (115).

43. The idea that women's bodies communicate their psychic states more directly than do men's continues today. See, for example, Dinora Pines, *A Woman's Unconscious Use of Her Body* (New Haven: Yale University Press, 1994), in which the author writes that her experience as an M.D. and psychoanalyst convinced her that "bodily expressions of unbearable feelings were more common in women patients. In

thinking about this observation I came to realize that a mature woman's body offers her a means of avoiding conscious thought and facing psychic conflict" (5).

44. G. J. Barker-Benfield argues forcefully in *The Culture of Sensibility: Sex and Society in Eighteenth-Century Britain* (Chicago: University of Chicago Press, 1992) that Mackenzie intended "to satirize such unrestrained sensibility in a man . . . but significantly for the history of the relations between gender and sensibility, the best-selling *The Man of Feeling* was 'consistently misread' from the date of its publication as a celebration of the character Mackenzie intended to spoof" (144).

45. Claudia L. Johnson's *Equivocal Beings: Politics, Gender, and Sentimentality in the 1790s* (Chicago: University of Chicago Press, 1995) offers a more skeptical view of this phenomenon by arguing that sensibility (at least during the decade she examines) co-opted traditionally feminine affects for men and thereby automatically categorized any displays of feeling by women as perverse and excessive. For Johnson, increased emotionalism and sensitivity for men became yet another way to denigrate women.

46. Claudia L. Johnson, "A 'Sweet Face as White as Death': Jane Austen and the Politics of Female Sensibility," *Novel* 22 (1989): 159–74, at 173.

47. Janet Todd, *Sensibility: An Introduction* (London, New York: Methuen, 1986), 9.

48. Mary Poovey, *The Proper Lady and the Woman Writer: Ideology as Style in the Works of Mary Wollstonecraft, Mary Shelley, and Jane Austen* (Chicago: University of Chicago Press, 1984).

49. Todd, *Sensibility,* 130–31. For an excellent examination of the conflict between "Radical" and "Conservative" sensibility see Chris Jones's "Radical Sensibility in the 1790s," in *Reflections of Revolution: Images of Romanticism,* ed. Alison Yarrington and Kelvin Everest (London: Routledge, 1993), 68–82.

50. Johnson, "Sweet Face," 173.

51. Dorothy Van Ghent's "Clarissa Harlowe," in *The English Novel: Form and Function* (New York: Harper and Row, 1953), is one well-known diagnosis of Richardson's fiction as antisexual. Discussion of Clarissa as heroine in particular often centers on her putative frigidity. William Beatty Warner, in a controversial interpretation, seems to find Lovelace's textual and sexual excesses a relief compared to the sterility (in his view) of Clarissa's moral and stylistic rigor. For Nancy K. Miller, although Clarissa is capable of passion for Lovelace, "loathing for female sexuality as it has been inscribed for her by Lovelace and her father" keeps her "in the dark about the nature of her desire" (*The Heroine's Text: Readings in the French and English Novel, 1722–1782* [New York: Columbia University Press, 1980], 95). Leo Braudy's "Penetration and Impenetrability in Clarissa," in *New Approaches to Eighteenth-Century Literature: Selected Papers from the English Institute,* ed. Philip Harth (New York and London: Columbia University Press, 1974), 177–206, is a particularly rich discussion of the struggle for self-definition in both Clarissa and Lovelace. See also William Beatty Warner, *Reading Clarissa: The Struggles of Interpretation* (New Haven: Yale University Press, 1979).

52. John Mullan, *Sentiment and Sociability: The Language of Feeling in the Eighteenth Century* (Oxford: Clarendon Press, 1988), 112–13.

53. Jean H. Hagstrum, *Sex and Sensibility: Ideal and Erotic Love from Milton to*

Mozart (Chicago and London: University of Chicago Press, 1980), 198.

54. In addition to the works cited elsewhere in this chapter, discussions of sensibility include Louis I. Bredvold, *The Natural History of Sensibility* (Detroit: Wayne State University Press, 1962). Carol Kay discusses the related topic of sympathy in "Sympathy, Sex, and Authority in Richardson and Hume," *Studies in Eighteenth-Century Culture* 12 (1983): 77–92. Jo Anne Lee Perry in "The Representation of Feeling in the Novels of Samuel Richardson" (Ph.D. diss., University of California at Santa Barbara, 1982) argues that Richardson uses physical expressiveness to show that "feeling comprehends a form of moral consciousness" (vii).

55. Quoted in R. F. Brissenden's *Virtue in Distress: Studies in the Novel of Sentiment from Richardson to Sade* (New York: Barnes & Noble, 1974), 103.

56. Mullan's *Sentiment and Sociability* and Brissenden's *Virtue in Distress* are invaluable for placing the "language" of the physical within the context of eighteenth-century theories about the sentiments. George Sherburn's "'Writing to the Moment': One Aspect," in *Restoration and Eighteenth-Century Literature: Essays in Honor of Alan Dugald McKillop,* ed. Carroll Camden (Chicago and London: University of Chicago Press, 1963), 201–9, traces many of the specific physical gestures of Richardson's characters to the author's "keen visual gift" (209). Lilian R. Furst points out the dangers to women in a feminine ideal that put too great an emphasis on sensibility in "The Man of Sensibility and the Woman of Sense," *Jahrbuch für Internationale Germanistik* 14 (1982): 13–26.

57. As Christopher Flint points out in "The Anxiety of Affluence: Family and Class (Dis)order in *Pamela; or, Virtue Rewarded, Studies in English Literature, 1500–1900* 29 (1989): 489–514, "[b]y fainting Pamela loses all active power. She would appear to be most vulnerable at this point and be what B most wants her to be— a completely passive body. Yet these moments frustrate B a great deal and he ascribes active agency to them" (513). Mr. B's epiphany comes when he moves from despising this agency as manipulative and hypocritical to honoring it as sincere and heartfelt.

58. Judith Laurence-Anderson, "Changing Affective Life in Eighteenth-Century England and Samuel Richardson's *Pamela,*" *Studies in Eighteenth-Century Culture* 10 (1981): 445–56, at 452.

Terry Castle's "P/B: *Pamela* as Sexual Fiction" gives a Freudian twist to the power relations in this novel by diagnosing Pamela's story as the Oedipal drama of Pamela's recognition of sexual difference and acceptance of female "castration" (*Studies in English Literature, 1500–1900* 22 [1982]: 469–89).

59. Robert Folkenflik argues in "*Pamela*: Domestic Servitude, Marriage, and the Novel," *Eighteenth-Century Fiction* 5 (1993): 253–68, that Pamela's imprisonment in the first volume of her story illustrates sociologist Erving Goffman's account of life in a "total institution," in which individuals are not allowed even the silent protest of facial expressions and body language.

60. Dolores Peters in "The Pregnant Pamela" discusses Pamela's "change in . . . personality" as a result of her intense fear of pregnancy (and adult sexuality in general) indicative of her "continued inability to assimilate her new roles" as wife and matron (448). This reading, however, bypasses "Mr. B's alienation" (448) from his wife as occurring only after her vapors indicate fears of his infidelity rather than terror of childbirth dangers.

61. R. F. Brissenden, *Samuel Richardson,* in *Writers and Their Work 101,* gen. ed., Geoffrey Bullough (London: Longmans, Green, 1958; reprint 1965), 17.

62. Ibid.

63. Cynthia Griffin Wolff, *Samuel Richardson and the Eighteenth-Century Puritan Character* (Hamden: Archon, 1972), 88.

64. John Mullan points out that Clarissa also illustrates her independent judgment through her mastery of the "'gaze' or 'look'" that is "the piercing expression of her virtue" and "a perturbation at the heart of even the most diabolical of Lovelace's scheming." Clarissa's penetrating gaze reveals her disdain for the unworthies around her. By this means she can manifest the severe judgments that conventions of feminine reticence and soft-spokenness inhibit in female speech. Unfortunately, although "defensive" this gaze is also "cut off from social application" because it cannot ultimately deflect "Lovelace's ruling desire" (76–77).

65. Johnson, "'Sweet Face,'" 160–61; Todd, 134–38.

66. Morris Golden, *Richardson's Characters* (Ann Arbor: University of Michigan Press, 1963), 121.

67. Janet Todd, *Women's Friendship in Literature,* (New York: Columbia University Press, 1980), 49, 57, 59.

68. Keiko Izubuchi, "Subversive or Not? Anna Howe's Function in *Clarissa,*" in *Samuel Richardson: Passion and Prudence,* ed. Valerie Grosvenor Myer (London: Vision and Totowa, N.J.: Barnes & Noble, 1986), 78–92, at 87.

69. Margaret R. Miles, "Textual Harassment: Desire and the Female Body," in *The Good Body: Asceticism in Contemporary Culture,* ed. Mary G. Winkler and Letha B. Cole (New Haven: Yale University Press, 1994), 49–63, at 52.

70. See, for example, Terry Eagleton's comparison of *Pamela* and *Clarissa* in *The Rape of Clarissa* (Minneapolis: University of Minnesota Press, 1982). For Eagleton, Pamela's "absolutism about sexuality . . . [is] contrived" (34), and the novel itself is "a cartoon version of *Clarissa,* simplified, stereotyped and comic in outcome" (37). *Clarissa,* on other hand, is "a devastating demystification" that gives us "the tragic reality" that *Pamela* obscures (39). Michael McKeon, by contrast, argues that "the choice between *Pamela* and *Clarissa* is a classic one between two strikingly and reciprocally imperfect alternatives: manifest material and social empowerment, which can be only fitfully acknowledged on the plane of discourse; and manifest discursive and imaginative empowerment, whose material register consists in nothing more substantial than the posthumous requital of one's persecutors" (*The Origins of the English Novel, 1600–1740* [Baltimore: Johns Hopkins University Press, 1987], 380).

71. Judith Laurence-Anderson ("Changing Affective Live in Eighteenth-Century England), in examining the conditions of servant life in the eighteenth century, forcibly reminds us how extraordinary such defiance is.

72. As McKeon points out, Mr. B's treatment of his sister makes her "obliged to recall that she is a woman first and a lady second" (379). Ruth Perry expands and develops the idea of a shift in class/gender priorities in her discussion of breast-feeding: "[T]he effect of erasing class differences among women in this matter [suckling] was to universalize the meanings and purposes of the female body and to reduce the degree of freedom in interpreting women's sex roles. Gender—not class—increasingly defined a woman's duties" (208).

73. Terry Castle, *Clarissa's Ciphers: Meaning and Disruption in Richardson's "Clarissa"* (Ithaca: Cornell University Press, 1982), 125.

74. Linda S. Kauffman, *Discourses of Desire: Gender, Genre, and Epistolary Fictions* (Ithaca: Cornell University Press, 1986). In this connection Mary G. Winkler in "Model Women" (in *The Good Body: Asceticism in Contemporary Culture,* ed. by Mary G. Winkler and Letha B. Cole [New Haven: Yale University Press, 1994], 215–31) makes the point that the "slender body (when it is achieved against nature) resists patriarchy by renouncing a 'purely reproductive destiny'" (219).

75. Margaret Anne Doody, *A Natural Passion: A Study of the Novels of Samuel Richardson* (Oxford: Clarendon Press, 1974), 179.

76. Ellen Pollak, *The Poetics of Sexual Myth: Gender and Ideology in the Verse of Swift and Pope* (Chicago: University of Chicago Press, 1985), 50, 58.

77. Rita Goldberg in *Sex and Enlightenment: Women in Richardson and Diderot* (Cambridge: Cambridge University Press, 1984), applying Jungian insights to Christian traditions (124–27), provides an interesting discussion of Clarissa's control over this new "symbolic existence" (124).

78. Clarissa's continuing concern for her body, including the explicit instructions she leaves for its handling after her death, suggests a more complex set of attitudes than Tony Tanner allows when he claims that Clarissa dies "purified of body" (*Adultery in the Novel: Contract and Transgression* [Baltimore and London: Johns Hopkins University Press, 1979], 109).

79. Arthur Friedman appropriately characterizes Clarissa's calm and triumphant certainty of salvation as an "end [that] is all that a Christian could hope for," "Aspects of Sentimentalism in Eighteenth-Century Literature," in *The Augustan Milieu: Essays Presented to Louis A. Landa,* ed. Henry Knight Miller, Eric Rothstein, and G. S. Rousseau (Oxford: Clarendon Press, 1970), 247–61, at 259. Margaret Doody in her invaluable work *A Natural Passion,* at 151–57 and 168–79, provides a fuller examination of Clarissa's "holy dying" (169).

80. Julie A. Storme, "'An Exit So Happy': The Deaths of Julie and Clarissa," *Canadian Review of Comparative Literature* 14 (1987): 191–210, at 201.

81. Johnson, "Sweet Face," 172–73.

82. Mark Kinkead-Weekes, *Samuel Richardson: Dramatic Novelist* (Ithaca: Cornell University Press, 1973), 275.

83. Samuel Richardson, *Selected Letters of Samuel Richardson,* ed. John Carroll (Oxford: Clarendon Press, 1964), 161.

CHAPTER 2: FRANCES BURNEY AND THE EMBODIMENT OF DELICACY

1. See, for instance, Susan Staves's "*Evelina;* or, Female Difficulties," *Modern Philology* 73 (1975–1976): 368–91; Judith Lowder Newton's chapter on *Evelina* in *Women, Power, and Subversion: Social Strategies in British Fiction, 1778–1860* (Athens: University of Georgia Press, 1981), 23–54; Kristina Straub's *Divided Fictions: Fanny Burney and Feminine Strategy* (Lexington: University Press of Kentucky, 1987); and Julia L. Epstein's *The Iron Pen: Frances Burney and the Politics of Women's Writing* (Madison: University of Wisconsin Press, 1989).

2. Jenni Calder, *Women and Marriage in Victorian Fiction* (New York: Oxford University Press, 1976), 16.

3. Juliet McMaster's "The Silent Angel: Impediments to Female Expression in Frances Burney's Novels," *Studies in the Novel* 21 (1989): 235–52, discusses "the issue of expression, and particularly the impediments to expression for a woman" as "a major concern in all Frances Burney's novels" (235). According to McMaster, "To examine Burney's concern with expression is to arrive at a . . . feminist reading" and a recognition of Burney's own incipient feminism (236).

4. Fanny Burney, *Evelina* [1778], ed. and intro. Edward A. Bloom with Lillian D. Bloom (Oxford: Oxford University Press, 1991), 244–46.

5. Fanny Burney, *Camilla* [1776], ed. and intro. Edward A. and Lillian D. Bloom (Oxford: Oxford University Press, 1989), 526–27.

6. Mr. Collins's infamous declaration appears in the nineteenth chapter of the first volume of *Pride and Prejudice.*

7. Joanne Cutting-Gray, *Woman as 'Nobody' and the Novels of Fanny Burney* (Gainesville: University Press of Florida, 1992), 14.

8. Ruth Bernard Yeazell, *Fictions of Modesty: Women and Courtship in the English Novel* (Chicago: University of Chicago Press, 1991).

9. Dr. James Fordyce, *Sermons to Young Women,* 3d ed. (London: A. Millar and T. Cadell, 1766), 99.

10. Joyce Hemlow, "Fanny Burney and the Courtesy Books," *PMLA* 65 (1950): 732–61.

11. See the note by Lillian and Edward Bloom on chapter 5 of volume 3, "A Sermon," in their edition of *Camilla* (941). Margaret Doody also mentions this fact (*Frances Burney: A Life in the Works* [New Brunswick: Rutgers University Press, 1988], 246) but differs sharply from the Blooms in her assessment of the chapter itself. To the Blooms "A Sermon" represents "the moralistic essence of the novel, setting forth an ideal of ethical conduct (941). Doody, meanwhile, condemns the "visibly imperfect" "judgment" of the chapter's advice-giver, remarking tartly that "Burney cannot be blamed for" readers' willingness to take the chapter as a guide (246).

12. Nancy Armstrong in *Desire and Domestic Fiction: A Political History of the Novel* (Oxford: Oxford University Press, 1987) offers an excellent assessment of the "powers" supposedly attained by the domestic (i.e. virtuous) woman. She however sees women assuming these powers through their increasing control over domestic discourse. For Armstrong the importance of the moral sentiments conveyed by women's words replaces the importance of women's bodies. My argument, by contrast, rests on the idea that women's bodies themselves can convey moral sentiments.

13. "On Shamefacedness," *New Lady's Magazine* (London), Feb. 1786, 27.

14. Fanny Burney, *Cecilia* [1782], intro. Judy Simons (London: Virago, 1986), 545–46.

15. Fanny Burney, *The Wanderer* [1814], ed. Margaret Anne Doody, Robert L. Mack, Peter Sabor; intro. Margaret Anne Doody (Oxford: Oxford University Press, 1991), 139–41.

16. See Hélène Cixous, "The Laugh of the Medusa," in *The Women and Language Debate: A Sourcebook* ed. Camille Roman, Suzanne Juhasz, and Christanne Miller (New Brunswick: Rutgers University Press, 1994), 78–93.

17. Jean-Jacques Rousseau, *Politics and the Arts: Letter to M. d'Alembert on the Theatre,* trans. and intro. Allan Bloom, (Ithaca: Cornell University Press, 1960), 84, 85.

18. John J. Richetti and Joanne Cutting-Gray see Evelina the narrator as essentially a separate character from the far less interesting young woman whose adventures the writing Evelina describes. See Richetti's "Voice and Gender in Eighteenth-Century Fiction: Haywood to Burney," *Studies in the Novel* 19 (1987): 263–72; and Cutting-Gray's "Writing Innocence: Fanny Burney's *Evelina,*" *Tulsa Studies in Women's Literature* 9 (1990): 43–57. David Oakleaf in "The Name of the Father: Social Identity and the Ambition of *Evelina,*" *Eighteenth-Century Fiction* 3 (1991): 341–58, attributes Evelina's silence to her having, despite a "distinctively meritorious" private identity (344), only "an uncertain social identity in a world where public views of identity were, though challenged, socially ascendent" (343).

19. Patricia Meyer Spacks, identifying fear as the driving force behind Burney's fiction and life, provides a biographical context for the formula to which she claims Burney subscribed: "Loss of modesty amounts to loss of virtue; only by strict decorum can a woman protect herself" (*Imagining a Self: Autobiography and Novel in Eighteenth-Century England* [Cambridge, Mass.: Harvard University Press, 1976], 166); see the chapter on Burney, 158–92.

20. See, for example, *Evelina* (97–100), *Camilla* (613–14, 624), and *The Wanderer* (139–42, 242–43, 688–90).

21. Cutting-Gray, *Woman as 'Nobody,'* 22.

22. The watchfulness of Burney's heroes may account for some of their unpopularity in a time when, as Beth Newman points out, "the 'gaze' has become an object of suspicion." Newman continues, however, with a point directly applicable to Burney's novels, "that being the object of someone's look can in some circumstances be pleasurable, even sustaining and necessary" ("Getting Fixed: Feminine Identity and Scopic Crisis in *The Turn of the Screw,*" *Novel* 25 [1992]: 44–63, at 44). Certainly Burney's heroines benefit from the perceptive attentiveness of the heroes as much as they suffer from the crude misreadings of various rakes and fops.

23. See, for example, 164, 235, 422, 538–39.

24. See, for example, Edward Bloom's dismissal of Lord Orville in his introduction to *Evelina* (xxiii), Doody's scathing description of *The Wanderer's* Harleigh (introduction, xxiii–xxiv), and Marjorie Dobbin's claim in "The Novel, Women's Awareness and Fanny Burney," *English Language Notes* 22.3 (1985): 42–52, for the general "flatness" of Burney's male characters (48). Yeazell, however, shrewdly remarks that while "to most readers [Orville] scarcely comes alive at all," his true role does not demand vivacity: he is not so much a lover as a "witness" (128–29).

25. Judith Newton argues, however, that even Orville's endless benignity serves ultimately oppressive ends: "too good to be true . . . his extraordinary virtues are not only compensation but justification for the way things are" (41). Burney does offer Orville what Newton calls "an exemplum of what male authority ought to be" (41), but I would argue that his presence only exposes more fully the "abuse of women" at the hands of more typical men.

26. Cutting-Gray, *Woman as 'Nobody,'* 22.

27. This reliance on nonverbal communication counters Huang Mei's claim in *Transforming the Cinderella Dream: From Frances Burney to Charlotte Brontë* (New

Brunswick: Rutgers University Press, 1990) that "we, and Evelina as well, know too little [of Orville] to shape any definite idea [of him] (our good-looking hero does nothing throughout the story except ask Evelina to dance, conduct a few dull conversations, and finally propose to her)" (38).

28. Claudia L. Johnson, *Equivocal Beings: Politics, Gender, and Sentimentality in the 1790s* (Chicago: University of Chicago Press, 1995), 27. Johnson offers a splendid analysis of the debate over male chivalry and female beauty, 26–29.

29. Rose Marie Cutting, for example, claims that "[it] is highly unlikely that Fanny Burney admitted, even to herself, the sympathy she conveyed for these unconventional females" ("Defiant Women: The Growth of Feminism in Fanny Burney's Novels," *Studies in English Literature* 17 [1977]: 519–30, at 521).

CHAPTER 3: "THE FEEDERS OF MEN"

1. Helena Michie, *The Flesh Made Word: Female Figures and Women's Bodies* (New York: Oxford University Press, 1987), 12. Michie entitles her chapter on women's eating in Victorian literature and society "Ladylike Anorexia: Hunger, Sexuality, and Etiquette in the Nineteenth Century," thus marrying the idea of anorexia as a norm for Victorian "ladies" with the sexual subtext that most recent commentators find in the subject of food.

2. Michie, 20. See also Joan Jacobs Brumberg's *Fasting Girls: The Emergence of Anorexia Nervosa as a Modern Disease* (Cambridge, Mass.: Harvard University Press, 1988), 175; and Carole M. Counihan's statement (in "An Anthropological View of Western Women's Prodigious Fasting: A Review Essay," *Food and Foodways* 3 [1989]: 357–75) that in Victorian times "denial of appetite stood for suppression of sexuality" (365).

3. Gail Houston, "Anorexic Dickens" (Ph.D. diss., University of California at Los Angeles, 1990), 19. Citations of Houston come from this work. She has expanded and developed her study into the book *Consuming Fictions: Gender, Class, and Hunger in Dickens's Novels* (Carbondale: Southern Illinois University Press, 1994).

4. See Raymond Hilliard's "*Clarissa* and Ritual Cannibalism," *PMLA* 105 (1990): 1083–97.

5. Lilian R. Furst, introduction to *Disorderly Eaters: Texts in Self-Empowerment*, ed. Lilian R. Furst and Peter W. Graham (University Park: Pennsylvania State University Press, 1992), 5.

6. At least one study that acknowledges the strenuous nineteenth-century efforts to combat anorexia nonetheless finds the period essentially accepting of the disease. Brumberg's *Fasting Girls* gives ample details in chapters 4 through 6 of the forceful methods doctors used in dealing with anorexics and the disapproval they bestowed upon "the manipulative politics of female invalidism" (153). At the same time, however, she claims that "as long as emaciation did not become too extreme or threatening, a sitophobic [anorexic] girl could exist 'on the outside,' because many Victorian women and girls were notoriously poor eaters and fragility was widely cultivated" and that there was "a general female fashion for sickness and debility" (110, 171). Brumberg devotes lengthy discussion to ways in which "Victorian society . . . promote[d] restrictive eating among privileged adolescent women," 178–88.

7. Susie Orbach, "Accepting the Symptom: A Feminist Psychoanalytic Treatment of Anorexia Nervosa," in *A Handbook of Psychotherapy for Anorexia Nervosa and Bulimia,* ed. David M. Garner and Paul E. Garfinkel (New York: Guilford Press, 1985), 87.

8. Harvey Peter Sucksmith, introduction to *Little Dorrit* by Charles Dickens (Oxford: Oxford University Press, 1982), xiii.

9. Wm. Alex McIntosh and Mary Zey, "Women as Gatekeepers of Food Consumption: A Sociological Critique," *Food and Foodways* 3 (1989): 317.

10. In "A 'Craving Vacancy': Women and Sexual Love in Four British Novelists, 1740–1880" (Ph.D. diss., Columbia University, 1987), Susan Ostrov Weisser argues that the Victorians dreaded female sexuality because they linked sexuality with aggressiveness: "The individual selfishly pursuing sexual gratification seemed totally irreconcilable with the woman whose role was giving humane support and sustenance" (61). Although Weisser's argument is plausible in explaining the Victorian insistence on female purity, I would emphasize that the Victorians dreaded any sign of "egoism" and "rapacious will" in women (61) that might hinder their ability to aid others—regardless of whether there were any sexual connotations to their selfishness.

11. This example appears in "The Roots of Honour" chapter of John Ruskin, *Unto This Last* (1860).

12. Frances Power Cobbe, "Female Charity—Lay and Monastic," *Fraser's* (1862), 779.

13. See, for instance, the article "Food and Fasting" in *Chamber's Edinburgh Journal* 57 (1880): 545–48. There the author cites a doctor who claims that "in hysterical states, . . . 'there is frequently a very remarkable disposition for abstinence and power of sustaining it'" (547).

14. Henry Thompson, "Food and Feeding," *The Nineteenth Century* 5 (1879): 980.

15. "Cooks," *The Cornhill Magazine* 6 (1861): 601–8.

16. See, for instance, the praise of Paris as "that centre of gastronomic intelligence" in "The Pleasures of the Table," *Bentley's Miscellany* 45 (1856): 52; and entreaty in "The Dinner Question," *Bentley's Miscellany* 45 (1856), that Englishwomen "deign to accept a hint from the French," whose culinary expertise the author goes on to commend (167).

17. In *Bleak House,* for example, Mrs. Jellyby is to blame for the dismal meal that her family and visitors endure, while in *David Copperfield* Dora's household ineptitude emerges most clearly through culinary disasters.

18. "The Poetry of Diet," *Chamber's Edinburgh Journal* 9 (1847): 25.

19. See, for example, "The Pleasures of the Table," *Bentley's Miscellany* 45 (1856): 40–52, in which the anonymous author protests that "we believe that all civilized nations join in the opinion that the one great purpose of life is having a good dinner daily" (40); "Theory of Human Food," *Eclectic Review* 99 (1854): 274–87, which begins by defining "man . . . as essentially a cooking animal" and goes on to state that it "may be very important for a politician and a statesman to have some knowledge of this subject [alimentation]" (274–75). Other representative articles include "A Few Words about Food Reform," *Chamber's Edinburgh Journal* 57 (1880): 359–61; "Food and Fasting," *Chamber's Edinburgh Journal* 57 (1880): 545–48; Henry Thompson,

"Food and Feeding," *The Nineteenth Century* 5 (1879): 971–91, and 6 (1879): 99–118; "Training in Relation to Health," *The Cornhill Magazine* 9 (1864): 219–32; "Over-Eating and Under-Eating," *The Cornhill Magazine* 8 (1863): 35–47; "Fat and Lean Food," *Irish Quarterly Review* 8 (1859): 865–84; "Food—How to Take It," *The Cornhill Magazine* 6 (1861): 281–94; "Cooks," *The Cornhill Magazine;* "Diet and Dyspepsy," *Quarterly Review* 65 (1840): 315–41.

20. "Over-Eating and Under-Eating," 35, 37.

21. "The Dinner Question Discussed by an Eight Hundred a Year Man," *Bentley's Miscellany* 45 (1856): 167.

22. Lyon Playfair, "On the Nature and Composition of Food," *Good Words* 6 (1865): 162.

23. Charles Kingsley, for example, describes Shelley's "physical distaste for meat" as "especially feminine" and one of many proofs that "Shelley's nature is utterly womanish" ("Thoughts about Shelley and Byron," *Fraser's* [1853], 572).

24. Quoted in "The Dinner Question," 168.

25. "Some Talk about Food," *Fraser's Magazine* 55 (1857): 474.

26. In *Oliver Twist* Dickens employs the popular notion that "meat" promotes a fierce spirit when Mr. Bumble blames flesh eating for Oliver's attack on Noah Claypole.

27. Bram Stoker's *Dracula,* of course, offers bloody-mouthed women as the ultimate horror of vampirism, particularly in the gruesome scene of the undead Lucy treating a baby as food. Many critical accounts of Stoker's novel have focused on the erotic threat of vampirism and on Dracula's bite as awakening women's sexuality. The literal bloodthirstiness of the vampiric women appears at least as important, however, and in both Lucy's case and an earlier scene at Dracula's castle, the women's victims are children—exactly the beings for whom women are supposed to be "natural" caretakers.

28. Charles Kingsley, *The Water Babies* [1863] (Philadelphia and London: Lippincott, 1917), 195, 185.

29. Hardy consistently associates Arabella with the slaughter of animals. Even her first overture to Jude involves throwing a pig's severed penis at him. Using any genital organ—amputated or connected, human or nonhuman—to attract attention clearly has sexual connotations, but in this instance the connotations of barnyard suffering are even stronger. The pig whose penis Arabella flings at her soon-to-be swain obviously has been slaughtered and processed into human food, his sexual organs meanwhile being discarded as one of the body parts that nineteenth-century Britain did not market for widespread consumption.

30. Thomas Hardy, *Jude the Obscure* [1895] (New York: Norton, 1978), 55.

31. See Gail Houston's "Anorexic Dickens" (22–24) for a brief discussion of psychoanalytic perspectives on the suckling breast as defining women's role—and therefore women—for the suckling child.

32. Charles Dickens, *David Copperfield* [1850] (Oxford: Oxford University Press, 1981), 522–23. (For those using other editions, this scene appears in the chapter "Our Housekeeping.")

33. James E. Marlow's "Social Harmony and Dickens' Revolutionary Cookery," *Dickens Studies Annual* 17 (1988): 145–78, points out that, for Dickens, good food and social harmony go together. Among the obstacles to this happy combination was the "false ideal . . . that superior status for a woman required culinary ignorance" (156). The

ineptitude of Dora and her ilk thus has ramifications beyond the individual household.

34. Charles Dickens, *Bleak House* [1853] (Harmondsworth: Penguin, 1971), 440.

35. Susan Schoenbauer Thurin discusses the "dry-feeding" process Pip endured in "To Be Brought Up 'By Hand'" in *Victorian Newsletter* (1983): 27–29. Mary Burgan devotes a much fuller study to the same subject in "Bringing Up By Hand: Dickens and the Feeding of Children," *Mosaic* 24.3/4 (1991): 69–88.

36. Charles Dickens, *Great Expectations* [1861] (Oxford: Oxford University Press: 1953), 58.

37. Barbara Hardy likewise has pointed out this defeminization of the domestic apron and also of the female breasts beneath it. See *The Moral Art of Charles Dickens* (London: Athalone, 1970), 149.

38. Lillian Nayder, "The Cannibal, the Nurse, and the Cook in Dickens's *The Frozen Deep,*" *Victorian Literature and Culture* 19 (1992): 3.

39. Robert Polhemus, *Comic Faith: The Great Tradition from Austen to Joyce* (Chicago: University of Chicago Press, 1980), 112.

40. Sarah Gilead, "Barmecide Feasts: Ritual, Narrative, and the Victorian Novel," *Dickens Studies Annual* 17 (1988): 233. One of the most striking instances of Dickens's keen sensitivity to the aggressive possibilities implicit in eating is his well-documented interest in (and revulsion of) cannibalism. Ian R. Stone in "'The Contents of the Kettles': Charles Dickens, John Rae and Cannibalism on the 1845 Franklin Expedition," *The Dickensian* 84 (1987): 6–16; and James E. Marlow's "English Cannibalism: Dickens after 1859," *Studies in English Literature, 1500–1900* 23 (1983): 647–66, offer valuable discussions of Dickens's strong response to the idea of cannibalism. Other works, aside from Lillian Nayder, "The Cannibal, the Nurse, and the Cook," include Angus Easson's "From Terror to Terror: Dickens, Carlyle and Cannibalism," in *Reflections of Revolution: Images of Romanticism,* ed. Alison Yarrington and Kelvin Everest (London: Routledge, 1993), 96–111; and the most massive single study: the first section, "Dickens and Cannibalism: The Unpardonable Sin" (1–268) of Harry Stone, *The Night Side of Dickens: Cannibalism, Passion, Necessity* (Athens: University of Ohio Press, 1994).

Thackeray as well sometimes plays with the idea of cannibalism, as his frequent Amina references indicate. In "Funeral Baked Meats: Thackeray's Last Novel," *Studies in the Novel* 8 (1981): 133–53, Juliet McMaster points out that in *The Adventures of Philip* "Thackeray develops the view of human relations as carnivorous, as a system of people devouring people" (138).

41. Charles Dickens, *Oliver Twist* [1838] (Oxford: Oxford University Press, 1966), 170.

42. For a discussion of "deference" as the most important offering that Victorian women could make to others, an offering that then returned to them as recognition of their feminine virtue, see Sarah Winter's "Domestic Fictions: Feminine Deference and Maternal Shadow Labor in Dickens's *Little Dorrit,*" *Dickens Studies Annual* 18 (1989): 243–54.

43. Diane Dewhurst Belcher, "Servants and Their Masters in the Novels of Charles Dickens" (Ph.D. diss., Ohio State University 1984), 133–34.

44. Charles Dickens, *Hard Times* [1854] (Harmondsworth: Penguin, 1969), 109.

45. Ian Watt, "Oral Dickens," *Dickens Studies Annual* 3 (1974): 167.

46. Charles Dickens, *Little Dorrit* [1857] (Harmondsworth: Penguin, 1867), 121.

47. William Makepeace Thackeray, *The Adventures of Philip* [1862], ed. George Saintsbury (London: Oxford University Press, n.d.), 619–23.

48. William Makepeace Thackeray, *The History of Pendennis* [1850] (Harmondsworth: Penguin, 1972), 135.

49. Leonee Ormond in "Cayenne and Cream Tarts: W. M. Thackeray and R. L. Stevenson," in *The Arabian Nights in English Literature,* ed. Peter L. Caracciolo (New York: St. Martin's Press, 1988), 178–96, points out that this story "particularly captured Thackeray's imagination" (184).

50. William Makepeace Thackeray, *The Fitz-Boodle Papers* [1842–43], in *The Great Hoggarty Diamond; Fitz-Boodle Papers; Men's Wives; etc.,* ed. George Saintsbury (London: Oxford University Press, n.d.), 312.

51. As if to demonstrate how inexhaustibly applicable Thackeray found the Amina comparison, he uses it again in *The Adventures of Philip*. Rejoicing in his escape from Agnes Twysden, Philip declares "'I might have been like that fellow in the *Arabian Nights,* who married Amina—the respectable woman, who dined upon grains of rice, but supped upon cold dead body'" (272). Here Amina is designated as the "respectable" woman—not the sexual outcast.

52. In "No Angel in the House: Victorian Mothers and Daughters in George Eliot and Elizabeth Gaskell," *The Midwest Quarterly* 24 (1983): 297–314, Carol A. Martin argues that women writers such as Gaskell and Eliot were far less inclined to idealize motherhood than male authors such as Dickens and Thackeray. Many critics, however, detect much subversive undercutting of sentimental maternity even in the latter writers. Critics of Dickens have been cited elsewhere. For Thackeray, Ina Ferris in "The Demystification of Laura Pendennis," *Studies in the Novel* 13 (1981): 122–31, traces Laura's increasing "distortions of perceptions," "arrogance," and "rapaciousness" (129) through the series of novels in which she appears. Robert Bledsoe's "*Pendennis* and the Power of Sentimentality: A Study of Motherly Love," *PMLA* 91 (1976): 871–83, takes a skeptical view of both Laura and Helen. In *Women and Marriage in Victorian Fiction* (New York: Oxford University Press, 1976), Jenni Calder notes an irony typical of Thackeray: before marriage to Pendennis, "Laura Bell . . . shares the name of one of the most notorious prostitutes of the Victorian era" (26). Micael M. Clarke, meanwhile, argues forcefully in *Thackeray and Women* (DeKalb: Northern Illinois University Press, 1995) that Thackeray displays steadily intensifying and consciously feminist attitudes throughout his fiction.

53. George Orwell, "Charles Dickens" [1939], in *Dickens, Dali & Others: Studies in Popular Culture* (New York: Reynal & Hitchcock, 1946), 73.

54. Cates Baldridge, "The Problems of Worldliness in *Pendennis,*" *Nineteenth-Century Literature* 44 (1990): 494.

55. Thackeray, letter of 12 Sept. 1855 to Rev. Whitwell Elwin, *The Letters and Private Papers of William Makepeace Thackeray,* vol. 3, ed. Gordon Ray, (Cambridge, Mass.: Harvard University Press, 1946), 469.

56. In "Oral Dickens" Ian Watt observes that "in Dickens, it is the women characters who present the strongest examples of individual and social pathology, and

almost without exception their symptoms are manifested through their attitudes to food" (172). His comment underscores the high proportion of female monstrosity to female virtue in Dickens's novels and also the importance of food as a vehicle for expressing monstrosity.

Many critics, of course, have questioned the demureness of Dickens's heroines. Esther Summerson in particular has been subject to a slew of revisionist readings, but other characters have also come under scrutiny for repressed rage. The point remains, however, that Dickens, even more than Thackeray, could not openly admit the existence of hostile feelings in his "good" women. Whatever his art might reveal about "good" women's potential for anger clashes sharply with the ideology of long-suffering feminine devotion his narrators consistently praise.

For a representative sampling of criticism on Esther, see Carol A. Senf's "*Bleak House*: Dickens, Esther and the Androgynous Mind," *Victorian Newsletter* 64 (1983): 21–27, and Valerie Kennedy's "More Trouble with Esther," *Journal of Women's Studies in Literature* 1 (1979): 330–47, both of which suggest that Dickens himself was aware of his heroine's limitations. Likewise, Lawrence Frank's "'Through a Glass Darkly': Esther Summerson and *Bleak House*," *Dickens Studies Annual* 4 (1975): 91–112, argues that "Dickens is working here . . . with a full awareness of the psychological predicaments of his characters" (93), with a resulting Esther whose "responses to the world she encounters . . . grow more inadequate, evasive, faintly self-righteous" (92) and finally reach a "self-abasing worst" (111). Alex Zwerdling, in "Esther Summerson Rehabilitated," in *Charles Dickens's Bleak House, Modern Critical Interpretations* (New York: Chelsea House, 1987): 37–56, sees her as convincing in everything except her goodness. Patricia R. Eldredge, in "The Lost Self of Esther Summerson: A Horneyan Interpretation of *Bleak House*," *Literary Review* 244 (2): 252–78, on the other hand, seeks "to explain an Esther who only seems (not is) genuinely open and loving" (255).

Meanwhile, in her chapter on *Little Dorrit* in *Dickens and the Broken Scripture* (Athens: University of Georgia Press, 1985), Janet Larson acknowledges Amy Dorrit's "compassionate fidelity toward other human beings" but considerably qualifies the "extravagant claims . . . made for [her] as a Christian figure" (257–58), seeing her rather as an "imperfect" (267), realistically flawed character. In "'As If She Had Done Him a Wrong': Hidden Rage and Object Protection in Dickens's Amy Dorrit," *English Studies* 4 (1991): 368–76, Richard A. Currie goes much further in attributing "angry feelings of resentment" to Amy and describing her "direction of anger at herself rather than at what caused it [as] a sign of emotional illness" (369). Likewise, Currie's "Doubles, Self-Attack, and Murderous Rage in Florence Dombey," *Dickens Studies Annual* 21 (1992): 113–29, provides an uncompromising assessment of the darkness lurking behind an apparently ideal feminine facade.

57. For John Hazard Wildman, Helen is not ambiguous. He vigorously denounces her in "Thackeray's Wickedest Woman," in *Essays in Honor of Esmond Linworth Marilla,* ed. Thomas Austin Kirby and William John Olive (Baton Rouge: Louisiana State University Press, 1970): 253–58. In *Women in the English Novel, 1800–1900* (New York: St. Martin's Press, 1984), Merryn Williams offers a subtler view by observing that "we are asked to believe [Helen] is a saintly woman; Thackeray says so emphatically more than once," yet his novels "shows how a woman who does love and pray can bully and damage those around her" (122). Thackeray's "lip-service to the

ideal of the Angel in the House" doesn't prevent his revealing "that these good passive wives and mothers had a bitter and empty existence" (125), but it does expose his own ambivalence about admitting what he seems to have known. Despite his protests in the preface to *Pendennis* that current prudery prevents authors from writing the truth about men, Thackeray seems to have felt less able to write frankly about women.

58. Letter of 25 Feb. 1852 to Mary Holmes (*Letters*, 3:13).

59. In a Marxist critique Camille Colatosti argues that this double standard for self-denial functions to support bourgeois capitalism. See her "Male vs. Female Self-Denial: The Subversive Potential of the Feminine Ideal in Dickens," *Dickens Studies Annual* 19 (1990): 1–24.

CHAPTER 4: SPINSTERS AND FOOD IN *CRANFORD* AND *VILLETTE*

1. Martin Dodsworth and Peter Keating, for example, view *Cranford* as essentially a study in female sexual frustration, although Keating's discussion is far more sympathetic and nuanced than Dodsworth's. See Dodsworth's "Women without Men at Cranford," *Essays in Criticism* 13 (1963): 132–45, and Keating's introduction to *Cranford/Cousin Phillis* by Elizabeth Gaskell (Harmondsworth: Penguin, 1976). John Maynard, in *Charlotte Brontë and Sexuality* (Cambridge: Cambridge University Press, 1984), offers a sensitive and richly rewarding analysis of *Villette* but nonetheless concentrates exclusively on sexual suppression and awakening as the crucial factors in Lucy's psychological and physical life.

2. Nina Auerbach, for example, presents both Lucy and Matty as triumphant in her chapter on *Villette* and *Cranford* in *Communities of Women: An Idea in Fiction* (Cambridge, Mass.: Harvard University Press, 1978). Judith Newton is similarly enthusiastic about Lucy's success in her chapter on *Villette* in *Women, Power, and Subversion: Social Strategies in British Fiction, 1778–1860* (Athens: University of Georgia Press, 1981). In contrast to Auerbach's celebration Patsy Stoneman's chapter on *Cranford* in *Elizabeth Gaskell* (Bloomington: Indiana University Press, 1987) offers a more cautious and persuasively balanced view of the Cranfordian community as "admirable, [but] . . . not triumphant" (91).

In "The Queerness of Lucy Snowe," *Nineteenth-Century Contexts* 18 (1995): 367–84, Ann Weinstone offers a different perspective on Lucy's situation by arguing that her most intense desire is to "enter into a chaste relationship of diffused eroticism with a male brother-mate" (367). Although Weinstone's argument is fascinating, it presupposes the oppressiveness of heterosexual relationships while assuming that an attainable alternative exists in Lucy's "queer" ideal of "passionate, yet chaste, brotherly equality between men and women"—more specifically, between Lucy and Paul (378). One wonders, however, whether Paul would be more egalitarian with a "sister" than with a wife.

3. Shirley Foster perceptively points out that, although Charlotte Brontë at numerous points in her letters insists on the need for women's employment, she at times implies "that work is merely a diversion from the emptiness of singlehood" (*Victorian Women's Fiction: Marriage, Freedom and the Individual* [Totowa, N.J.: Barnes & Noble Books, 1985], 75). Brontë herself detested both governessing and teaching, two jobs through which she tried to gain at least financial independence. Perhaps

Brontë's awareness that not all work is fulfilling added to her emphasis on the "emotional needs which a single life failed to meet" (75). For a fuller discussion of Brontë's complex and ambivalent attitudes toward female singleness, see Foster's entire chapter on Brontë, 71–109. Deirdre Lashgari's "What Some Women Can't Swallow: Hunger as Protest in Charlotte Brontë's *Shirley*," in *Disorderly Eaters: Texts in Self-Empowerment,* ed. Lilian R. Furst and Peter W. Graham (University Park: Pennsylvania State University Press, 1992), 141–52, examines the single woman's plight as an example of social dislocation.

4. Margaret Buchmann's "Charlotte Brontë, *Villette,* and Teaching" (in *From Socrates to Software: The Teacher as Text and the Text as Teacher,* pt. 1, ed. Philip W. Jackson and Sophie Haroutunian-Gordon [Chicago: University of Chicago Press, 1989], 60–85) traces the parallel between Brontë's own distaste for teaching and Lucy's reluctant entry into the profession.

5. Sarah Stickney Ellis, *The Women of England: Their Social Duties and Domestic Habits* (London, 1839), 155.

6. Charlotte Brontë, *Villette* [1853] (Harmondsworth: Penguin, 1979), 450–51.

7. "Queen Bees or Working Bees?" *Saturday Review* 8 (1859): 576–77.

8. [W. G. Hamley], "Old Maids," *Blackwood's Edinburgh Magazine* 112 (1872): 101.

9. Elizabeth Gaskell, *Cranford* [1853] (Harmondsworth: Penguin, 1976), 213.

10. Jill L. Matus, *Unstable Bodies: Victorian Representations of Sexuality and Maternity* (Manchester: Manchester University Press, 1995), 133.

11. Linda C. Hunt, "Sustenance and Balm: The Question of Female Friendship in *Shirley* and *Villette*," *Tulsa Studies in Women's Literature* 1 (1982): 56. See also her chapter on Charlotte Brontë in *A Woman's Portion: Ideology, Culture, and the British Female Novel Tradition* (New York: Garland, 1988).

12. Hunt in *A Woman's Portion,* 96.

13. Despite the contrast between Matty's sweetness and Lucy's acerbity, the two women share one stereotypically "feminine" attitude: indifference to intellectual pursuits. "On me school-triumphs shed but a cold lustre," Lucy comments (225), and she adds later that "I could read little; there were few bound and printed volumes that did not weary me—whose perusal did not fag and blind" (472). Significantly, she declares that M. Paul's "mind was indeed my library" (472): it is only through listening to him that she can "read" with pleasure. In this assessment I disagree with Brenda R. Silver's claim that Lucy's "pride of intellect . . . is great"; see "The Reflecting Reader in *Villette*" (*The Voyage In: Fictions of Female Development,* ed. Elizabeth Abel, Marianne Hirsch, and Elizabeth Langland [Hanover: University Press of New England, 1983], 90–111, at 97). Miss Matty reads even less than Lucy (201) and aspires to no higher mental excitement than that gained by playing cards.

14. Lucy remarks that one of her fellow-teachers "once, as a mark of high favour, . . . showed me a hoard . . . about fifteen guineas, in five-franc pieces. . . . These were her savings. She would come and talk to me about them with an infatuated and persevering dotage, strange to behold in a person not yet twenty-five" (194). However repellant Lucy finds this greed, it has its pathos as a form of self-defense against the exigencies of a financially insecure life. One can say the same about the other teachers' self-deluding claims that they attract masculine admiration.

15. W. R. Greg, "Why Are Women Redundant?" *National Review* 14 (1862): 451.

16. Eileen Gillooly, "Humor as Daughterly Defense," *English Literary History* 59 (1992): 892.

17. In *Communities of Women* Nina Auerbach acknowledges as much when she describes the ideal Cranfordian man as "a patient and polite provider"—in this case, one whose only known characteristic is his "good estate in Scotland" and consequent ability to "give a home" to a woman who is "unable to support herself" (81–82).

18. Gaskell's treatment of men here fits in neatly with the attitude Francis L. and Monica A. Fennell ascribe to Charlotte Brontë. According to the Fennells, "[f]or Brontë the test regarding a male character is simple: can a man at least on occasion relinquish his society-given 'rights' and prepare food, especially for a woman? If so, according to Brontë's implicit social philosophy he has an innate goodness and humility which will compensate for his sins, whatever they may be" ("'Ladies—Loaf Givers': Food, Women, and Society in the Novels of Charlotte Brontë and George Eliot," in *Keeping the Victorian House: A Collection of Essays* ed. Vanessa D. Dickerson [New York: Garland, 1995], 235–58, at 245).

19. Susan Anne Carlson, "Brontë's Morbid Heroine: Reading Lucy Snowe as an Incest Survivor," talk at meetings of the M/MLA, Minneapolis, 4–6 Nov. 1993. Carlson develops this theme in "Unveiled Rage and Unspoken Fear: A Study of Emotional, Physical and Sexual Abuse in the Juvenilia and Novels of Charlotte Brontë" (Ph.D. diss., Ohio State University, 1992). Other critics examining Lucy's morbidity have focused on her place within Victorian theories of neurosis. See, for example, Sally Shuttleworth's "'The Surveillance of a Sleepless Eye': The Constitution of Neurosis in *Villette,*" in *One Culture: Essays in Science and Literature,* ed. George Levine (University of Wisconsin Press, 1987), 313–35; and Athena Vrettos's "From Neurosis to Narrative: The Private Life of the Nerves in *Villette* and *Daniel Deronda,*" *Victorian Studies* 33 (1990): 551–79.

20. Roslyn Belkyn argues that in *Shirley* Brontë "gives the lie direct to the fallacy, still perpetuated in modern literature, that the chief problems of single, older women are sexual rather than social and economic" ("Rejects of the Marketplace: Old Maids in Charlotte Brontë's *Shirley,*" *International Journal of Women's Studies* 4 [1981]: 50–66, at 52). She points to the yearning for meaningful occupation expressed by both of *Shirley*'s central women. These women do eventually marry and apparently assume only the traditional occupation of middle-class matron. Thus it is especially interesting that Lucy, who must work and whose work largely shapes her life, does not perceive in it any possibilities for deep or sustained pleasure.

21. Elizabeth Gaskell, *The Life of Charlotte Brontë* [1857] (London: Oxford University Press, 1961), 402. The article to which Brontë refers as on women's "emancipation" appeared anonymously in the July 1851 *Westminster Review* under the title "The Enfranchisement of Women." This essay frequently has been attributed to John Stuart Mill, who reprinted it in 1859 in his *Dissertations and Discussions.* Mill himself credited his wife Harriet Taylor with the essay's authorship. For a full discussion of the essay see chapter 6, "The Enfranchisement of Women—The Essay and the M.P." in Gail Tulloch's *Mill and Sexual Equality* (Hemel Hempstead: Harvester Wheatsheaf, 1989).

22. The ambivalent relationship between Ginevra and Lucy complicates Robert Bernard Martin's claim in *Charlotte Brontë's Novels: The Accents of Persuasion* (New York: Norton, 1966) that *Villette* displays unambiguously "the reconciliatory, even amatory, powers of food." Certainly, *Villette* has "a fairly common usage of shared meals as indication of personal harmony," but Lucy's sharing of her food with Ginevra "expresses" feelings considerably more complex than a simple "preference" (185). However much Lucy coddles Ginevra, the younger woman obviously inspires her with as much contempt as affection.

23. Helena Michie, *The Flesh Made Word: Female Figures and Women's Bodies* (New York: Oxford University Press, 1987), 25.

24. See Elizabeth Rigby, review of *Jane Eyre: An Autobiography* [1848], in *Critical Essays on Charlotte Brontë*, ed. Barbara Timm Gates (Boston: Hall, 1990), 139–42; reprint from *Quarterly Review* 84 (1848): 173–76.

25. Dickens's Sairey Gamp in *Martin Chuzzlewit* is one supremely comic example of the untrustworthy nurse. Lillian Nayder neatly summarizes "the pernicious effect of the nurse [as] defined in terms of social class as well as gender—as a threat posed to employers by immoral and ignorant female workers," "The Cannibal, the Nurse, and the Cook in Dickens's *The Frozen Deep*," *Victorian Literature and Culture* 19 (1992): 1–24, at 11–12.

26. Winifred Gerin, *Charlotte Brontë: The Evolution of Genius* (London: Oxford University Press, 1967), 143.

27. See Jeanne Peterson's "Status Incongruence in Family and Society," in *Suffer and Be Still*, ed. Martha Vicinus (Bloomington: Indiana University Press, 1972), 3–19.

28. Mary Poovey, *Uneven Developments: The Ideological Work of Gender in Mid-Victorian England* (Chicago: University of Chicago Press, 1988), 127.

29. Charles Dickens, *A Tale of Two Cities* [1859] (Harmondsworth: Penguin, 1970), 126.

30. It is also possible, of course, to see Lucy's relationship with Ginevera as incipiently lesbian, an idea Sara Putzell-Korab explores in "Passion between Women in the Victorian Novel," in *Sexuality and Victorian Literature,* ed. Don Richard Cox (Knoxville: University of Tennessee Press, 1984), 180–95. In his introduction to the Penguin edition of *Villette* Tony Tanner likewise alludes to the possibility of "a latent lesbianism," although he dismisses the matter as "an open question" (35).

31. Patricia Beer, *Reader, I Married Him: A Study of the Women Characters of Jane Austen, Charlotte Brontë, Elizabeth Gaskell and George Eliot* (New York: Barnes & Noble, 1974), 92.

CHAPTER 5: WOMEN'S WORK AND WORKING WOMEN

1. For a sociological exposition of this point of view, see Lorna Duffin's "The Conspicuous Consumptive: Woman as an Invalid," in *The Nineteenth-Century Woman: Her Cultural and Physical World*, ed. Sara Delamont and Lorna Duffin (London: Croom Helm, 1978), 25–56. In *The Sickroom in Victorian Fiction: The Art of Being Ill* (Cambridge: Cambridge University Press, 1994), Miriam Bailin more specifically discusses the idealization of illness in Victorian literature. Paula Marantz Cohen, mean-

while, argues for the "functionality" of female illness and death in the domestic novel in "The Anorexic Syndrome and the Nineteenth-Century Domestic Novel," in *Disorderly Eaters: Texts in Self-Empowerment*, ed. Lilian R. Furst and Peter W. Graham (University Park: Pennsylvania State University Press, 1992), 125–39, at 129 (this article contains material that she develops further in her book *The Daughter's Dilemma*). Bram Dijkstra pushes this idea to an extreme in his book *Idols of Perversity: Fantasies of Feminine Evil in Fin-de-Siècle Culture* (New York: Oxford University Press, 1986); despite the subtitle he covers most of the nineteenth century. According to Dijkstra "[f]or many a Victorian husband his wife's physical weakness came to be evidence to the world and to God of her physical and mental purity" (25). Dijkstra further claims, "Death became a woman's ultimate sacrifice of her being to the males she had been born to serve. To withhold from them this last gesture of her exalted servility was, in a sense, an act of insubordination, of 'self-will'" (29).

2. Critics have been particularly prone to see Dickens's heroines as "deathly" figures, because they either die without explicable physical cause or are generally associated with death. Little Nell in *The Old Curiosity Shop* is perhaps the most striking example of the former phenomenon. Among the discussions of her death's significance are Marilyn Georgas's "Little Nell and the Art of Holy Dying: Dickens and Jeremy Taylor," *Dickens Studies Annual* 20 (1991): 35–56, and Patrick J. McCarthy, "The Curious Road to Death's Nell," in ibid., 17–34. Simon Edwards in "Anorexia Nervosa versus the Fleshpots of London: Rose and Nancy in *Oliver Twist*," *Dickens Studies Annual* 19 (1990): 49–64, discerns not anorexia nervosa but the "'meaning' of anorexia" behind Rose Maylie's otherwise unexplained illness in *Oliver Twist* (58). More generally, Alexander Welsh discusses the Dickensian angelic woman as a death-associated figure in *The City of Dickens* (Oxford: Clarendon Press, 1971). In *The Daughter's Dilemma: Family Process and the Nineteenth-Century Domestic Novel* (Ann Arbor: University of Michigan Press, 1991), Paula Marantz Cohen encapsulates a widespread view when she declares that "Dickens's heroines are generally frail if not outright ailing creatures" (26)—a statement this chapter is devoted partly to disproving.

3. As Sheila Smith points out in *The Other Nation: The Poor in English Novels of the 1840s and 1850s* (Oxford: Clarendon Press, 1980), even such an apparent iconoclast as Arthur J. Munby, who sought to prove "that women like hard work and are capable of it" (147), was motivated by an extreme version of the "contemporary approval of servitude in those who ministered to the business and comfort of the Victorian middle and upper classes" (146).

4. Catherine Gallagher provides a brief discussion of Lord Ashley's position in *The Industrial Reformation of English Fiction: Social Discourse and Narrative Form 1832–1867* (Chicago: University of Chicago Press, 1985), 121–25.

5. See W. R. Greg's "Why Are Women Redundant?" *National Review* 14: (1862): 451.

6. See Patricia Branca, *The Silent Sisterhood: Middle-Class Women in the Victorian Home* (Pittsburgh: Carnegie-Mellon Press, 1975).

7. Branca (22–35) discusses some of the criticisms of and demands upon women's housekeeping skills.

8. Charles Dickens, *Nicholas Nickleby* [1839] (Oxford: Oxford University Press, 1981), 265.

9. For a brief overview of the "tradition" of the "swoon" in particular as a "weapon . . . of guile and manipulative ambition," see pages 106–8 of Douglas Thorpe's "'I Never Knew My Lady Swoon Before': Lady Dedlock and the Revival of the Victorian Fainting Woman," *Dickens Studies Annual* 20 (1991): 103–25.

10. Elizabeth Gaskell, *North and South* [1855] (Harmondsworth: Penguin, 1970), 44.

11. Anthony Trollope, *Doctor Thorne* [1858] (London: Dent, 1949), 128.

12. Elizabeth Gaskell, *Mary Barton* [1848] (New York: Norton, 1958), 194.

13. See Elaine Scarry, *The Body in Pain: The Making and Unmaking of the World* (New York: Oxford University Press, 1985), 30.

14. Often the only value of the "invalid" woman is to demonstrate to other women what behavior to avoid. Dolly Varden in Dickens's *Barnaby Rudge* [1841] (Harmondsworth: Penguin, 1973) learns what *not* to be from her mother, who stages bouts of ill-being to dramatize and avenge her grievances against her husband. Dolly, by contrast, "was by no means accustomed to displays of this sort, rather learning from her mother's example to avoid them as much as possible" (228–29).

15. Helena Michie in *The Flesh Made Word: Female Figures and Women's Bodies* (New York: Oxford University Press, 1987) posits an alternative explanation for heroines' illnesses when she suggests that "the disease begins when . . . the heroine realizes her own sexuality" and that it is "a predictable malady that will end either in marriage or death" (25). Susan Zlotnick, focusing on *Mary Barton,* argues forcefully that while the novel as a whole valorizes action (including female action), Gaskell reduces Mary after her illness "to a state of infantile dependence" because "the virtues of work and the values of ladyhood are not reconcilable after all." (Zlotnick delivered these comments during her talk "The Curse of Leisure: Unemployment in *Mary Barton*" as part of the panel, *Gaskell and the Social Novel,* presented 7 May 1993 at the Second Annual Conference on Women Writers of Eighteenth- and Nineteenth-Century Britain, held in Seattle at the University of Washington.)

16. A typical strategy is for writers to emphasize the combination of feminine delicacy with the strength born of female love. Thus, for example, Florence Dombey wins plaudits from other characters and the narrator of *Dombey and Son* for her courage in facing a servantless life on shipboard and enduring childbirth under austere conditions. In the same novel, however, the narrator assumes working-class hardiness, so that Mr. Toots's exhortations to his pregnant, originally lower-class wife to "remember the medical man" when she exerts herself just show his infatuation (Charles Dickens, *Dombey and Son* (1846) [Harmondsworth: Penguin, 1970], 946–49). His wife, always more sensible than he, knows better than to worry about herself. Most striking of all, Mary Smith in *Cranford* is dumbfounded by the maid Martha's tears and tremors late in her pregnancy. Apparently Mary considers such sensitivity in a working-class woman an anomaly that can provoke puzzlement but not stir compassion, much less win respect.

17. One significant exception to this general pattern appears in the novels of Charlotte Brontë, whose Lucy Snowe and Caroline Helstone suffer prolonged and enervating bouts of illness (whether psychosomatic or not). The most energetic of domestic heroines appear in stories exalting domesticity, so Brontë's heroines (who typically appear in novels more ambivalent about the domestic ideal) may indeed be more susceptible to general malaise.

18. Catherine Barnes Stevenson, "'What Must Not Be Said': *North and South* and the Problem of Women's Work," *Victorian Literature and Culture* 19 (1992): 68.

19. Charles Dickens, *Our Mutual Friend* [1865] (Oxford: Oxford University Press, 1989), 818.

20. Elizabeth Langland, *Nobody's Angels: Middle-Class Women and Domestic Ideology in Victorian Culture* (Ithaca: Cornell University Press, 1995), 81.

21. For an excellent discussion of the ambiguities involved in marrying the "middle-class work ethic" to representations of women's domestic labor "that does not acknowledge its status as work," see Martin A. Danahay's "Housekeeping and Hegemony in Dickens's *Bleak House*," in *Keeping the Victorian House: A Collection of Essays,* ed. Vanessa D. Dickerson (New York: Garland, 1995), 3–25, at 6–7. These ambiguities, of course, arise largely because of the "separate sphere" doctrine that tried rigidly to separate the public and private arenas of human experience. Barbara Gottfried, in "Household Arrangements and the Patriarchal Order in *Bleak House*," *Journal of Narrative Technique* 24 (1994): 1–17, suggests that the novel ultimately is unable to maintain the pretense of a "beneficent separation between the public, impersonal (male) realm . . . and the private, domestic (female) sphere" (1).

22. Sarah Stickney Ellis, *The Women of England: Their Social Duties and Domestic Habits* (London, 1839), 34.

23. See Sarah Winter's "Domestic Fictions: Feminine Deference and Maternal Shadow Labor in Dickens's *Little Dorrit*," *Dickens Studies Annual* 18 (1989): 243–54.

24. George Gissing, "The Foolish Virgin" [1896], in *The Yellow Book: Quintessence of the Nineties,* ed. Stanley Weintraub (New York: Doubleday, 1964), 227.

25. Charles Dickens, *A Tale of Two Cities* (Harmondsworth: Penguin, 1970), 304.

26. The actual importance of women's household and social management and the satisfactions it provided for women themselves are still a source of debate. Such nineteenth-century proponents of "women's mission" as Sarah Lewis, Sarah Stickney Ellis, and Mrs. John Sandhurst emphasized the crucial role that women played in national life through their domestic responsibilities. On the other hand, Florence Nightingale's "Cassandra" [1852] (New York: Feminist Press, 1979) denounced "[t]hose conventional frivolities, which are called [women's] 'duties'" (37), while Thorstein Veblen devised the theory of conspicuous leisure to account for middle-class women's unproductive lives. The sociologist Leonore Davidoff, however, while acknowledging the popular view that Victorian women created ways to waste time, argues that "sociology . . . should alert us to be wary [of assuming] . . . that large numbers of people living far above a poverty line would have continued to accept, much less passionately defend, a system which was without meaning and without goals" (*The Best Circles: Society Etiquette and the Season* [London: Croom Helm, 1973], 14).

27. W. R. Greg makes this point abundantly clear when he refers to the "unfulfilled destinies" in "the highest ranks of all": "women who have gay society, but no sacred or sufficing home, whose dreary round of pleasure is yet sadder, less remunerative, and less satisfying, than the dreary round of toil trodden by their humbler sisters" (437).

28. Dante Gabriel Rossetti makes the same ostensibly daring move in "Jenny" [1870] when the poem's speaker muses over the physical and emotional similarities

between Jenny, the streetwalker he has picked up for the evening, and his well-born, well-protected cousin Nell (185–202).

29. William Makepeace Thackeray, *The Adventures of Philip,* ed. George Saintsbury (London: Oxford University Press, n.d.), 111.

30. Robert Newsom, "Embodying *Dombey*: Whole and in Part," *Dickens Studies Annual* 18 (1989): 206.

31. Maria Nicholls, "Lady Dedlock's Sin," *The Dickensian* 89 (1993): 43.

32. I use these terms from Lyn Pykett's "*Dombey and Son*: A Sentimental Family Romance," *Studies in the Novel* 24 (1987): 20, although I disagree with her application of them, since she does perceive sexuality as the essence of the contrast between Florence and Edith Dombey.

33. For example, in her talk Susan Zlotnick remarked that Mary Barton "is subject to the intense eroticization all working-class women underwent." Laura Yavitz in her paper "Work Fit for a Woman: Elizabeth Gaskell and Working Women," given at the 1994 Midwest Victorian Studies Association Conference, agrees that "such sexualized images" exist but goes on to examine how Gaskell complicates them.

34. The serious stature given Lizzie works against Dickens's general tendency to link the lower-class body with comedy. At the same time, however, Lizzie is the most dramatic example of a trend that becomes increasingly important in Dickens's later novels: the joining of a lower-class heroine with a middle- or upper-class hero.

35. Here again, see Catherine Gallagher, *The Industrial Reformation of English Fiction: Social Discourse and Narrative Form 1832–1867* (Chicago: University of Chicago Press, 1985), 121–25. In "Lost Mothers: The Challenge to Paternalism in *Mary Barton*," *Nineteenth Century Studies* 6 (1992): 19–35, Kristin Flieger Samuelian describes Chartist "conservatism . . . in the area of gender relations, akin to middle-class assumptions." Samuelian also alludes to nineteenth-century fears of "'cotton mill morality' [as] essentially a middle-class myth based on a fear of increasing equality between the sexes and of destruction of the social order caused by women abandoning their households to become breadwinners" and suggests that "the move to keep married women out of factory work" was a step toward bringing the working-class family "'much closer to the bourgeois ideal'" (22). Even working-class men's interest in traditional gender roles then is figured in Samuelian's argument as quintessentially bourgeois.

36. In "Crossing the Gulfs: The Importance of the Master-Servant Relationship in Dickens's *Bleak House*," *The Dickensian* 85 (1989): 150–60, R. Ann Smalley offers a positive interpretation of the idea that rather than "family limited to blood relations, Dickens seems to be indicating that desirable and comparable loyalties can exist between different classes in the form of certain master-servant bonds." Smalley argues that this "symbolic relationship" is "beneficial for both groups," although one benefit for the working class participants is apparently the opportunity "to do what they do best . . . [give] devoted service under reassuring guidance and direction" (160).

37. Charles Dickens, *David Copperfield* [1850] (Oxford: Oxford University Press, 1981), 10.

38. There is a parallel lack of typical masculinity in Gaskell's working-class men. Higgins in *North and South* and Barton in *Mary Barton* are both physically depleted men, worn out by the vicissitudes of working-class life (and in John's case eventually, by opium addiction). Jem (also in *Mary Barton*) is more powerfully built, but his sta-

tus makes all the other characters in the book assume that he is physically unappealing to women, especially when compared to the well-bred Harry Carson.

39. Esther Summerson in *Bleak House* occupies a similar position as Mr. Jarndyce's housekeeper and Ada's companion for most of the book. That her status is as ambiguous as it is—she at once performs a servant's tasks and enjoys the emotional bonds of an (adoptive) family member—testifies to the blurring of the division between a servant's and a domestic woman's duties.

40. In "High Life below Stairs, or, Cribbage in the Kitchen," *English Language Notes* 23 (1985): 45–61, Lynn C. Bartlett points out that Dickens also employs "condescending" humor in his treatment of the Marchioness in *The Old Curiosity Shop* to differentiate her from the novel's solemnly treated heroine. The "comic name" bestowed on this waif by her future husband "mark[s] her as someone whom we are not expected to take as seriously as, say, Little Nell" (61).

41. See "Family Romances" [1909], in *The Standard Edition of the Complete Psychological Works of Sigmund Freud,* ed. James Strachey, Anna Freud, Alix Strachey, and Alan Tyson, vol. 9, (London: Hogarth Press, 1959), 235–41.

42. Hands are *so* gendered, in fact, that in Robert Browning's poem "Andrea del Sarto" the eponymous speaker tells his wife, "Your soft hand is a woman of itself / And mine the man's bared breast she curls inside" (ll. 21–22). The reddening and roughening of hands by manual labor is the subject of many allusions in nineteenth-century literature, of which one striking example is Lizzie Hexam's account in *Our Mutual Friend* of the change Eugene Wrayburn has made in her life. Speaking of her apparently hopeless love for her social superior, Lizzie says "'he has done me nothing but good since I have known him, and . . . he has made a change within me, like—like the change in the grain of these hands, which were coarse, and racked, and hard, and brown when I rowed on the river with father, and are softened and made supple by this new work as you see them now'" (527). Lizzie's status even at this point is not that of a "lady," but she clearly is rising on the social scale—and moving towards her eventual position as Eugene's wife.

43. Patsy Stoneman argues more optimistically that in *Mary Barton* at least there is a deliberate conflation of "female/nurturing/working-class as a 'package' in opposition to male/authoritarian/middle-class" (*Elizabeth Gaskell* [Bloomington: Indiana University Press, 1987], 119). In Stoneman's argument Gaskell's "'feminisation' of working-class life" is a type of endorsement and empowerment. This is an attractive idea, but I would argue that Stoneman overstates the authority with which Gaskell invests her nurturing working-class men.

44. Toodle nonetheless maintains his dignity in many respects, his deep love for his wife and children acting particularly in his favor compared to Mr. Dombey's cold self-centeredness. It is, however, his domestic affections—the most "feminine" side of his personality—that establish him as a sympathetic and admirable figure.

Robert Newsom in his excellent article "Embodying *Dombey:* Whole and in Part" argues that the heartlessness of many of the novel's women, coupled with the number of "tender" and "delicate" men, "blur[s] conventionally masculine and feminine qualities" (209–10). Aside from the mentally deficient Toots, however, the tenderest and therefore most androgynous—or feminine—men come from the working class.

45. Ironically, earlier in the novel Martha's response when told to serve ladies

before gentlemen at dinner is that she "like[s] lads best" (68). Her ultimate loyalty, however, is emphatically to a "lady" rather than a "lad."

46. This is not to deny, of course, that some obviously erotic working-class women appear in Victorian fiction: Fanny Bolton in Thackeray's *Pendennis* is one of the most obvious examples.

47. Dickens and Gaskell were not alone in these sentiments, of course. Thomas Carlyle, Charles Kingsley, and John Ruskin are among the many other Victorians who advocated fellow feeling as an important element in ending class strife.

48. Rosemarie Bodenheimer, on the other hand, reads this scene much more hopefully than I do. See her *The Politics of Story in Victorian Social Fiction* (Ithaca: Cornell University Press, 1988), 59. She also is more optimistic about the implications of Higgins's adopting the Boucher children (61).

49. Although *Our Mutual Friend* satirizes the sanctity of "Shares" and the parasitism of such genteel sharpsters as the Lammles, it does not exempt the lower classes from scorn. Silas Wegg is one of the novel's paramount examples of someone who is "constitutionally of a shirking temperament, [and] . . . well enough pleased to stump away, without doing what he had come to do, and was paid for doing" (191).

CHAPTER 6: THE SERVANT'S BODY IN *PAMELA* AND *LADY CHATTERLEY'S LOVER*

1. As many critics have pointed out, novels often symbolically reconcile opposing social forces "by a marriage which brings together in the person of the hero and heroine the two sets of values," Mary Eagleton and David Pierce, *Attitudes to Class in the English Novel from Walter Scott to David Storey* (London: Thames and Hudson, 1979), 18. A cross-class marriage, however, is relatively infrequent compared to one between two social peers but ideological opposites, such as that between Margaret Hale and Mr. Thornton in Gaskell's *North and South*. Their union aptly illustrates the paradigm that Eagleton and Pierce describe, in which "elements from a rural world are presented as tempering and humanizing the more brutal and acquisitive values of the industrial world" (18).

2. There has been some dispute over whether Lawrence was an authentic member of the working classes, but Lawrence himself certainly claimed a working-class background. Colin Holmes's "Lawrence's Social Origins" in *D. H. Lawrence: New Studies,* ed. Christopher Heywood (New York: St. Martin's Press, 1987), 1–15, briefly summarizes claims for the Lawrence family's middle-class standing—claims Holmes attempts to refute.

3. See Peter Scheckner's *Class, Politics, and the Individual: A Study of the Major Works of D. H. Lawrence* (Rutherford: Associated University Press, 1985), 146–47, 160–61.

4. Pamela Horn, *The Rise and Fall of the Victorian Servant* (Dublin: Gill and Macmillan, 1975), 1.

5. Bruce Robbins, *The Servant's Hand: English Fiction from Below* (New York: Columbia University Press, 1986), x–xi. Robbins's book, incidentally, stands out amid a surprising scarcity of literary criticism specifically on servants as opposed to other members of the working class. Critics from Patrick Brantlinger to Catherine Gallagher

to Rosemarie Bodenheimer have written on the novels inspired by nineteenth-century industrialism, yet this focus has excluded representations of domestic servants. Likewise, P. J. Keating states in the preface to his much-cited book, *The Working Classes in Victorian Fiction* (New York: Barnes & Noble, 1971) that "I have omitted entirely fiction about agricultural workers and (allowing for one or two special cases) domestic servants" (xii), a statement that also holds true for Sheila M. Smith, *The Other Nation: The Poor in English Novels of the 1840s and 1850s* (Oxford: Clarendon Press, 1980). There is the same paucity in criticism on eighteenth-century fiction. Several relatively recent dissertations on this topic, however, suggest that this might be a field ripe for exploration. In addition to Diane Belcher's "Servants and Their Masters in the Novels of Charles Dickens" (Ohio State University, 1984), already cited, there are Rebecca Estelle Rumbo's "Subversive Servitude: *Pamela* and Conduct Books for Servants" (University of Southern California, 1992), Ann Frankland's "Maids and Maiden Ladies: A Study of Selected Secondary Characters in the Six Major Novels of Elizabeth Gaskell" (East Texas State University, 1988) and Natalie Hess, "A Hole in the Whole of the Familial Narrative: Dickens' and Freud's Intrusive Servants" (University of Arizona, 1993).

6. Bruce Robbins notes, for example, that modern critics have observed the same "collapse of a paternalistic model of mutual obligation and the rise of a self-interested, contractual view [of service] . . . both in Dickens and in Shakespeare." Critics, therefore, should beware of "stak[ing] everything on claims for what is specific to one 'historical moment'" (40). Of course, this is not to deny the reality of material changes in the lives of actual servants and employers. Studies of those material conditions include J. Jean Hecht, *The Domestic Servant Class in Eighteenth-Century England* (London: Routledge & Kegan Paul, 1956); Theresa MacBride, *The Domestic Revolution: The Modernisation of Household Service in England and France, 1820–1920* (London, 1976); Jonathan Gathorne-Hardy, *The Rise and Fall of the Victorian Nanny* (London, 1972); Pamela Horn, *The Rise and Fall of the Victorian Servant;* Leonore Davidoff and Catherine Hall, *Family Fortunes: Men and Women of the English Middle Class 1780–1850* (Chicago: University of Chicago Press, 1987); and Randolph Trumbach, *The Rise of the Egalitarian Family: Aristocratic Kinship and Domestic Relations in Eighteenth-Century England* (New York: Academic Press, 1978).

7. William Hazlitt, "On Footmen," in *Uncollected Essays,* vol. 17 of *The Complete Works of William Hazlitt,* ed. P. P. Howe, (New York: AMS Press, 1967), 356.

8. Daniel Defoe, *Religious Courtship,* 5th ed. (London, 1737), 310–11.

9. Janice Thaddeus, "Swift's *Directions to Servants* and the Reader as Eavesdropper," *Studies in Eighteenth-Century Culture* 16 (1986): 107–23.

10. Jonathan Swift, *Directions to Servants and Miscellaneous Pieces 1733–1742,* in *The Prose Works of Jonathan Swift,* ed. Herbert Davis (Oxford: Basil Blackwell, 1964) 12:61.

11. See, for instance, Frank Dawes, *Not in Front of the Servants: A True Portrait of English Upstairs/Downstairs Life* (New York: Taplinger, 1973), 27–29; Horn, 110–12.

12. Dinah Mulock's "Female Servants," in *A Woman's Thoughts about Women* (Philadelphia: Peterson & Brothers, n.d [original London edition published in 1841]), 86–113, offers a classic example of the informal sumptuary regulations an employer might impose. As one instance of her friendly concern for her parlour-maid, Mulock

writes that "I like to see her prettily dressed, and never scruple to tell her when she sets my teeth on edge by a blue bow on a green-cotton gown" (91).

13. Frank E. Huggett, *Life below Stairs: Domestic Servants in England from Victorian Times* (London: Book Club Associates, 1977), 69–70.

14. *The Female Servant's Adviser,* or *The Service Instructor* (London: Sherwood, Gilbert, and Piper, 1829 [?]), 21.

15. Helena Michie, *The Flesh Made Word: Female Figures and Women's Bodies* (New York: Oxford University Press, 1987), 30.

16. Barbara Ehrenrich and Dierdre English, *For Her Own Good: 150 Years of the Experts' Advice to Women* (New York: Doubleday Books, 1979), 114.

17. For some discussion of this motif in writings about servants, see pages 52–53 of Mitzi Meyers's "'Servants As They Are Now Educated': Women Writers and Georgian Pedagogy," *Essays in Literature* 16 (1989): 51–69; and pages 178–79 of Anthea Trodd's "Household Spies: The Servant and the Plot in Victorian Fiction," *Literature and History* 13 (1987): 175–76. Trodd also discusses servants' surveillance of employers and intimidation of the children in their charge in chapters 3 and 4 of her book *Domestic Crime in the Victorian Novel* (New York: St. Martin's Press, 1989). The relevant chapters are "Household Spies: Servants and Crimes" (45–68) and "Nurses' Stories: Servant Interpreters" (69–95). Theresa MacBride examines Victorian fears about contact between middle-class children and coarse servants in "'As the Twig Is Bent': The Victorian Nanny," in *The Victorian Family: Structure and Stresses,* ed. Anthony S. Wohl (New York: St. Martin's Press, 1978), 44–58.

18. "Ladies in Service," *The Spectator,* 16 July 1892, 92.

19. Both John Richetti and Bruce Robbins see a distinction between what they perceive as Fielding's egalitarian-spirited fiction and the extreme conservatism of his political and judicial pamphlets. *Shamela* seems to be an instance of his combining fictional (and comic) form with extreme conservatism. See Robbins, 12–13, and Richetti, "Class Struggle without Class: Novelists and Magistrates," *The Eighteenth-Century* 32 (1991): 203–18.

20. Tom Jones's love for the wellborn Sophia Western only apparently challenges class structures, since Tom, although illegitimate, comes from a squire's family. Only Squire Western's invective upon discovering Tom's love for his daughter *before* knowing the secret of Tom's ancestry makes Tom's seemingly low birth appear an obstacle to the romance.

The chaste and sensitive Fanny Goodwill in *Joseph Andrews* is an exception to the usual promiscuity of Fielding's lower-class women, such as *Tom Jones's* Molly and *Joseph Andrews's* Betty. Fanny, Pamela's long-lost sister, seems intended to embody the genuine modesty that Fielding finds lacking in Richardson's Pamela. She strikingly differs from Pamela, however, in that Fielding consistently arranges for masculine protectors, whether Joseph or Parson Adams, to shield her from assault. Always meek and usually silent, she never exhibits the sometimes brash consciousness of merit that allows Pamela to transcend class differences to assert herself and to condemn Mr. B. It is this assertiveness that Fielding seems to have found particularly grating. Actually his parodic aping of Richardson's original breaks down most blatantly when his Shamela turns into a temper-throwing shrew after marriage. One would think that the almost painful obsequiousness of Richardson's postmarital Pamela would be one of Fielding's choicest satiric targets, but instead he chooses to develop in burlesque form a theme that simply does not appear in Richardson.

21. Henry Fielding, *Shamela,* in *Pamela/Shamela,* intro. John M. Bullitt (New York: Signet, 1980), 538.

22. Fielding apparently had no such reservations about the impeccably born Clarissa's desire to preserve *her* chastity. The contrast between his extreme skepticism about Pamela's "virtue" and his faith in Clarissa's nobility, when both women's moral struggles hinge on their defense of their bodily integrity, suggests a greater willingness to believe in a "lady's," as opposed to a servant's, purity. See G. J. Barker-Benfield, *The Culture of Sensibility: Sex and Society in Eighteenth-Century Britain* (Chicago: University of Chicago Press, 1992), 141.

23. Betty Schellenberg points out that in volume 2 of *Pamela* the "proper bride" retracts the scorn of the "harassed servant-girl" by recollecting Mr. B as almost irresistible seducer rather than contemptible intriguer ("Enclosing the Immovable: Structuring Social Authority in *Pamela* Part II," *Eighteenth-Century Fiction* 4 [1991]: 26–42, at 33).

24. Another servant also poses a sexual threat to Pamela: the Swiss monster Colbrand. Like Mrs. Jewkes Colbrand objectifies the grotesquerie and degradation of Mr. B's sexual impulses toward Pamela. It is typical of Mrs. Jewkes's greater importance, however, that she becomes the means through which Colbrand's dangerousness becomes apparent. Mrs. Jewkes informs Pamela that Mr. B plans to marry her forcibly to Colbrand, who will then sell her to his master. By this point Mr. B is tacitly admitting Pamela's ability to defy class hierarchy, since this plan depends not on a master's status but a husband's: once married, Pamela theoretically will have to obey Colbrand's commands to submit to Mr. B (1:156). This plan, of course, also assumes that Colbrand lacks sexual agency of his own since he is only to be a means toward Mr. B's satisfaction.

25. Janet Todd offers a shrewd analysis of how "the maid becomes the mistress by exaggerating servility" in "*Pamela*: Or the Bliss of Servitude," *British Journal for Eighteenth-Century Studies* 6 (1983): 135–48, at 139.

26. See *Sir Charles Grandison,* 2:229, in which Harriet Byron writes that "I never saw love and reverence so agreeably mingled in servants' faces in my life" as in "the attention paid to [Sir Charles] by the servants as they waited at table."

27. See *Selected Letters of Samuel Richardson,* ed. John Carroll (Oxford: Oxford University Press, 1964), 171.

28. Elaine Showalter in *Sexual Anarchy: Gender and Culture at the Fin-de-Siècle* (New York: Viking, 1990) discusses the fears of gender ambiguity prevalent at the turn of the century.

29. George Gissing, *The Emancipated* (New York: AMS Press, 1969), 3:266.

30. George Gissing, "The Foolish Virgin," in *The Yellow Book: Quintessence of the Nineties,* ed. Stanley Weintraub (New York: Doubleday, 1964), 214, 234.

31. W. R. Greg, "Why Are Women Redundant?" *National Review* 14 (1862): 451 (Greg's emphasis).

32. See David Ellis's "Lawrence and the Biological Psyche," in *D. H. Lawrence: Centenary Essays,* ed. Mara Kalnins, (Bristol: Bristol Classical Press, 1986), 89–109; Christopher Heywood's "'Blood-Consciousness' and the Pioneers of the Reflex and

Ganglionic Systems" in *D. H. Lawrence: New Studies,* 104–23; and James Cowan's *Journey with Genius: D. H. Lawrence's American Journey* (London: Case Western Reserve University Press, 1970), 15–24.

33. Graham Holderness, *D. H. Lawrence: History, Ideology and Fiction* (Dublin: Gill and Macmillan, 1982), 226.

34. Donald Gutierrez, on the other hand ("D. H. Lawrence and Sex," *Liberal and Fine Arts Review* 3 [1983]: 43–56), sees *Lady Chatterley's Lover* as primarily a social document, which "embodies disease, diagnosis, and cure, for the body social (incarnated in the literal bodies of the three prime characters) is what is at stake in the novel." To Gutierrez, therefore, Connie Chatterley is "the Body of England" (51) rather than a representative of "Woman."

35. Kate Millett, in her highly controversial attack on Lawrence in *Sexual Politics* (New York: Doubleday, 1970), claims that "[t]he lovers have not so much bridged class as transcended it into an aristocracy based presumably on sexual dynamism rather than on wealth or position" (244). Millett's discussion of *Lady Chatterley's Lover* is on pages 237–45.

36. D. H. Lawrence, *Lady Chatterley's Lover,* ed. Michael Squires, The Cambridge Edition of the Letters and Works of D. H. Lawrence (Cambridge: Cambridge University Press, 1993), 6.

37. Ed Jewinski ("The Phallus in D. H. Lawrence and Jacques Lacan," *D.H. Lawrence Review* 21 [1989]: 7–24) points out that Lawrence's reliance on the intense symbolic significance of the phallus continues (in a different form) in Jacques Lacan's psychological theories. For Lacan, as for Lawrence, "phallic imagery [is] the only possible vehicle for exploring *the necessary distinctness of beings*" (7). Jewinski argues that noticing this parallel "can put the reader at ease with Lawrence's repeated emphasis" on such imagery (7); however, he ignores the possibility of readers who find Lacan's theories less than convincing.

38. G. R. Strickland, "The First *Lady Chatterley's Lover,*" in *D. H. Lawrence: A Critical Study of the Major Novels and Other Writings,* ed. A. H. Gomme (Sussex: Harvester and New York: Barnes & Noble, 1978), 172.

39. H. M. Daleski goes so far as to call Mellors a "preponderantly 'female' character"—an assessment with which I would disagree. See *The Forked Flame: A Study of D. H. Lawrence* (Evanston: Northwestern University Press, 1965), 300–3, at 301.

40. Several studies of the three different versions of *Lady Chatterley's Lover* comment on Lawrence's gradual shift of attention away from political commitment and toward personal regeneration through sexuality. See, for instance, Scheckner, 137–70; Richard Wasson, "Class and the Vicissitudes of the Male Body in Works by D. H. Lawrence," *D. H. Lawrence Review* 14 (1981): 289–305; Scott Sanders, *D. H. Lawrence: The World of the Five Major Novels* (New York: Viking Press, 1973), 179–80; and Holderness, 220–27.

41. Joseph Brennan ("Male Power in the Work of D. H. Lawrence," *Paunch* 63–64 [1990]: 199–207) notices and applauds this aspect (as well as others) of Lawrence's emphasis on "male power" (199). Brennan argues that in Lawrence "masculine power . . . can give the woman her sexual body" and thus constitutes a "profoundly liberating" force (203–4). Neither Brennan nor Lawrence, however, convinc-

ingly explains why women must depend on men to gain their own bodies.

42. James C. Cowan in "D. H. Lawrence and the Resurrection of the Body," in *Healing Arts in Literature: Medicine and Literature,* ed. Joanne Trautmann (Carbondale: Southern Illinois University Press, 1981), 55–69, argues that Lawrence's "reaffirmation of intuitive, subjective knowledge validated experientially in the body is an attempt to redeem the feminine, the inward, the mutable" as opposed to "masculine . . . scientific law" (57). If such knowledge is "feminine," however, Lawrence "redeems" it only by wresting it from women and bestowing it exclusively upon men.

43. Mark Spilka's "Lawrence and the Clitoris," in *The Challenge of D. H. Lawrence,* ed. Michael Squires and Keith Cushman (Madison: University of Wisconsin Press, 1990), 176–86, argues strenuously for the essential justice of Lawrence's tactics here.

44. Mark Spilka points out that "Mellors too has his wilful occasions" and cites his diatribe against Bertha as one example ("On Lawrence's Hostility to Wilful Women: The Chatterley Solution," in *Lawrence and Women,* ed. Anne Smith [New York: Barnes & Noble, 1978], 189–211). Yet although Spilka argues that Lawrence presents "mutual love . . . without . . . male mastery or female subjection" in the relationship between Connie and Mellors (205), he does admit that the relationship is predicated on supposedly innate differences between the "wills" of the two sexes. In Lawrence's vision, Spilka argues, "a strong woman can always outwill [a man]. But, if she is a caring woman who wants to keep their love intact, she can also yield more easily, presumably from her position of greater strength" (208). Rosemary Reeves Davies ("The Eighth Love Scene: The Real Climax of *Lady Chatterley's Lover,*" *D. H. Lawrence Review* 15 [1982]: 167–76) similarly finds strength in a woman's submission when she argues that Connie's acquiescence during the sodomy scene and elsewhere "avoids . . . injury to [Mellors's] pride" (170), and consequently "the bond between them is strengthened rather than weakened by her submissiveness" (172). While Davies is far less explicit than Spilka in claiming that innate female strength allows women to "submit" without injury to *themselves,* such an assumption seems implicit in her argument. One can only observe that such a theory of female strength is most convenient—though not to women.

45. One classic example is the account that John Cleland gives of Fanny Hill's initiation by Phoebe, her brothel companion, rapidly followed by Fanny's dissatisfaction with "this foolery from woman to woman" and her hunger for "the essential specific" (*The Memoirs of a Woman of Pleasure* [1750], ed. Peter Sabor [London: Oxford University Press, 1985], 10–34, at 34).

46. Richard Wasson, "Class and the Vicissitudes of the Male Body in Works by D. H. Lawrence," *D. H. Lawrence Review* 14 (1981): 303, 302.

47. As any student of D. H. Lawrence will recognize, almost no statement—including this one—can apply fully to all his writings. The particulars of this claim apply specifically to Lawrence's final version of his last major novel, but using the proper relations between the sexes as a model and basis for general social renewal is a recurring theme in Lawrence's work. Nonetheless, at numerous points in his literary output Lawrence focuses with tremendous intensity on the benefits of masculine bonding. Cornelia Nixon's *Lawrence's Leadership Politics and the Turn against Women* (Berkeley: University of California Press, 1986) is one of the most rewarding investigations of this particular aspect of Lawrence's gender theories.

CONCLUSION

1. It is far beyond the limits of this conclusion to outline and discuss the various histories and theories of the novel that have emerged over the decades. Obviously the generalizations that I offer here are meant to be suggestive rather than definitive; I do not presume to apply them across the whole novelistic spectrum. I do propose them, however, as a useful way to approach many examples of the bildungsroman that played so prominent a role in eighteenth- and nineteenth-century literature. My debt to Ian Watt's classic *The Rise of the Novel* (Berkeley: University of California Press, 1964) is obvious, as is my agreement with E. M. Forster's contention that the traditional novel employs love, like death, as a convenient means of closure (*Aspects of the Novel* [New York: Harcourt, Brace, 1957], 55).

2. Richardson's Sir Charles Grandison is, of course, as much a static paragon as the most improbably virtuous female character—and his static perfection is often cited as a reason for the book's artistic failure.

3. I speak here of the terms in which the book is constructed, not necessarily of the way in which individual readers do indeed respond. Many traditional novels base much of their hold upon the reader on the assumption that readers will identify with the protagonist. Judith Fetterley in *The Resisting Reader* (Indiana University Press, 1978) argues cogently that such identification is exactly what female readers must avoid, lest they absorb patriarchal biases against their own sex. Although I agree with many of Fetterley's points, her stance does not alter the fact that most eighteenth- and nineteenth-century novels attempt to induce sympathy for and empathy with the protagonist: Fetterley simply argues that we should fend off these attempts.

4. See Nancy Chodorow's *The Reproduction of Mothering* (Berkeley: University of California Press, 1978) and Janice Radway's *Reading the Romance* (Chapel Hill: University of North Carolina Press, 1984) for two investigations whose findings provide a sharp and often poignant commentary on the optimistic assumptions of this particular developmental model. Chodorow's work focuses on the socially induced perpetuation of feminine "mothering" qualities while Radway's book examines the expectations and attitudes of female romance readers. Both authors conclude, however, that the emphasis on women's provision and men's reception of nurture is a major component in the emotional hunger and dissatisfaction with actual relationships that many women experience.

5. See Joan Scott, pt. 3, "Gender in History," of *Gender and the Politics of History* (Columbia University Press, 1988), in particular chapter 7, "'L'ouvrière! Mot impie, sordide . . .': Women Workers in the Discourse of French Political Economy, 1840–1860," 139–63.

6. Here, as throughout this chapter (and book), I am deeply indebted to Dorothy Dinnerstein's *The Mermaid and the Minotaur: Sexual Arrangements and Human Malaise* (New York: Harper & Row, 1976).

Selected Bibliography

Armstrong, Nancy. *Desire and Domestic Fiction: A Political History of the Novel.* Oxford: Oxford University Press, 1987.

Auerbach, Nina. *Communities of Women: An Idea in Fiction.* Cambridge, Mass.: Harvard University Press, 1978.

———. *Woman and the Demon: The Life of a Victorian Myth.* Cambridge, Mass.: Harvard University Press, 1982.

Badinter, Elisabeth. *Mother Love, Myth and Reality: Motherhood in Modern History.* New York: Macmillan, 1981.

Bailin, Miriam. *The Sickroom in Victorian Fiction: The Art of Being Ill.* Cambridge: Cambridge University Press, 1994.

Baldridge, Cates. "The Problems of Worldliness in *Pendennis.*" *Nineteenth Century Literature* 44 (1990): 492–513.

Barker-Benfield, G. J. *The Culture of Sensibility: Sex and Society in Eighteenth-Century Britain.* Chicago: University of Chicago Press, 1992.

Bartlett, Lynn C. "High Life below Stairs, or, Cribbage in the Kitchen." *English Language Notes* 23 (1985): 45–61.

Bassil, Veronica. "The Faces of Griselda: Chaucer, Prior, and Richardson." *Texas Studies in Literature and Language* 26 (1984): 157–82.

Beer, Patricia. *Reader, I Married Him: A Study of the Women Characters of Jane Austen, Charlotte Bronte, Elizabeth Gaskell and George Eliot.* New York: Barnes & Noble, 1974.

Belcher, Diane. "Servants and Their Masters in the Novels of Charles Dickens." Ph.D. diss., Ohio State University, 1984.

Belkyn, Roslyn. "Rejects of the Marketplace: Old Maids in Charlotte Brontë's *Shirley.*" *International Journal of Women's Studies* 4 (1981): 50–66.

Bledsoe, Robert. "*Pendennis* and the Power of Sentimentality: A Study of Motherly Love." *PMLA* 91 (1976): 871–83.

Bloom, Edward and Lillian. "Introduction." In *Camilla* by Fanny Burney, edited by Edward and Lillian Bloom. Oxford: Oxford University Press, 1972.

Bodenheimer, Rosemarie. *The Politics of Story in Victorian Social Fiction.* Ithaca: Cornell University Press, 1988.

Bowers, Toni. "'A Point of Conscience': Breastfeeding and Maternal Authority in *Pamela 2.*" *Eighteenth-Century Fiction* 7 (1995): 259–78.

Branca, Patricia. *The Silent Sisterhood: Middle-Class Women in the Victorian Home.* Pittsburgh: Carnegie-Mellon Press, 1975.

Braudy, Leo. "Penetration and Impenetrability in *Clarissa.*" In *New Approaches to Eighteenth-Century Literature: Selected Papers from the English Institute,* edited by Philip Harth. New York and London: Columbia University Press, 1974.

Brennan, Joseph. "Male Power in the Work of D. H. Lawrence." *Paunch* 63/64 (1990): 199–207.

Brissenden, R. F. *Samuel Richardson.* In *Writers and Their Work 101,* gen. ed., Geoffrey Bullough. London: Longmans, Green, 1958; reprint 1965.

———. *Virtue in Distress: Studies in the Novel of Sentiment from Richardson to Sade.* New York: Barnes & Noble, 1974.

Brontë, Charlotte. *Villette.* Harmondsworth: Penguin, 1979.

Brumberg, Joan Jacobs. *Fasting Girls: The Emergence of Anorexia Nervosa as a Modern Disease.* Cambridge, Mass.: Harvard University Press, 1988.

Buchmann, Margaret. "Charlotte Brontë, *Villette,* and Teaching." In *From Socrates to Software: The Teacher as Text and the Text as Teacher,* Part 1, edited by Philip W. Jackson and Sophie Haroutunian-Gordon. Chicago: University of Chicago Press, 1989.

Burgan, Mary. "Bringing Up by Hand: Dickens and the Feeding of Children." *Mosaic* 24.3/4 (1991): 9–88.

Burney, Frances. *Camilla.* Edited and introduced by Edward A. and Lillian Bloom. Oxford: Oxford University Press, 1989.

———. *Cecilia.* Introduced by Judy Simons. London: Virago, 1986.

———. *Evelina.* Edited and introduced by Edward A. Bloom with Lillian D. Bloom. Oxford: Oxford University Press, 1991.

———. *The Wanderer.* Edited by Margaret Anne Doody, Robert L. Mack, and Peter Sabor. Oxford: Oxford University Press, 1991.

Calder, Jenni. *Women and Marriage in Victorian Fiction.* New York: Oxford University Press, 1976.

Castle, Terry. *Clarissa's Ciphers: Meaning and Disruption in Richardson's "Clarissa."* Ithaca: Cornell University Press, 1982.

———. "P/B: *Pamela* as Sexual Fiction." *Studies in English Literature, 1500–1900* 22 (1982): 469–89.

Chodorow, Nancy. *The Reproduction of Mothering: Psychoanalysis and the Sociology of Gender.* Berkeley: University of California Press, 1978.

Cixous, Hélène. "The Laugh of the Medusa." In *The Women and Language Debate: A Sourcebook,* edited by Camille Roman, Suzanne Juhasz, Christanne Miller. New Brunswick: Rutgers University Press, 1994.

Cleland, John. *The Memoirs of a Woman of Pleasure.* Edited by Peter Sabor. London: Oxford University Press, 1985.

Cobbe, Frances Power. "Female Charity—Lay and Monastic." *Fraser's Magazine* 66 (1862): 774–88.

Cohen, Paula Marantz. "The Anorexic Syndrome and the Nineteenth-Century Domestic Novel." In *Disorderly Eaters: Texts in Self-Empowerment,* edited by Lilian R. Furst and Peter W. Graham. University Park: Pennsylvania State University Press, 1992.

———. *The Daughter's Dilemma: Family Process and the Nineteenth-Century Domestic Novel.* Ann Arbor: University of Michigan Press, 1991.

Colatosti, Camille. "Male vs. Female Self-Denial: The Subversive Potential of the Feminine Ideal in Dickens." *Dickens Studies Annual* 19 (1990): 1–24.

Contratto, Susan Weisskopf. "Maternal Sexuality and Asexual Motherhood." In *Women: Sex and Sexuality,* edited by Catharine R. Stimpson and Ethel Spector Person. Chicago: University of Chicago Press, 1980.

Cosslett, Tess. *Woman to Woman: Female Friendship in Victorian Fiction.* Atlantic Highlands, N.J.: Humanities Press International, 1988.

Counihan, Carole M. "An Anthropological View of Western Women's Prodigious Fasting: A Review Essay." *Food and Foodways* 3 (1989): 357–75.

Cowan, James. "D. H. Lawrence and the Resurrection of the Body." In *Healing Arts in Literature: Medicine and Literature,* edited by Joanne Trautmann. Carbondale: Southern Illinois University Press, 1981.

Currie, Richard A. "'As If She Had Done Him a Wrong': Hidden Rage and Object Projection in Dickens's Amy Dorrit." *English Studies* 4 (1991): 368–76.

———. "Doubles, Self-Attack, and Murderous Rage in Florence Dombey." *Dickens Studies Annual* 21 (1992): 113–29.

Cutting, Rose Marie. "Defiant Women: The Growth of Feminism in Fanny Burney's Novels." *Studies in English Literature* 17 (1977): 519–30.

Cutting-Gray, Joanne. *Woman as 'Nobody' and the Novels of Fanny Burney.* Gainesville: University Press of Florida, 1992.

Daleski, H. M. *The Forked Flame: A Study of D. H. Lawrence.* Evanston: Northwestern University Press, 1965.

Daly, Mary. *Gyn/Ecology: The Metaethics of Radical Feminism.* Boston: Beacon Press, 1978.

Danahay, Martin A. "Housekeeping and Hegemony in Dickens's *Bleak House.*" In *Keeping the Victorian House: A Collection of Essays,* edited by Vanessa D. Dickerson. New York: Garland, 1995.

Davidoff, Leonore. *The Best Circles: Society Etiquette and the Season.* London: Croom Helm, 1973.

Davidoff, Leonore, and Catherine Hall. *Family Fortunes: Men and Women of the English Middle Class, 1780–1850.* Chicago: University of Chicago Press, 1987.

Davies, Rosemary Reeves. "The Eighth Love Scene: The Real Climax of *Lady Chatterley's Lover.*" *D. H. Lawrence Review* 15 (1982): 167–76.

Dawes, Frank. *Not in Front of the Servants: A True Portrait of English Upstairs/Downstairs Life.* New York: Taplinger, 1973.

Defoe, Daniel. *Religious Courtship.* 5th ed. London, 1737.

Demetrakopoulos, Stephanie. "The Nursing Mother and Feminine Metaphysics: An Essay on Embodiment." *Soundings* 65 (1982): 430–43.

Dickens, Charles. *Bleak House.* Harmondsworth: Penguin, 1971.

———. *David Copperfield.* Oxford: Oxford University Press, 1981.

———. *Dombey and Son.* Harmondsworth: Penguin, 1970.

———. *Great Expectations.* Oxford: Oxford University Press, 1953.

———. *Hard Times.* Harmondsworth: Penguin, 1969.

———. *Little Dorrit.* Harmondsworth: Penguin, 1967.

———. *Nicholas Nickleby.* Oxford: Oxford University Press, 1981.

———. *Oliver Twist.* Oxford: Oxford University Press, 1966.

———. *Our Mutual Friend.* Oxford: Oxford University Press, 1989.

———. *A Tale of Two Cities.* Harmondsworth: Penguin, 1970.

Dijkstra, Bram. *Idols of Perversity: Fantasies of Feminine Evil in Fin-de-Siècle Culture.* New York: Oxford University Press, 1986.

"The Dinner Question Discussed by an Eight Hundred a Year Man." *Bentley's Miscellany* 45 (1856).

Dinnerstein, Dorothy. *The Mermaid and the Minotaur: Sexual Arrangements and Human Malaise.* New York: Harper & Row, 1976.

Dobbin, Marjorie. "The Novel, Women's Awareness and Fanny Burney." *English Language Notes* 22.3 (1985): 42–52.

Dodsworth, Martin. "Women without Men at Cranford." *Essays in Criticism* 13 (1963): 132–45.

Doody, Margaret Anne. *Frances Burney: A Life in the Works.* New Brunswick: Rutgers University Press, 1988.

———. *A Natural Passion: A Study of the Novels of Samuel Richardson.* Oxford: Clarendon Press, 1974.

Duffin, Lorna. "The Conspicuous Consumptive: Woman as an Invalid." In *The Nineteenth-Century Woman: Her Cultural and Physical World,* edited by Sara Delamont and Lorna Duffin. London: Croom Helm, 1978.

Eagleton, Mary, and David Pierce. *Attitudes to Class in the English Novel from Walter Scott to David Storey.* London: Thames and Hudson, 1979.

Eagleton, Terry. *The Rape of Clarissa.* Minneapolis: University of Minnesota Press, 1982.

Edwards, Simon. "Anorexia Nervosa versus the Fleshpots of London: Rose and Nancy in *Oliver Twist.*" *Dickens Studies Annual* 19 (1990): 49–64.

Ehrenrich, Barbara and Dierdre English. *For Her Own Good: 150 Years of the Experts' Advice to Women.* New York: Doubleday Books, 1979.

Eldredge, Patricia R. "The Lost Self of Esther Summerson: A Horneyan Interpretation of *Bleak House.*" *Literary Review* 24 (1981): 252–78.

Ellis, David. "Lawrence and the Biological Psyche." In *D. H. Lawrence: Centenary Essays,* edited by Mara Kalnins. Bristol: Bristol Classical Press, 1986.

Ellis, Sarah Stickney. *The Women of England: Their Social Duties and Domestic Habits.* London, 1839.

Epstein, Julia L. *The Iron Pen: Frances Burney and the Politics of Women's Writing.* Madison: University of Wisconsin Press, 1989.

Erickson, Robert A. *Mother Midnight: Birth, Sex, and Fate in Eighteenth-Century Fiction (Defoe, Richardson, and Sterne).* New York: AMS Press, 1986.

Female Servant's Adviser, or The Service Instructor. London: Sherwood, Gilbert, and Piper, 1829 [?].

Fennell, Francis L. and Monica A. "'Ladies—Loaf Givers': Food, Women, and Society in the Novels of Charlotte Brontë and George Eliot." In *Keeping the Victorian House: A Collection of Essays,* edited by Vanessa D. Dickerson, 235–58. New York: Garland, 1995.

Ferris, Ina. "The Demystification of Laura Pendennis." *Studies in the Novel* 13 (1981): 122–31.

Fielding, Henry. *Shamela.* In *Pamela/Shamela.* Introduced by John M. Bullitt. New York: Signet, 1980.

Flint, Christopher. "The Anxiety of Affluence: Family and Class (Dis)order in *Pamela; or, Virtue Rewarded.*" *Studies in English Literature, 1500–1900* 29 (1989): 489–514.

Flynn, Carol Houlihan. "The Pains of Compliance in *Sir Charles Grandison.*" *Samuel Richardson: Tercentenary Essays,* edited by Margaret Anne Doody and Peter Sabor. Cambridge: Cambridge University Press, 1989.

Folkenflik, Robert. "*Pamela:* Domestic Servitude, Marriage, and the Novel." *Eighteenth-Century Fiction* 5 (1993): 253–68.

"Food and Fasting." *Chamber's Edinburgh Journal* 57 (1880).

Fordyce, James. *Sermons to Young Women.* 3d ed. London: A. Millar and T. Cadell, 1766.

Forster, E. M. *Aspects of the Novel.* New York: Harcourt, Brace, 1927.

Foster, Shirley. *Victorian Women's Fiction: Marriage, Freedom and the Individual.* Totowa, N.J.: Barnes & Noble, 1985.

Fraiman, Susan. *Unbecoming Women: British Women Writers and the Novel of Development.* New York: Columbia University Press, 1993.

Francus, Marilyn. "The Monstrous Mother: Reproductive Anxiety in Swift and Pope." *English Literary History* 4 (1994): 829–51.

Frank, Lawrence. "'Through a Glass Darkly': Esther Summerson and *Bleak House.*" *Dickens Studies Annual* 4 (1975): 91–112.

Freud, Sigmund. "Family Romances." [1909] In *The Standard Edition of the Complete Psychological Works of Sigmund Freud,* edited by James Strachey, Anna Freud, Alix Strachey, and Alan Tyson. Vol. 9. London: Hogarth Press, 1959.

Friedman, Arthur. "Aspects of Sentimentalism in Eighteenth-Century Literature." In *The Augustan Milieu: Essays Presented to Louis A. Landa,* edited by Henry Knight Miller, Eric Rothstein, and G. S. Rousseau. Oxford: Clarendon Press, 1970.

Furst, Lilian R. Introduction. *Disorderly Eaters: Texts in Self-Empowerment,* edited by Lilian R. Furst and Peter W. Graham. University Park: Pennsylvania State University Press, 1992.

Gallagher, Catherine. *The Industrial Reformation of English Fiction: Social Discourse and Narrative Form, 1832–1867.* Chicago: University of Chicago Press, 1985.

Gaskell, Elizabeth. *Cranford.* Harmondsworth: Penguin, 1976.

———. *The Life of Charlotte Brontë.* London: Oxford University Press, 1961.

———. *Mary Barton.* New York: Norton, 1958.

———. *North and South.* Harmondsworth: Penguin, 1970.

Gilead, Sarah. "Barmecide Feasts: Ritual, Narrative, and the Victorian Novel." *Dickens Studies Annual* 17 (1988): 225–47.

Gillooly, Eileen. "Humor as Daughterly Defense." *English Literary History* 59 (1992): 883–910.

Gissing, George. *The Emancipated.* New York: AMS Press, 1969.

————. "The Foolish Virgin." In *The Yellow Book: Quintessence of the Nineties.* Edited by Stanley Weintraub. New York: Doubleday, 1964.

Goldberg, Rita. *Sex and Enlightenment: Women in Richardson and Diderot.* Cambridge: Cambridge University Press, 1984.

Golden, Morris. *Richardson's Characters.* Ann Arbor: University of Michigan Press, 1963.

Gottfried, Barbara. "Household Arrangements and the Patriarchal Order in *Bleak House.*" *Journal of Narrative Technique* 24 (1994): 1–17.

Greg, W. R. "Why Are Women Redundant?" *National Review* 14 (1862).

Griffin, Susan. *Woman and Nature: The Roaring Inside Her.* New York: Harper & and Row, 1978.

Gutierrez, Donald. "D. H. Lawrence and Sex." *Liberal and Fine Arts Review* 3 (1983): 43–56.

Gwilliam, Tassie. *Samuel Richardson's Fictions of Gender.* Stanford: Stanford University Press, 1993.

Hagstrum, Jean H. *Sex and Sensibility: Ideal and Erotic Love from Milton to Mozart.* Chicago and London: University of Chicago Press, 1980.

[Hamley, W. G.] "Old Maids." *Blackwood's Edinburgh Magazine* 112 (1872).

Hardy, Barbara. *The Moral Art of Charles Dickens.* London: Athalone, 1970.

Hardy, Thomas. *Jude the Obscure.* New York: Norton, 1978.

Harris, Adrienne, and Ynestra King. *Rocking the Ship of State: Toward a Feminist Peace Politics.* Boulder: Westview Press, 1989.

Hazlitt, William. "On Footmen." In *Uncollected Essays,* vol. 17 of *The Complete Works of William Hazlitt.* Edited by P. P. Howe. New York: AMS Press, 1967.

Hemlow, Joyce. "Fanny Burney and the Courtesy Books." *PMLA* 65 (1950): 732–61.

Hilliard, Raymond. "*Clarissa* and Ritual Cannibalism." *PMLA* 105 (1990): 1083–97.

Holderness, Graham. *D. H. Lawrence: History, Ideology, and Fiction.* Dublin: Gill and Macmillan, 1982.

Holmes, Colin. "Lawrence's Social Origins." In *D. H. Lawrence: New Studies,* edited by Christopher Heywood. New York: St. Martin's Press, 1987.

Horn, Pamela. *The Rise and Fall of the Victorian Servant.* Dublin: Gill and Macmillan, 1975.

Houston, Gail. "Anorexic Dickens." Ph.D. diss., University of California at Los Angeles, 1990.

Huggett, Frank E. *Life below Stairs: Domestic Servants in England from Victorian Times.* London: Book Club Associates, 1977.

Hunt, Linda C. "Sustenance and Balm: The Question of Female Friendship in *Shirley* and *Villette.*" *Tulsa Studies in Women's Literature* 1 (1982): 55–66.

————. *A Woman's Portion: Ideology, Culture, and the British Female Novel Tradition.* New York: Garland, 1988.

Izubuchi, Keiko. "Subversive or Not? Anna Howe's Function in *Clarissa.*" In *Samuel Richardson: Passion and Prudence,* edited by Valerie Grosvenor Myer. London: Vision and Totowa, N.J.: Barnes & Noble, 1986.

Jewinski, Ed. "The Phallus in D. H. Lawrence and Jacques Lacan." *D. H. Lawrence Review* 21 (1989): 7–24.

Johnson, Claudia L. *Equivocal Beings: Politics, Gender, and Sentimentality in the 1790s.* Chicago: University of Chicago Press, 1995.

———. "A 'Sweet Face as White as Death': Jane Austen and the Politics of Female Sensibility." *Novel* 22 (1989): 159–74.

Jones, Chris. "Radical Sensibility in the 1790s." In *Reflections of Revolution: Images of Romanticism,* edited by Alison Yarrington and Kelvin Everest. London: Routledge, 1993.

Kauffman, Linda S. *Discourses of Desire: Gender, Genre, and Epistolary Fictions.* Ithaca: Cornell University Press, 1986.

Keating, P. J. *The Working Classes in Victorian Fiction.* New York: Barnes & Noble, 1971.

Kingsley, Charles. "Thoughts about Shelley and Byron." *Fraser's Magazine* (1853): 568–76.

———. *The Water Babies.* [1863] Philadelphia and London: Lippincott, 1917.

Kinkead-Weekes, Mark. *Samuel Richardson: Dramatic Novelist.* Ithaca: Cornell University Press, 1973.

Kristeva, Julia. *Powers of Horror: An Essay on Abjection.* Translated by Leon S. Roudiez. New York: Columbia University Press, 1982.

"Ladies in Service." *The Spectator,* 16 July 1892, 92.

Langland, Elizabeth. *Nobody's Angels: Middle-Class Women and Domestic Ideology in Victorian Culture.* Ithaca: Cornell University Press, 1995.

Laqueur, Thomas. *Making Sex: Body and Gender from the Greeks to Freud.* Cambridge, Mass.: Harvard University Press, 1990.

Larson, Janet. *Dickens and the Broken Scripture.* Athens: University of Georgia Press, 1985.

Lashgari, Deirdre. "What Some Women Can't Swallow: Hunger as Protest in Charlotte Brontë's *Shirley.*" In *Disorderly Eaters: Texts in Self-Empowerment,* edited by Lilian R. Furst and Peter W. Graham. University Park: Pennsylvania State University Press, 1992.

Laurence-Anderson, Judith. "Changing Affective Life in Eighteenth-Century England and Samuel Richardson's *Pamela.*" *Studies in Eighteenth-Century Culture* 10 (1981): 445–56.

Lawrence, D. H. *Lady Chatterley's Lover.* Edited by Michael Squires. The Cambridge Edition of the Letters and Works of D. H. Lawrence. Cambridge: Cambridge University Press, 1993.

LeGates, Marlene. "The Cult of Womanhood in Eighteenth-Century Thought." *Eighteenth-Century Studies* 10 (1976): 21–39.

Love, Barbara, and Elizabeth Shanklin. "The Answer Is Matriarchy." *Mothering: Essays in Feminist Theory,* edited by Joyce Trebilcot. Totowa, N.J.: Rowman & Allenheld, 1983.

MacBride, Theresa. "'As the Twig Is Bent': The Victorian Nanny." In *The Victorian Family: Structure and Stresses,* edited by Anthony S. Wohl. New York: St. Martin's Press, 1978.

McIntosh, Wm. Alex, and Mary Zey. "Women as Gatekeepers of Food Consumption: A Sociological Critique." *Food and Foodways* 3 (1989): 317–32.

McKeon, Michael. *The Origins of the English Novel, 1600–1740.* Baltimore: Johns Hopkins University Press, 1987.

McLaren, Dorothy. "Marital Fertility and Lactation, 1570-1720." In *Women in English Society, 1500-1800,* edited by Mary Prior. London: Methuen, 1985.

McMaster, Juliet. "Funeral Baked Meats: Thackeray's Last Novel." *Studies in the Novel* 8 (1981): 133–53.

———. "The Silent Angel: Impediments to Female Expression in Frances Burney's Novels." *Studies in the Novel* 21 (1989): 235–252.

Maddox, James H., Jr. "Lovelace and the World of Ressentiment in *Clarissa.*" *Texas Studies in Literature and Language* 24 (1982): 271–92.

Marlowe, James E. "Social Harmony and Dickens' Revolutionary Cookery." *Dickens Studies Annual* 17 (1988): 145–78.

Martin, Robert Bernard. *Charlotte Bronte's Novels: The Accents of Persuasion.* New York: Norton, 1966.

Matus, Jill L. *Unstable Bodies: Victorian Representations of Sexuality and Maternity.* Manchester: Manchester University Press, 1995.

Maynard, John. *Charlotte Brontë and Sexuality.* Cambridge: Cambridge University Press, 1984.

Mei, Huang. *Transforming the Cinderella Dream: From Frances Burney to Charlotte Bronte.* New Brunswick: Rutgers University Press, 1990.

Meisel, Martin. *Realizations: Narrative, Pictorial, and Theatrical Arts in Nineteenth-Century England.* Princeton: Princeton University Press, 1983.

Michie, Helena. *The Flesh Made Word: Female Figures and Women's Bodies.* New York: Oxford University Press, 1987.

Miles, Margaret R. "Textual Harassment: Desire and the Female Body." In *The Good Body: Asceticism in Contemporary Culture,* edited by Mary G. Winkler and Letha B. Cole. New Haven: Yale University Press, 1994.

Miller, Nancy K. *The Heroine's Text: Readings in the French and English Novel, 1722–1782.* New York: Columbia University Press, 1980.

Millett, Kate. *Sexual Politics.* New York: Doubleday, 1970.

Moon, Elaine. "'Sacrific'd to My Sex': The Marriages of Samuel Richardson's Pamela and Mr. B, and Mr. and Mrs. Harlowe." *AUMLA: Journal of the Australasian Universities Language and Literature Association* 63 (1985): 19–32.

Moynihan, Robert D. "Clarissa and the Enlightened Woman as Literary Heroine." *Journal of the History of Ideas* 36 (1975): 159–66.

Mullan, John. *Sentiment and Sociability: The Language of Feeling in the Eighteenth Century.* Oxford: Clarendon Press, 1988.

Mulock, Dinah. "Female Servants." In *A Woman's Thoughts about Women.* Philadelphia: Peterson & Brothers, n.d. [Original London edition 1841].

Nayder, Lillian. "The Cannibal, the Nurse, and the Cook in Dickens's *The Frozen Deep.*" *Victorian Literature and Culture* 19 (1992): 1–24.

Nelson, Claudia. *Invisible Men: Fatherhood in Victorian Periodicals, 1850–1910.* Athens: University of Georgia Press, 1995.

Newman, Beth. "Getting Fixed: Feminine Identity and Scopic Crisis in *The Turn of the Screw.*" *Novel* 25 (1992): 44–63.

Newsom, Robert. "Embodying *Dombey:* Whole and in Part." *Dickens Studies Annual* 18 (1989): 197–219.

Newton, Judith Lowder. *Women, Power, and Subversion: Social Strategies in British*

Fiction, 1778–1860. Athens: University of Georgia Press, 1981.

Nicholls, Maria. "Lady Dedlock's Sin." *The Dickensian* 89 (1993): 39–44.

Nightingale, Florence. "Cassandra." [1852] New York: Feminist Press, 1979.

Nussbaum, Felicity. "'Savage' Mothers: Narratives of Maternity in the Mid-Eighteenth Century." *Eighteenth-Century Life* 16, n.s. 1 (1992): 163–84.

Oakleaf, David. "The Name of the Father: Social Identity and the Ambition of *Evelina.*" *Eighteenth-Century Fiction* 3 (1991): 341–58.

"On Shamefacedness." *New Lady's Magazine* (London). Feb. 1786, 27.

Orbach, Susie. "Accepting the Sympton: A Feminist Psychoanalytic Treatment of Anorexia Nervosa." In *A Handbook of Psychotherapy for Anorexia Nervosa and Bulimia,* edited by David M. Garner and Paul E. Garfinkel. New York: Guilford Press, 1985.

Ormond, Leonee. "Cayenne and Cream Tarts: W. M. Thackeray and R. L. Stevenson." In *The Arabian Nights in English Literature,* edited by Peter L. Caracciolo. New York: St. Martin's Press, 1988.

Orwell, George. "Charles Dickens." [1939] In *Dickens, Dali & Others: Studies in Popular Culture.* New York: Reynal & Hitchcock, 1946.

"Over-Eating and Under-Eating." *The Cornhill Magazine* 8 (1863): 35–47.

Patnaik, Eira. "The Succulent Gender: Eat Her Softly." In *Literary Gastronomy,* edited by David Bevan. Amsterdam: Rodopi, 1988.

Perry, Jo Anne Lee. "The Representation of Feeling in the Novels of Samuel Richardson." Ph.D. diss., University of California at Santa Barbara, 1982.

Perry, Ruth. "Colonizing the Breast." *Eighteenth-Century Life* 16, n.s. 1 (1992): 185–213.

Peters, Dolores. "The Pregnant Pamela: Characterization and Popular Medical Attitudes in the Eighteenth Century." *Eighteenth-Century Studies* 14 (1981): 432–51.

Peterson, Jeanne. "Status Incongruence in Family and Society." In *Suffer and Be Still,* edited by Martha Vicinus. Bloomington: Indiana University Press, 1972.

Pines, Dinora. *A Woman's Unconscious Use of Her Body.* New Haven: Yale University Press, 1994.

Playfair, Lyon. "On the Nature and Composition of Food." *Good Words* 6 (1865): 24–31, 156–64.

"Pleasures of the Table." *Bentley's Miscellany* 45 (1856): 40–52.

Polhemus, Robert. *Comic Faith: The Great Tradition from Austen to Joyce.* University of Chicago Press, 1980.

Pollak, Ellen. *The Poetics of Sexual Myth: Gender and Ideology in the Verse of Swift and Pope.* Chicago: University of Chicago Press, 1985.

Poovey, Mary. *The Proper Lady and the Woman Writer: Ideology as Style in the Works of Mary Wollstonecraft, Mary Shelley, and Jane Austen.* Chicago: University of Chicago Press, 1984.

———. *Uneven Developments: The Ideological Work of Gender in Mid-Victorian England.* Chicago: University of Chicago Press, 1988.

Pykett, Lyn. "*Dombey and Son:* A Sentimental Family Romance." *Studies in the Novel* 24 (1987): 16–30.

"Queen Bees or Working Bees?" *Saturday Review* 8 (1859): 575–76.

Richardson, Samuel. *Clarissa.* Introduction by W. Lyon Phelps. 4 vols. Everyman's Library. London: Dent and New York: Dutton, 1932; reprint 1950.

———. *Pamela.* Introduction by George Saintsbury. 2 vols. Everyman's Library. London: Dent and New York: Dutton, 1914; reprint 1926.

———. *Selected Letters of Samuel Richardson.* Edited by John Carroll. Oxford: Clarendon Press, 1964.

———. *Sir Charles Grandison.* 7 vols. Oxford: Oxford University Press, 1972.

Rigby, Elizabeth. Review of *Jane Eyre: An Autobiography.* In *Critical Essays on Charlotte Brontë,* edited by Barbara Timm Gates. Boston: Hall, 1990. Reprinted from *Quarterly Review* 84 (1848): 173–76.

Rivero, Albert J. "The Place of Sally Godfrey in Richardson's *Pamela.*" *Eighteenth-Century Fiction* 6 (1993): 29–46.

Robbins, Bruce. *The Servant's Hand: English Fiction from Below.* New York: Columbia University Press, 1986.

Rousseau, Jean-Jacques. *Politics and the Arts: Letter to M. d'Alembert on the Theater.* Translated and introduced by Allan Bloom. Ithaca: Cornell University Press, 1960.

Samuelian, Kristin Flieger. "Lost Mothers: The Challenge to Paternalism in *Mary Barton.*" *Nineteenth-Century Studies* 6 (1992): 19–35.

Sanders, Scott. *D. H. Lawrence: The World of the Five Major Novels.* New York: Viking, 1973.

Scarry, Elaine. *The Body in Pain: The Making and Unmaking of the World.* New York: Oxford University Press, 1985.

Scheckner, Peter. *Class, Politics, and the Individual: A Study of the Major Works of D. H. Lawrence.* Rutherford: Associated University Press, 1985.

Schellenberg, Betty. "Enclosing the Immovable: Structuring Social Authority in *Pamela* Part II." *Eighteenth-Century Fiction* 4 (1991): 26–42.

Scott, Joan. *Gender and the Politics of History.* New York: Columbia University Press, 1988.

Sherburn, George. "'Writing to the Moment': One Aspect." In *Restoration and Eighteenth-Century Literature: Essays in Honor of Alan Dugald McKillop,* edited by Carroll Camden. Chicago and London: University of Chicago Press, 1963.

Showalter, Elaine. *Sexual Anarchy: Gender and Culture at the Fin-de-Siècle.* New York: Viking, 1990.

Shuttleworth, Sally. "Demonic Mothers: Ideologies of Bourgeois Motherhood in the Mid-Victorian Era." In *Rewriting the Victorians: Theory, History, and the Politics of Gender,* edited by Linda M. Shires. New York: Routledge, 1992.

Silver, Brenda R. "The Reflecting Reader in *Villette.*" In *The Voyage In: Fictions of Female Development,* edited by Elizabeth Abel, Marianne Hirsch, and England Langland. Hanover: University Press of New England, 1983.

Smalley, R. Ann. "Crossing the Gulfs: The Importance of the Master-Servant Relationship in Dickens's *Bleak House.*" *The Dickensian* 85 (1989): 150–60.

Smith, Sheila M. *The Other Nation: The Poor in English Novels of the 1840s and 1850s.* Oxford: Clarendon Press, 1980.

"Some Talk About Food." *Fraser's Magazine* 55 (1857): 474–84.

Spacks, Patricia Meyer. *Imagining a Self: Autobiography and Novel in Eighteenth-Century*

England. Cambridge, Mass.: Harvard University Press, 1976.

Spilka, Mark. "Lawrence and the Clitoris." In *The Challenge of D. H. Lawrence,* edited by Michael Squires and Keith Cushman. Madison: University of Wisconsin Press, 1990.

————. "On Lawrence's Hostility to Wilful Women: The Chatterley Solution." In *Lawrence and Women,* edited by Anne Smith. New York: Barnes & Noble, 1978.

Staves, Susan. "*Evelina;* or, Female Difficulties." *Modern Philology* 73 (1975–1976): 368–91.

Stevenson, Catherine Barnes. "'What Must Not Be Said': *North and South* and the Problem of Women's Work." *Victorian Literature and Culture* 19 (1992): 67–84.

Stone, Lawrence. *The Family, Sex, and Marriage in England 1500–1800.* New York: Harper, 1977.

Stone, Marjorie. "Taste, Totems, and Taboos: The Female Breast in Victorian Poetry." *Dalhousie Review* 64 (1985): 748–70.

Stoneman, Patsy. *Elizabeth Gaskell.* Bloomington: Indiana University Press, 1987.

Storme, Julie. "'An Exit So Happy': The Deaths of Julie and Clarissa." *Canadian Review of Comparative Literature* 14 (1987): 191–210.

Straub, Kristina. *Divided Fictions: Fanny Burney and Feminine Strategy.* Lexington: University Press of Kentucky, 1987.

Strickland, G. R. "The First *Lady Chatterley's Lover.*" In *D. H. Lawrence: A Critical Study of the Major Novels and Other Writings,* edited by A. H. Gomme. Sussex: Harvester and New York: Barnes & Noble, 1978.

Stuber, Florian. "On Fathers and Authority in *Clarissa.*" *Studies in English Literature, 1500–1900* 25 (1985): 557–74.

Swift, Jonathan. *Directions to Servants and Miscellaneous Pieces, 1733–1742.* In *The Prose Works of Jonathan Swift.* Edited by Herbert Davis. Oxford: Basil Blackwell, 1964.

Tanner, Tony. *Adultery in the Novel: Contract and Transgression.* Baltimore and London: Johns Hopkins University Press, 1979.

————. "Introduction." In *Villette* by Charlotte Bronte. Harmondsworth: Penguin, 1979.

Taylor, Jeremy. *The Life of Our Blessed Lord and Saviour Jesus Christ.* In *The Whole Works.* Edited by Reginald Heber and Rev. Charles Page Eden. 10 vols. Vol. 2. Hildesheim and New York: G. Olms Verlag, 1969.

Thackeray, William Makepeace. *The Adventures of Philip.* Edited by George Saintsbury. London: Oxford University Press, n.d.

————. *The Fitz-Boodle Papers.* In *The Great Hoggarty Diamond; Fitz-Boodle Papers; Men's Wives; Etc.* Edited by George Saintsbury. London: Oxford University Press, n.d.

————. *The History of Pendennis.* Harmondsworth: Penguin, 1972.

————. *The Letters and Private Papers of William Makepeace Thackeray.* Edited by Gordon Ray. Cambridge: Harvard University Press, 1946.

Thaddeus, Janice. "Swift's *Directions to Servants* and the Reader as Eavesdropper." *Studies in Eighteenth-Century Culture* 16 (1986): 107–23.

"Theory of Human Food." *Eclectic Review* 99 (1854): 274–87.

Thompson, Henry. "Food and Feeding. *The Nineteenth Century* 5 (1879): 971–91.

Thorpe, Douglas. "'I Never Knew My Lady Swoon Before': Lady Dedlock and the Revival of the Victorian Fainting Woman." *Dickens Studies Annual* 20 (1991): 103–25.

Thurin, Susan Schoenbauer. "To Be Brought Up 'By Hand.'" *Victorian Newsletter* 64 (1983): 27–29.

Tillotson, John. *The Golden Book of Tillotson: Selections from the Writings of the Rev. John Tillotson, D.D., Archbishop of Canterbury.* Edited by James Moffatt. Westport, Conn.: Greenwood, 1926; reprint 1971.

Todd, Janet. "*Pamela:* Or the Bliss of Servitude." *British Journal for Eighteenth-Century Studies* 6 (1983): 135–48.

———. *Sensibility: An Introduction.* London, New York: Methuen, 1986.

———. *Women's Friendship in Literature.* New York: Columbia University Press, 1980.

Trodd, Anthea. *Domestic Crime in the Victorian Novel.* New York: St. Martin's Press, 1989.

Trollope, Anthony. *Doctor Thorne.* [1858] London: Dent, 1949.

Tullock, Gail. *Mill and Sexual Equality.* Hemel Hempstead: Harvester Wheatsheaf, 1989.

Van Ghent, Dorothy. "Clarissa Harlowe." In *The English Novel: Form and Function.* New York: Harper and Row, 1953.

Van Sant, Ann Jessie. *Eighteenth-Century Sensibility and the Novel: The Senses in Social Context.* Cambridge: Cambridge University Press, 1993.

Warner, Marina. *Alone of All Her Sex: The Myth and the Cult of the Virgin Mary.* New York: Knopf, 1976.

Warner, William Beatty. *Reading Clarissa: The Struggles of Interpretation.* New Haven: Yale University Press, 1979.

Wasson, Richard. "Class and the Vicissitudes of the Male Body in Works by D. H. Lawrence." *D. H. Lawrence Review* 14 (1981): 289–305.

Watt, Ian. "Oral Dickens." *Dickens Studies Annual* 3 (1974): 165–81.

———. *The Rise of the Novel: Studies in Defoe, Richardson and Fielding.* Berkeley: University of California Press, 1964.

Weinstone, Ann. "The Queerness of Lucy Snowe." *Nineteenth-Century Contexts* 18 (1995): 367–84.

Weisser, Susan Ostrov. "A 'Craving Vacancy': Women and Sexual Love in Four British Novelists, 1740–1880." Ph.D. diss., Columbia University, 1987.

Welsh, Alexander. *The City of Dickens.* Oxford: Clarendon Press, 1971.

———. *From Copyright to Copperfield: The Identity of Dickens.* Cambridge, Mass.: Harvard University Press, 1987.

Wildman, John Hazard. "Thackeray's Wickedest Woman." In *Essays in Honor of Esmond Linworth Marilla,* edited by Thomas Austin Kirby and William John Olive. Baton Rouge: Louisiana State University Press, 1970.

Williams, Merryn. *Women in the English Novel, 1800–1900.* New York: St. Martin's Press, 1984.

Wilt, Judith. "He Could Go No Further: A Modest Proposal about Lovelace and Clarissa." *PMLA* 92 (1977): 19–32.

Winkler, Mary G. "Model Women." In *The Good Body: Asceticism in Contemporary*

Culture, edited by Mary G. Winkler and Letha B. Cole. New Haven: Yale University Press, 1994.

Winter, Sarah. "Domestic Fictions: Feminine Deference and Maternal Shadow Labor in Dickens's *Little Dorrit.*" *Dickens Studies Annual* 18 (1989): 243–54.

Wolff, Cynthia Griffin. *Samuel Richardson and the Eighteenth-Century Puritan Character.* Hamden: Archon, 1972.

Yavitz, Laura. "'Work Fit for a Woman': Elizabeth Gaskell and Working Women." Paper presented at the 1994 Midwest Victorian Studies Association Meeting, St. Louis, Mo., April 1994.

Yeazell, Ruth Bernard. *Fictions of Modesty: Women and Courtship in the English Novel.* Chicago: University of Chicago Press, 1991.

Zlotnick, Susan. "The Curse of Leisure: Unemployment in *Mary Barton.*" Paper presented at the Second Annual Conference on Women Writers of Eighteenth- and Nineteenth-Century Britain, Seattle, Wash., May 1993.

Index